WITHDRAWN

HARVARD LIBRARY

WITHDRAWN

Equal Consideration

Equal Consideration

A THEORY OF MORAL JUSTIFICATION

D. W. Haslett

NEWARK: UNIVERSITY OF DELAWARE PRESS
LONDON AND TORONTO: ASSOCIATED UNIVERSITY PRESSES

© 1987 by Associated University Presses, Inc.

Associated University Presses
440 Forsgate Drive
Cranbury, NJ 08512

Associated University Presses
25 Sicilian Avenue
London WC1A 2QH, England

Associated University Presses
2133 Royal Windsor Drive
Unit 1
Mississauga, Ontario
Canada L5J 1K5

The paper used in this publication meets the requirements of the American National Standard for Permanence of Paper for Printed Library Materials Z39.48-1984.

Library of Congress Cataloging-in-Publication Data

Haslett, D. W.
   Equal consideration.

   Bibliography: p.
   Includes index.
   1. Ethics. I. Title.
BJ1012.H343   1987   171'.5   86-40379
ISBN 0-87413-314-9 (alk. paper)

Printed in the United States of America

TO BETH

Contents

Preface   11

Part I *The Method*

1 Introduction   21
   1.1 Some Questions   21
   1.2 Norms and Values   22
   1.3 Beliefs That Should Never Be Acted Upon   25

2 Self-Interest   29
   2.1 Self-Interest and the Ideal Choice   29
   2.2 The Ideal Choice under Conditions of Risk   32
   2.3 Qualified and Unqualified Self-Interest   36

3 Equal Consideration of Everyone's Interests   40
   3.1 The Utilitarian Norm   40
   3.2 Three Types of Objections   43
   3.3 Two Conceptual Objections   45
   3.4 Preference Utilitarianism   49
   3.5 The Utilitarian Standard   50

4 Social-Pressure Systems   52
   4.1 The Standard of Evaluation   52
   4.2 Social-Pressure Combinations   54
   4.3 Three-Dimensional Evaluation   56
   4.4 Practical Applications   57
   4.5 The Equal Consideration System   60
   4.6 Why Philosophy Yields No Final Answers   65
   4.7 If Everyone Adopted the Utilitarian Standard   67

Part II *Personal Morality*

5 The Direct Utilitarian Code   75
   5.1 What the Utilitarian Standard Does *Not* Justify   75
   5.2 Hare's Two-Level Theory   80

6 The EC Code   88
   6.1 Requirements Any Moral Code Must Meet   88

6.2 Standard Objections the EC Code Avoids	90
6.3 Why General Beneficence Is Not Mandatory	91
6.4 Why Not an Elitist Code?	94
6.5 Exceptions	95
6.6 Conflict Cases	100
6.7 The Catch-All Secondary Norm	102
6.8 Borderline Cases	104
6.9 The Bridge Norm	108

Part III *Political Morality*

7 Human Rights	113
7.1 Personal and Political Morality Compared	113
7.2 The Structure of the Argument for Rights	117
7.3 Freedom of Speech: An Application of the Argument	120
7.4 Positive Rights	123
7.5 Consistency with Common Beliefs	125
7.6 How Not to Justify Reverse Discrimination	129
7.7 Human Fallibility: One More Natural Fact	131
7.8 A Possible Misinterpretation	133
7.9 Other Norms of Political Morality	135
8 The General Welfare Norm	138
8.1 The Need for a General Welfare Norm	138
8.2 The Spatial Division of Governmental Labor	139
8.3 But What about Great Need Elsewhere?	144
8.4 The Temporal Division of Governmental Labor	145
8.5 But What about Future Generations?	148
9 Judicial Reasoning	151
9.1 The Traditional View	151
9.2 Criticisms of the Traditional View	154
9.3 The Role of Preemptive Moral Norms	158
9.4 Why Judges May Have to Legislate After All	160
9.5 Reflective Equilibrium and Moral Justification	163

Part IV *The Rationale*

10 Equal Consideration and Self-Interest	169
10.1 The Project and the Strategy	169
10.2 Some Observations about Discrimination	174
10.3 The Premises	177
10.4 The Conclusion	180
10.5 The Practical Effect	182
10.6 Future Generations and Animals	184
11 Why We Should Act Morally	188
11.1 Two Versions of the Question	188

11.2 Noncompliance for Reasons of Greed	189
11.3 Noncompliance for Reasons of Conscience	195
11.4 And the Second Version of the Question	199
12 Utilitarian Standard vs. Original Position	201
12.1 How to Formulate a Utilitarian Original Position	201
12.2 Less Significant Differences	205
12.3 Primary Goods: First Objection	206
12.4 Primary Goods: Second Objection	212
12.5 The Veil of Ignorance and the Maximin Rule	217
12.6 Final Remarks	220
References	223
Index	227

Preface

These days it is fashionable in moral philosophy to focus upon specific moral problems—ones concerning the morality of controversial practices such as abortion, censorship, and reverse discrimination. This trend is, for the most part, a good thing; for too long specific moral problems had been ignored by philosophers, and left to those who attempt to solve them by doing little more than parading before us their own unexamined moral intuitions, intuitions inevitably found to be in hopeless conflict with those of numerous other people. Unfortunately, however, many of the philosophers now focusing upon these specific moral problems are doing exactly the same thing; they too, arrogantly or naively, are relying upon little more than their own unexamined moral intuitions. This is indeed unfortunate because philosophers are in a position to provide the one ingredient missing in most attempts to solve specific moral problems, this missing ingredient being a moral theory—a theory of moral justification—in terms of which people's conflicting moral intuitions can be adjudicated. It is just such a moral theory that this book attempts to provide—a moral theory that addresses itself to the major philosophic problem underlying all these specific moral problems: the problem of what differentiates the morally right from the morally wrong *in general*.

For appreciating the moral theory proposed here, it is not necessary to be familiar with current moral philosophy. But for those who are, it may be useful to locate roughly where this theory lies relative to other theories. Perhaps the best way to do this, as well as to indicate in broad terms what I take to be the contributions of this theory, is to compare it briefly with the moral theories put forth recently in two outstanding books—*A Theory of Justice*, by John Rawls, and *A Theory of the Good and the Right*, by Richard B. Brandt.

In one respect, the theory proposed here is not as broad in scope as that proposed by either Brandt or Rawls. Both Brandt and Rawls propose an original theory that encompasses not only the right, but also the good, while I am content to accept, after only minimal argument, a view of the good already widely held, and proceed from there. The view I accept is similar to that proposed by Rawls, although I introduce this view as one not about "the good" in general, but about "self-interest" only (see chap. 2 below). Yet in another respect the theory proposed here is broader in scope than that proposed by either Brandt or Rawls. Brandt, aside from a brief chapter on distributive justice, focuses only on personal morality, and Rawls focuses only on political morality, while the theory proposed here encompasses both, with the final result being a theory about not only *moral* norms, but also norms of etiquette, aesthetic norms, linguistic norms; in short, a theory about informal, social norms of *any* sort. Indeed, this theory extends even beyond norms to social values as well (i.e., virtues, ideals, etc.; see sec. 4.5).

I agree with both Brandt and Rawls in rejecting "act" utilitarianism. Although both Brandt's theory and the one proposed here can, in the broadest sense, be said to be utilitarian theories, neither is, however, a "rule" utilitarian theory; neither focuses upon a utilitarian evaluation of rules. Brandt's theory focuses upon what he calls "moral systems," while the theory proposed here focuses upon what I call "social-pressure combinations," which are, I think, similar to, yet importantly different from, Brandt's moral systems. Since the utilitarian theory proposed here focuses not upon rules, but upon social-pressure combinations and, finally, upon entire *systems* of social-pressure combinations (see sec. 4.5), it may be referred to as a version of "indirect" utilitarianism. This focus upon social-pressure combinations rather than rules is significant. As explained in chapter 4, this somewhat unorthodox focus enables us to evaluate moral codes along each of three equally important dimensions, rather than along just the one or two dimensions recognized by most utilitarian theories. And, as I try to show in chapters 5 through 9, the result is a utilitarian theory that succeeds in capturing all the advantages that rule utilitarian theories are supposed to have over act utilitarian theories, while avoiding what is often thought to be the main weakness of rule utilitarianism: a "collapse" back into act utilitarianism (see Lyons 1977). This "three-dimensional" evaluation is all part of a shift, proposed in this book, in the overall general perspective from which we do moral philosophy; a shift from the general perspective of compliance with moral norms to that of support through social pressure (sec. 4.4).

Rawls, as is well-known, adamantly rejects utilitarian theories of any kind. On the other hand, both Rawls's theory and the one proposed here are "ideal-chooser" theories of a variety adamantly rejected by Brandt (Brandt 1979, chap. 12). They are ideal-chooser theories in the sense that both specify an allegedly *ideal* standpoint for choosing moral codes, one that is such that any two individuals choosing from this standpoint would choose identically (see Rawls 1971, chap. 3, for the Rawlsian ideal standpoint, and chap. 3 below for the one proposed here). Rawls's ideal standpoint, known as the "original position," and the very different one proposed here are compared in chapter 12 below.

Finally, the theory set out here, but that of neither Rawls nor Brandt, attempts something that (owing, perhaps, to the long and dark shadow cast over moral philosophy by Kant) is rarely attempted these days: to show that morality is, in the end, justified in terms of individual self-interest (Part IV below). Rawls is far indeed from appealing to self-interest for purposes of justification, claiming, as he does, that the right is logically prior to the good, and thus to self-interest (1971, 30–33). Brandt's position is not quite so far from the one defended here as this; he does not claim that the right is logically prior to any aspect of the good. But Brandt attempts to derive the right from what it is allegedly rational to choose, not from what it is in our self-interest to choose; and, although Brandt allows that rationality and self-interest might coincide, he is careful to point out that, on his view, by no means do they necessarily coincide (Brandt 1979, chap. 17).

I do not claim that my attempt to demonstrate that morality is, in the end, justified in terms of individual self-interest is conclusive—for one thing, the relevant facts are no doubt much too complex for any conclusive demonstration without more factual investigation than can be undertaken here. But I hope this attempt is convincing enough at least to stimulate the skeptic to take the possibility of ethical justification in terms of self-interest somewhat more seriously. For if the connection between morality and self-interest cannot be made, we are, may I suggest, in real trouble. I am convinced, however, that the connection can indeed be made, and in this book I try to show how.

Let me indicate, roughly, what I take the nature of this connection to be. Morality is, I argue, connected to self-interest by means of certain *norms* of self-interest that it is in our best interests to comply with, sometimes even when complying with them is not what we believe to be in our best interests, and is in fact *not* in our best interests (see esp. chaps. 10 and 11). This apparent paradox is resolvable in terms of a crucial distinction: a distinction between "qualified" and "unqualified" self-interest (sec. 2.3 below). I argue that, even when it is not in our *unqualified* best interests to comply with these norms, it may still be in our *qualified* best interests to do so. All this will, I trust, become clear enough in due course.

None of the chapters in this book stands on its own; a full appreciation of any chapter requires an understanding of at least some material from other chapters. This is because, in moral theory, there are no quick answers; we can, I think, only proceed patiently, point by point, until the entire picture eventually emerges. The smallest combination of chapters short of the whole that, *taken together,* comes reasonably close to standing on its own are chapters 1 through 4 and 10, along with perhaps section 12.6; these five chapters, taken together, constitute, as it were, a mini-theory. But a word of caution: although from just these five chapters one may be able to gain a general idea of the full theory proposed here, many important features of this theory—ones necessary for a full appreciation of even these five chapters—are found only in the other chapters. Take, for example, the relationship, as explained at the beginning of chapter 5, between Parts II and III of this book on the one hand, and Part IV on the other.

Let me turn now from matters of substance to a matter of style. Footnotes are of two types: reference and content. Reference footnotes serve the purposes of revealing one's sources, indicating where further information may be found, and providing cross-references. This type of note is indispensable. Content footnotes, on the other hand, serve the purpose of amplifying what is found in the text. The rationale for this type of note is that the information it contains is not important enough to interrupt the line of reasoning in the text, yet is important enough not to be excluded altogether, thus calling for the compromise of being stuck in a footnote. This rationale seems to me to be flawed. A reader cannot afford simply to ignore a content footnote, for then he or she might miss something that really is important; the reader must, consequently, pause, look down at the bottom of the page or, worse yet, at the back of the book, read the footnote and, finally, locate again the place in the text where he or she left off. Thus the interruption that the content footnote was supposed to avoid is actually emphasized. My view, therefore, is that if some information is important enough to take up the reader's time, then it is important enough to be integrated into the text itself (with the help of parentheses, if necessary); otherwise, the information is best omitted altogether. Accordingly, the only notes found in this book are reference, not content notes. And so as further to avoid interrupting the reader's progress, each of these is placed not at the bottom of the page or the back of the book, but in parentheses within, or immediately after, the sentence to which it is most relevant.

None of the sections of this book has been published before, with the exception of section 5.2 (Haslett 1983). I am grateful to the editors and publishers of the *Journal of Value Inquiry* for permission to use this material here, in revised form. Also, certain parts of chapter 7 are the outgrowth of an article that appeared under the title "The General Theory of Rights" (Haslett 1980). In an earlier book, entitled *Moral Rightness* (Haslett 1974), I tried to accomplish two things: interpret the moral philosophy of C. I. Lewis, and sketch a position of my own. The position proposed here, although superficially similar in some respects to the one sketched there, is very different in decisive ways; my views, as well as my manner of expressing them, have both evolved considerably since that publication from early in my career.

I wish to thank David Cole, R. M. Hare, Joel J. Kupperman, Eric Von

Magnus, Edgar Page, and Roy Sorensen for many useful comments on earlier typescripts. In particular, I wish to thank my colleague Norman Bowie, who not only read an earlier typescript in its entirety, but discussed each chapter with me. These people deserve credit for pointing out many problems in the typescript, but bear no responsibility for my solutions; I am sure that, in many cases, they could have worked out better solutions themselves.

I also wish to thank the University of Delaware for having provided me with a sabbatical during which part of this book was written.

Finally, I dedicate this book to my wife, Beth, out of gratitude not only for her helpful criticism of my work, but also for her invaluable support in many other ways.

Equal Consideration

Part I
THE METHOD

1
Introduction

1.1 SOME QUESTIONS

Giving equal consideration to the interests of everyone is fundamental to morality. In making decisions of morality, special consideration ought not to be given to the interests of whites as opposed to blacks, males as opposed to females, Christians as opposed to Jews, oneself as opposed to others, and so on; rather *equal* consideration ought to be given to *everyone's* interests.

Yet, are the meaning and the significance of equal consideration fully appreciated by us? There are reasons for believing that they are not. These reasons include the vast disparity between rich and poor that we are willing to tolerate, and the vicious racial, sexual, and religious discrimination we still have not eliminated. But perhaps nothing reveals our lack of appreciation more than the fact that, as Robert S. McNamara recently pointed out (1979; see also Sivard 1978):

> Public expenditures on weapons research and development now approach $30 billion a year, and mobilize the talents of half a million scientists and engineers throughout the world. That is a greater research effort than is devoted to any other activity on earth, and it consumes more public research money than is spent on the problems of energy, health, education and food combined.

With our nuclear weapons and chemical poisons, we human beings can already kill one another with previously unheard of efficiency; yet, as millions are suffering agonizing deaths from want of cures for diseases and remedies for starvation, our governments are spending far more upon learning how to kill even more efficiently than upon finding these cures and remedies. There is much talk about the need for a strong national defense, and so on, but what it comes down to is simply this: we, throughout the world, cannot get along with one other well enough to enable these vast sums to be used for relieving suffering, rather than for creating it. And why can we not get along with one other well enough? Perhaps in part at least it is because, throughout the world, too many of us persist always in giving the interests of those in our own "group" *special* consideration, because we do not yet appreciate fully when it is appropriate to give the interests of everyone *equal* consideration.

But then exactly when *is* it appropriate to give everyone's interests equal consideration, and when not? Does this requirement of equal consideration represent a norm (or principle) of morality? If so, then when, and when not, ought this norm of morality to have priority over other norms of morality, ones forbidding such things as lies, theft, and murder? Suppose, for example, that what we would choose to do, were we to give everyone's interests equal consideration, would be to steal from the rich so as to give to the poor (contrary to norms of morality forbidding theft). Ought we really to do this? Consider another example. Some philosophers (e.g., Dworkin 1977, chap. 9; Singer 1978) have argued that a moral norm requiring equal consideration has priority over any moral norm forbidding racial discrimination. Therefore, according to these philosophers, the moral norm requiring equal consideration may be appealed to for justifying racial discrimination of a certain sort—namely, that which is known as "reverse" discrimination, the sort of discrimination that is designed to reverse damage from prior discrimination. But can reverse discrimination really be justified in this way, simply by appealing to a norm requiring equal consideration? In fact, is such a norm a norm of morality at all? Perhaps a norm requiring equal consideration is fundamental to morality not because it is itself a norm of morality, but because it is that norm to which we should appeal for *justifying* norms of morality, the most justified moral norms being whichever ones we would "choose" were we to give equal consideration to the interests of everyone. But then why should equal consideration have anything to do with the justification of moral norms? In other words, does giving everyone's interests equal consideration in "choosing" moral norms itself have any justification? And what sort of moral norms would be "chosen"? Finally, what exactly should "giving everyone's interests equal consideration" mean anyway?

A consideration of these questions quickly leads to the most fundamental question of all in moral philosophy: What distinguishes moral beliefs that are justified from ones that are not? The purpose of this book is to propose an answer to this question; to propose, in other words, a theory of moral justification—a theory that, it will turn out, is built around giving everyone's interest "equal consideration."

1.2 NORMS AND VALUES

Moreover, it will turn out that the theory of justification proposed here is applicable not just to moral reasoning but to "practical" reasoning in general, of which moral reasoning is only one variety. Practical reasoning is carried out by appeal to criteria. These criteria take many forms: rules, principles, values, ideals, and so on. It will be useful to begin by devising for these criteria a rough classificatory scheme. Criteria of practical reasoning, as I see it, fall into either of two broad categories: either they are (1) criteria in the form of general prescriptions purporting to distinguish that which is right from that which is wrong (rules, principles, etc.), or they are (2) criteria purporting to distinguish that which is good from that which is bad (virtues, ideals, etc.). I propose that we call criteria of the first kind "norms," and those of the second kind "values." Examples of norms would be the rule "Always tell the truth," and the principle "Always choose the alternative you would choose if you were to give equal consideration to the interests of everyone." The only difference between rules and principles, both of which are general prescriptions, is that rules, typically, are more specific. Examples of values would be the virtues of kindliness and generosity, and the ideals of freedom and equality. Virtues are, typically, attributable to persons, whereas ideals are, typically, attributable to things, states of affairs, and so on.

Notice that every value forms the basis for a standard in terms of things may be *comparatively* evaluated. The value itself, and the standard of (comparative) evaluation corresponding to it are perhaps most usefully viewed as being, in a sense, distinct criteria, but "distinct" only in the sense that two sides of the same coin are distinct. As I see it, *values* are criteria in terms of which absolute evaluations may be made—evaluations of the form "X is good," whereas *standards* (at least as I am using this term) are criteria in terms of which comparative evaluations may be made—evaluations of the form "X is better than Y." Take, for example, "utility," utility being that which a utilitarian values. Utility, a value, is not identical with, but forms the basis for, a standard of comparative evaluation according to which the more utility that results from X, the higher X is to be evaluated relative to alternatives (other things being equal). Notice also that this standard—the "utilitarian" standard—is distinct from the so-called *principle* of utility. The utilitarian standard, being a criterion for making comparative evaluations, may indeed influence our behavior indirectly, but the standard does not itself *prescribe* anything. The principle of utility, on the other hand, *does* prescribe something—namely, that we always do that which maximizes utility; therefore it is a norm rather than a standard. (Both the utilitarian standard and the principle of utility will be formulated more precisely in chapter 3.) Thus there is a subtle, yet, I think, genuine distinction between (1) utility, which is a value, (2) the utilitarian standard corresponding to this value, and (3) the principle of utility, which is a norm. In general, norms, values, and standards clearly are related, although the relationship between norms and values is not the same as the close, "logical" relationship that exists between values and the standards of comparative evaluation corresponding to them; yet norms, values, and standards are also distinct, and should not be confused with one another.

Accordingly, I propose that, throughout this inquiry, we adhere to the following rough classificatory scheme:

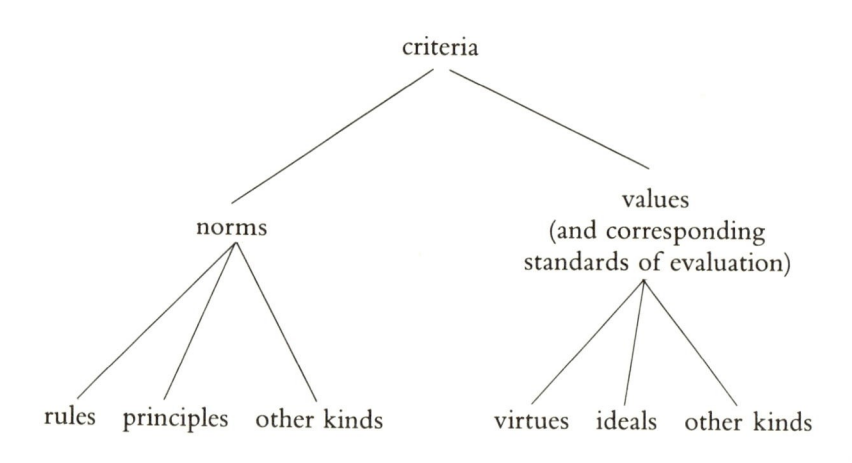

```
                          criteria
                         /        \
                        /          \
                       /            values
                    norms        (and corresponding
                                 standards of evaluation)
                   / | \            / | \
                  /  |  \          /  |  \
              rules principles other kinds   virtues ideals other kinds
```

Roughly speaking, norms *prescribe,* whereas values serve as bases for *evaluations.* Norms are the sort of criteria of which we might, typically, say that they had been "complied with," but not that they had been "exemplified," whereas values are the sort of criteria of which we might, typically, say that they had been "exemplified," but not that they had been "complied with." Norms and values are, of course, closely interrelated in many important ways.

This way of classifying criteria has certain advantages. It is probably as consistent with ordinary usage as any such rough classificatory scheme could be expected to be. It is also consistent with terminology prevalent in the social sciences today. Take, for example, what Robin M. Williams, Jr., says about the difference between norms and values in his useful article on values in the *International Encyclopedia of the Social Sciences:*

> Values are not the same as norms for conduct. Norms are rules for behaving: they say more or less specifically what should or should not be done by particular types of actors in given circumstances. Values are standards of desirability that are more nearly independent of specific situations. The same value may be a point of reference for a great many specific norms; a particular norm may represent the simultaneous application of several separate values. Thus the value premise "equality" may

enter into norms for relationships between husband and wife, brother and brother, teacher and student, and so on; on the other hand, the norm "a teacher must not show favoritism in grading" may in a particular instance involve the values of equality, honesty, humanitarianism, and several others. (Williams 1968, 16:84)

Throughout this inquiry I shall be focusing upon moral reasoning, as opposed to other varieties of practical reasoning, and upon rules and principles, as opposed to other kinds of criteria. But the theory that emerges extends in scope beyond just rules and principles to informal, social criteria of any sort (see sec. 4.5). Finally, so as to avoid unnecessary complications, all rules and principles will, throughout this inquiry, be referred to simply by means of the generic term *norms*.

1.3 BELIEFS THAT SHOULD NEVER BE ACTED UPON

As we shall see, the theory proposed here allows us, for purposes of moral justification, to make use of factual beliefs that cannot be established through the rigorous methods of scientific experimentation. Ethical, as well as practical, barriers prevent the relevant experiments from being performed. But making use of such factual beliefs does not make moral justification mere speculation; there is no reason why moral justification, even though largely beyond the scope of science, cannot nevertheless be rigorous, and yield conclusions that are well founded.

In previous centuries all of this would have been too obvious to mention. In our present century of spectacular scientific triumphs, however, there are those who appear to be so impressed with experimental methods, along with numbers, symbols, and graphs, that they think moral justification, since it is largely beyond the scope of science, must therefore be either arbitrary, or based upon mysterious, nonempirical intuitions of some sort. They appear to think that, if moral norms cannot be justified by the methods of science, then our beliefs about matters of fact must play no role in their justification at all. We do not, they claim, want something as important as, say, the moral right not to be made a slave depend upon something as uncertain as our beliefs about matters of fact, beliefs such as, say, those about what the consequences of slavery are.

Is it not extraordinary, however, to find complaints about uncertainty coming from those who base moral norms upon fundamental moral intuitions, considering how much these so-called intuitions conflict from one person to another? To be sure, people's beliefs about facts sometimes conflict too; but there is a difference; no matter how difficult conflicting factual beliefs may be to resolve in practice, how to resolve the conflict will at least be tolerably clear in principle, thus making it possible for the job of doing so to begin, while with conflicting, fundamental moral intuitions, how to resolve them is not even tolerably clear in principle. In short: before complaining about a splinter in the eye of another, the intuitionist should, as the proverb says, remove the log from his own eye.

Yet, as we shall see, at certain points in our moral reasoning an appeal to certain *kinds* of factual beliefs is indeed objectionable, although for reasons different from those recognized by the intuitionist. These kinds of beliefs are ones that, morally speaking, should never be acted upon. That certain kinds of factual beliefs should never be acted upon is, in fact, one of the underlying themes of this book.

Perhaps an illustration, not from morality, but from law, will help make clear what I mean by factual beliefs that should never be acted upon. A certain blood test can be administered to a man, which, with an accuracy of 99 percent, excludes the possibility of his being the father of a child with a certain blood type. Whenever a defendant in some legal proceeding has "passed" this blood test—whenever, that is, the test indicates that he could not be the father of a child he is accused of having fathered—what weight should the test be given? (Whenever the test merely indicates that the defendant *could* be the father, it should, of course, be given no weight at all.) Let us assume that the cases in question are ones where a woman is suing a man for support of a child she alleges he fathered, and that in none of these cases does the man either confess to being the father or admit to there having existed any extraordinary circumstances that make it certain he is the father (that is, he does not admit to having been, say, snowbound along with the woman the year during which the child was conceived). Let us assume furthermore that, in these cases, incorrect decisions against mothers are no better or worse than incorrect decisions against alleged fathers. Finally, let us (merely for simplicity) assume that cases of this sort are decided entirely by a judge without the help of a jury. Given these assumptions, Alf Ross reaches this conclusion: even though these tests, when they indicate that the defendant could not be the father, *are only 99 percent accurate,* they should, in all such cases, be viewed as "unconditional and absolute proof" (1958, 482). In other words, he concludes that, from among defendants who "pass" the blood test, a judge should not, on a case-by-case basis, try to pick out those few who are really the fathers after all; instead, he should simply assume that *none* are. The reason for this conclusion is not hard to guess. The probabilities tell us that, from among those defendants who "pass" the blood test, only one in a hundred (on the average) really is the father after all. Now, say a judge believes that the defendant before him in some particular case just happens to be this one defendant. What is the probability of this belief being correct? We know the probability will be *somewhat* higher than one in a hundred—that is, it will be somewhat higher than the .01 probability that the blood test provides, this .01 probability being what we may refer to as the "antecedent" probability. It will be somewhat higher because the judge's belief will be based upon evidence other than just the blood test—evidence such as the plaintiff's and defendant's testimony—and this additional evidence (or, in other words, the judge's own powers of discrimination when confronted with this evidence) counts for something. But *how much* higher than .01 will be judge's powers of discrimination cause the probability to be? We must remember that (we are to assume) none of the defendants who "pass" the blood test will confess; each will continue to insist upon his "innocence," and do his utmost to convince the judge. We must remember also that judges, like all human beings, are always subject to misinformation, rationalizations, deceptions, and so forth; judges are, in other words, fallible. If then we consider the low antecedent probability of .01 in conjunction with the judge's human fallibility, it becomes apparent that, even taking into account his powers of discrimination, the probability of his belief being correct still will not be very high. We cannot, of course, be sure about what the *exact* probability figure will be, but we can be sure of at least this: even taking into account the judge's powers of discrimination, the probability of his being correct in believing the defendant before him is the one in a hundred who is the father will still be something less than fifty-fifty, probably much less. That is to say, if a defendant has "passed" the blood test, yet the judge believes he is the father nevertheless, then it is always more probable that this belief is mistaken than that it is correct. Thus, in the interest of deciding as many cases correctly as possible, a judge should always act upon the assumption that the blood-test evidence in question is conclusive, no matter *how* convincing he takes the contrary evidence to be. A judge's powers of discrimination are simply not great enough to justify his trying to pick out the one defendant in a hundred who, in spite of the blood test, is really the father after all. So, because of his human fallibility, a judge should never act upon a certain kind of belief about the facts: a belief that the defendant before him is the father in spite of this blood test.

I shall argue in this book that what we have just seen to be true about decision-making in law is true about decision-making in other areas as well. In particular, it is true about decision-making in morality; because of human fallibility, we should never act upon certain kinds of factual beliefs if we want to do what is morally right. And I shall argue that, because of human fallibility once again, we should never act upon certain other kinds of factual beliefs if we want to do what is in our best interests. In fact, failure to recognize what *kinds* of beliefs should never be acted upon may well be responsible for more mistakes, both of morality and of self-interest, than is anything else. It is as Socrates said: he is truly wise who knows what he does not know.

The arguments for showing that certain kinds of beliefs should never be acted upon—arguments crucial for the theory of moral justification proposed here—will be presented in due course (see chaps. 7–11). Meanwhile, let us turn immediately to other, equally crucial, ingredients of this theory, starting in the next chapter with the fundamental norm of personal welfare, or self-interest. We shall then, in chapter 3, build upon this discussion of self-interest in formulating what will be meant here by giving "equal consideration" to everyone's interests. The stage will then be set for proposing, in chapter 4, a method of moral justification—that is, a method for justifying moral norms, or entire codes of morality. This "method" will involve giving equal consideration to everyone's interests, but that is not all it will involve. It will also involve evaluating moral norms from a particular "perspective," one that focuses upon social pressure in support of the norms, rather than merely upon compliance with them. That certain kinds of factual beliefs should never be acted upon is, as I said, one of the underlying themes of this book. That moral justification—indeed, the justification of informal social criteria in general—needs to proceed from the perspective of social pressure rather than that of compliance is the other underlying theme of this book.

2
Self-Interest

2.1 SELF-INTEREST AND THE IDEAL CHOICE

The theory of moral justification being proposed here is built upon a foundation of self-interest. It is, therefore, with self-interest that I shall begin. I shall try to formulate, in this chapter, a criterion for deciding which, from any given set of alternatives, is in a person's best interests, no matter *who* that person is.

What might such a perfectly *general* criterion of personal welfare as this be? Let us try to answer this question by taking some hypothetical person, say Jones, and asking: From the standpoint of Jones's own best interests, what would count as an "ideal" choice for him to make. What I mean here by an *ideal* choice is one made under conditions where anything that might conceivably cause the choice to be erroneous is absent. Thus, in order to characterize an ideal choice for Jones, we must isolate what the possible causes of error are for choices of this sort, ones from the standpoint of self-interest.

What then might cause a choice of the sort we are supposing Jones must make to go wrong? First of all, it might go wrong through being influenced by something irrelevant, or through failing to be influenced by something relevant. But then exactly what is, and what is not, in this context, a "relevant" influence? The main thing to keep in mind here is what Jones is *not* supposed to be choosing. He is *not* supposed to be choosing what is moral, what is rational, or what is best overall. He is not even supposed to be choosing what, all things considered, he would *want* most to choose. This last point is especially important; not even what a person wants or desires most to do—say, sacrifice himself for his children or for posterity—need be what is, or what he thinks is, in his *personal* best interests. Since then Jones is supposed to be choosing only what is in his *own best interests*—not any of these other things—his sole concern must be to choose the alternative that makes his own life as desirable as possible *for him,* not for others. So what really counts is how the alternatives affect *his* life and *only* his life.

It is, of course, true that how an alternative affects a person's life often does depend upon how it affects the lives of certain others, such as his loved ones. A person will often have relationships with others that are such that his greatest joys and sorrows are derived vicariously from the joys and sorrows of these others, so much so that rather than see them suffer or die he would gladly suffer or die himself. I happen to think that the person with such relationships is very fortunate; by means of them he will probably gain much more than he loses. But all this is beside the point. The point is that, although how an alternative affects Jones's life will undoubtedly depend upon how it affects the lives of certain others, its effects upon the lives of these others can, by hypothesis, be only *instrumentally* valuable for him—that is, valuable only as a means to the one and only *final* end we are, for purposes of argument, allowing him to recognize—that of making his own life as desirable as possible for himself. Accordingly, the alternative in Jones's best interests is simply the one whose effects upon *his* life would be of most value to him. More precisely, it is the alternative whose effects upon his life would be of most value to him *in themselves*, rather than as a means to something outside the scope of his own life. To the extent that their value for him was as a means to something outside the scope of his own life, their value for him would not, once again, be solely in terms of his own self-interest. This, it seems to me, follows simply from what we mean by a person's own "self-interest" as distinct from what that person, morally speaking, *should* do, most *wants* to do (all things considered), and so on.

What value then would the effects of the alternatives upon Jones's life have for him in themselves? I assume the only value the effects upon his life could have for him *in themselves* would lie entirely in what it would be like for him actually to experience them. Say one of the effects upon his life of some alternative A would be his having a toothache, while one of the effects of some alternative B would be his falling in love. Knowing what it is like to experience toothaches and love, I would tentatively suppose that, as between these two alternatives, B is the one in his best interests, although, of course, still other effects could always, in the final analysis, tip the balance in favor of A after all. In any case, the one and only crucial element in his personal-welfare calculations would have to be what he thought it would be like for him to experience—to actually *live* through—the effects upon his life. Any other influence upon his choice, by anything else whatsoever—anything such as his neuroses, his superstitions, his prejudices—might cause his choice to be in error. (I am thus adopting what L. W. Sumner calls an "experience" model, rather than what he calls a "desire" model. At least for purposes of elucidating *personal welfare,* an experience model is, as Sumner shows, superior. For the arguments for some kind of experience model, see Sumner 1981, sec. 21.)

So far then, my position is as follows: only to the extent that Jones's choice is influenced by and only by exactly what he thinks it would be like for him to experience, for each alternative, its effects upon *his* life, can his choice be said to be ideal from the standpoint of self-interest. But obviously his choice could go wrong in still another way: what he thinks the effects upon his life would be, or what he thinks it would be like to experience them, could be mistaken. So, to assure that Jones's choice will be ideal, we must not only rule out its being influenced by something other than what he thinks it would be like to experience these effects, but must also stipulate that what he thinks these effects would be, and what he thinks it would be like to experience them, is in fact correct. Indeed, his knowledge of the effects upon his life must be as perfect as it would be if he had already experienced each of these effects, and had retained perfect memory of the experiences. Another way of stating this requirement is that Jones must know exactly what effects each alternative would have upon his future experience—"experience" in the broad sense of consciousness or sentience—and, for present purposes, his future experience would even have to include any connected with any life he might have after his life on earth (i.e., any afterlife).

From this characterization of what an ideal choice for Jones to make from the standpoint of his personal welfare would be, we can now derive the following general criterion of personal welfare. That alternative which is in an individual's best interests is the one he would choose if (1) he knew exactly what effects each alternative would have upon his future experience, and (2) he was, in making his choice, influenced by, and only by, this knowledge. This criterion will become more complex shortly, so as to make it applicable to choosing under conditions of risk—that is, under conditions where probabilities differ. But before turning to this matter of differing probabilities, let me, as follows, formulate the criterion as a norm, a general norm of personal welfare.

> Choose that alternative which you would choose if:
> (1) you knew exactly what effects each alternative would have upon your future experience; and
> (2) you were influenced by, and only by, this knowledge.

In theory it is, of course, possible for two or more alternatives to be found *equally* choiceworthy from the ideal standpoint specified by this norm. And, in order to provide for this theoretical possibility, I could have formulated the norm as follows: "Choose that alternative which is such that there is no alternative you would choose over it (except arbitrarily) if . . ." But the theoretical possibility of these "ties" is, I should think, of little practical importance, of so little practical importance, in fact, that it does not warrant our struggling with this more complex formulation.

The theory of the good, or of personal welfare, underlying this norm can be traced at least as far back as Sidgwick (1907, see esp. 111–12). One of the most fully worked out versions of this theory of the good has been put forth by C. I. Lewis (1946). Today something similar to, even though not the same as, this norm would, I think it fair to say, be accepted by philosophers with views otherwise as different as those of R. M. Hare, who defends a utilitarian moral theory (1981), and John Rawls, who defends a modified Kantian moral theory (1971). As Rawls himself points out, what in the final analysis constitutes a person's good "is not in dispute" between himself and utilitarians (1971, 92). As we shall see later, from this theory of the good Rawls attempts to derive what he calls "primary goods," the use of which *is* in dispute between himself and utilitarians, but we need not go into this complication until chapter 12.

2.2 THE IDEAL CHOICE UNDER CONDITIONS OF RISK

The alternative most in our best interests is, I have argued, the one we would choose from a standpoint where we knew, for each alternative, what its effects upon our future experience would be. This ideal standpoint is thus one of *perfect* foresight. Yet, in real life, choices must always be made from a standpoint of *imperfect* foresight. So we need a solution to the problem of which alternative it is in our best interests to choose from *this* standpoint, a standpoint where only probabilities are known. Which, for example, should we choose as between an alternative with possible effects that are *excellent* but have a *low* probability of occurring, and one with possible effects that are only *fair* but have a *high* probability of occurring? We need, in other words, a solution to the problem of which alternative it is in our best interest to choose under "conditions of risk."

The usual solution found in current decision theory—the solution that will be adopted here—is to choose according to the rule: "Always maximize expected utility." The expected utility of some alternative is found through a two-step procedure: the first step is, for each of the alternative's possible sets of effects, to multiply the probability of the set's occurring by the utility it would yield if it did occur; the second step is to add together each of the products obtained in step one; the resulting sum is the alternative's expected utility. For example, say Jane is faced with having to choose between the following two alternatives: asking John for a kiss, and not doing so. Let us assume that the alternative of asking for the kiss has, under the circumstances, only two relevant possible effects (or, in other words, has only two possible sets of effects, each set having only one member). The first possible effect, which is 80 percent probable, is a kiss, which would yield Jane 100 units of utility. The second possible effect, which is 20 percent probable, is despondency at being turned down, which would yield Jane 200 units of *dis*utility. Given these figures, the *expected* utility for Jane of the first alternative—asking for the kiss—is (100 × .8) + (−200 × .2), or 40 units. If we assume (unrealistically) that the second alternative—not asking for the kiss—would result in no utility or disutility at all, it has, of course, an expected utility of zero. The first alternative with its 40 units of expected utility is then the one that, according to the rule of maximizing expected utility, should be chosen.

Among the objections one might encounter to using the rule of maximizing expected utility for decision-making under risk is that we are, at present, unable to calculate probabilities with anywhere near the precision assumed in my example. This is very true; but the same objection would be applicable to any alternative rules as well—all rules for decision-making under risk are more or less in the same boat—and, in any case, usually our rough "intuitive" estimates of the main probabilities in question are far from being so arbitrary as to be of no practical value whatever.

What appears to be the more serious objection to using this rule, the objection some variant of which one encounters most frequently in philosophical writing, is as follows. Utility and disutility, at least of the sort we are interested in, comes in the form of satisfying or dissatisfying experiences or sentient states—everything from warm baths and stubbed toes to the much more subtle, but significant joys and sorrows of life. Now we all know what it is for an experience or sentient state to be satisfying or positive—in other words, for it to have "utility" for us. We also know what it is to value (for its own sake) one experience or sentient state over another, and thus for the one to have *more* utility for us than the other. Since we can thus rank experiences in terms of their relative utility for us, a so-called *ordinal* measurement of the utility of experiences—one that simply ranks them relative to one another—is in principle quite possible. Unfortunately, for determining what the rule of maximizing expected utility calls for, a mere ordinal measurement of utility appears not to be sufficient. Determining what this rule calls for would appear to require that the mathematical operations of multiplication and addition be performed upon units of utility, and for performing these operations nothing less than a so-called *cardinal measurement* of utility would suffice—a measurement that yields the sort of numerical values upon which these mathematical operations can be performed meaningfully. But it is far from clear whether cardinal measurements of the utility of experiences are possible. This problem is particularly serious with respect to measurements that have to be *intersubjectively* valid—that is, valid not just relative to other experiences of the same person, but relative to experiences of other persons. Some would go so far as to say that an intersubjectively valid measurement not only cannot be done, but does not even make sense. I myself would not go so far as to say that the very idea is senseless, but it cannot be denied that at present we have little idea of how to make such measurements. For purposes of calculating *personal,* not *general* welfare, a measurement that is intersubjectively valid is not crucial. We shall soon be concerned, however, with calculating general welfare also, so this problem is one that we must face.

But having introduced this problem about cardinal measurements of utility, I want now to bring the discussion of it to an abrupt halt since, contrary to first appearances, a cardinal, as opposed to an ordinal, measurement is not really necessary for determining expected utility after all. Another rule can be formulated that always prescribes exactly what the original rule of maximizing expected utility set out above would prescribe, but that does not necessitate mathematical operations of any sort. It will be easier to grasp my abstract statement of this alternate rule if I first provide a concrete illustration of how it works. This illustration is not, of course, designed to reflect how people typically do reason, but is designed to show what, as far as personal welfare is concerned, would constitute a *perfect*, or *ideal* choice under conditions of risk, a choice arrived at by a process of reasoning that is, for most ordinary purposes, far more exact than is either necessary or (because of our limited knowledge) possible. Keeping this in mind consider, once again, the example where Jane must choose between asking and not asking John for a kiss. The alternative of asking for the kiss has two and only two relevant possible effects. The first possible effect—the pleasure of a kiss—has an 80 percent probability of occurring, and the second possible effect—the despondency of a rejection—has a 20 percent probability of occurring. In calculating this alternative's expected utility, instead of multiplying these probability figures by numerical values that represent the utility of the possible effects if they occur, we are, according to the nonmathematical variant of our original rule, to do the following. First, for each alternative, we state all the probabilities in question as fractions with a single common denominator; the lowest common denominator would be the simplest. In this case, it would mean stating the probability of the first possible effect as $4/5$ and that of the second as $1/5$. Now, since the common denominator is five, we simply assume for purposes of our calculations that this same alternative—that of asking for the kiss—will be chosen on five different occasions. Furthermore, since with this choice a kiss has a probability of occurring four out of five times and a rejection one out of five times, we assume that on four of these occasions Jane will in fact get a kiss and on one of these occasions, a rejection. The expected utility for Jane of this alternative is then equivalent to the utility of getting four kisses (each, of course, exactly the same without any diminishing returns) and one rejection. Now, just because the probabilities are what they are, this does not guarantee that if Jane actually did choose this same alternative on five different occasions the results would be four kisses and one rejection; this is merely what is to be assumed for purposes of calculating Jane's expected utility, and for these purposes only. Turning now to the second alternative—

not asking for the kiss—it, as will be recalled, would result in no utility or disutility at all. The alternate rule I am now illustrating tells us that, of the two alternatives, the one that has the greatest expected utility for Jane depends upon which, from an ideal standpoint that includes perfect knowledge of the effects in question, Jane would choose as between a "packaged" combination of four kisses and one rejection (which represents the expected utility of the first alternative) and nothing at all (which represents the expected utility of the second alternative). Notice that at nowhere throughout these calculations are any mathematical operations upon units of utility necessary. (Similar methods for determining expected utility without recourse to any mathematical operations upon utility have been suggested by Lewis 1946, 547–49; and Smart 1973, 37–42.)

For another illustration of how this alternate rule works, take the following—which, again for convenience, has been made simpler than real life. Assume that you are offered a million dollars for winning the following game of Russian roulette. Blindfolded, you are to spin the cylinder of a revolver, put the revolver against your temple, and pull its trigger once; of the six bullet chambers in the revolver's cylinder, only two contain a bullet; if your pulling the trigger does not discharge one of the two bullets, you win; otherwise, you lose. Thus, if you do pull the trigger you have a $\frac{4}{6}$ chance of winning, thereby assuring yourself a life of great luxury, but you also have a $\frac{2}{6}$ chance of losing, thereby assuring yourself instant death. Finally, assume that the (100% certain) effect of your playing it safe instead—that is, of your not pulling the trigger—would be a life of not great, but of modest luxury (and, to keep the illustration simple, assume there is no afterlife). If we give the probability fractions in question here—namely, $\frac{4}{6}$, $\frac{2}{6}$, and $\frac{1}{1}$—a lowest common denominator, they become $\frac{2}{3}$, $\frac{1}{3}$, and $\frac{3}{3}$. So, according to the rule in question, whether you should pull the trigger depends upon which, from an ideal standpoint that includes perfect knowledge of these lives, you would choose as between (a) enjoying the very luxurious life *two* times (along with nothing—i.e., instant death—one time, so to speak) and (b) enjoying the moderately luxurious life *three* times. And in making this choice you must, of course, assume that your enjoyment of the successive lives would be without any diminishing returns at all. (Before you jump to the conclusion that you would not risk instant death for any amount of money, remember that when riding in an automobile you are, in effect, risking instant death merely for the sake of convenience.)

Having illustrated how the nonmathematical variant of the rule of maximizing expected utility works, I shall now attempt an abstract statement of this rule, or norm. It is as follows.

Choose that alternative which you would choose if:
(1) you knew, for each alternative, exactly what all of its possible sets of

effects were upon your future experience, along with each set's probability of occurring;

(2) you assumed that, for whichever alternative you chose, each of its possible sets of effects upon your future experience would be experienced by yourself n times, where n is the numerator of a fraction that represents the set's probability of occurring; and

(3) you were influenced by, and only by, this knowledge, and this assumption.

For purposes of the above norm, all of the probability fractions must of course have, or else be given, a *common denominator*. Take, for example, an alternative that has two possible sets of effects; one set, composed of worthwhile experiences, has a ¾ probability of occurring, while the other, composed of unpleasant experiences, has a 6/24 probability of occurring. We are to assume that, if we chose this alternative, we would experience each of its possible sets of consequences n times, where n is the numerator of the set's probability of occurring fraction. If we did not give these fractions a common denominator, we would then have to assume that we would experience the worthwhile experiences three times, and the unpleasant ones six times. But obviously three and six do not even come close to accurately reflecting the difference in the probabilities of occurrence of these experiences (which, of course, is what these numbers are supposed to reflect). Thus a common denominator is necessary.

The above norm, which will be my final formulation of the personal welfare norm, is simply the personal welfare norm set out in the previous section, appropriately modified so as to allow differing probabilities of occurring to be taken into account.

Closely related to the fundamental norm of personal welfare is a *standard* for comparing alternatives with respect to how much they are in our interests. (Recall the distinction between norms and standards set out in sec. 1.2.) According to this standard, some alternative A is more in our interests than some other alternative B if and only if A would be chosen over B by us, were we choosing from the ideal standpoint delineated by the fundamental norm of personal welfare. We may call this the fundamental "standard" of personal welfare. I shall make use of this standard later, in Part IV, when discussing the connection between equal consideration and self-interest.

2.3 QUALIFIED AND UNQUALIFIED SELF-INTEREST

One final, and very important matter concerning the norm (and thus the standard) of personal welfare delineated above must be discussed. The ideal standpoint delineated by this norm requires perfect knowledge of what each possible set of effects upon our future experience is for each alternative, and what that set's probability of occurring is. But probabilities are always relative to what the *information* or *evidence* is upon which the probabilities are based. Relative to certain information—information to the effect that, say, an individual is a 40-year-old human being—the probability of the individual living to age 80 might be .5, but relative to certain other more extensive information—information that, say, the individual is female, in good health, and has parents both of whom are over 80—the probability of living to 80 might be .75 instead. Consider now those probabilities which are supposed to be known from the ideal standpoint delineated by the personal welfare norm. What we must try to decide is to what information exactly these probabilities are relative. Let us call a hypothetical individual choosing from this ideal standpoint an *ideal chooser,* and let us (for convenience) assume that those probabilities which an ideal chooser is supposed to know are calculated by this hypothetical chooser himself. If then we assume that the ideal chooser calculates these probabilities, we may formulate the question before us as: What information, or knowledge, is an ideal chooser to have for basing these probabilities upon? One possibility is to give him complete knowledge of all particular facts about the universe, past and present, along with knowledge of all possible sound laws of nature. This will not do, however, since whatever is based upon information this perfect would, it seems, no longer be probable, but certain. Another possibility is to stipulate that if it is Jones's personal welfare that is in question, the probabilities are to be based upon whatever information is currently possessed by Jones, while if it is Smith's personal welfare that is in question, the probabilities are to be based upon whatever information is currently possessed by Smith, and so on. But this stipulation will not do either, since the information possessed by individuals is very limited; and if the probabilities that the ideal chooser is to know were relative to such limited information, then the standpoint of this hypothetical chooser could hardly be said to be ideal. So, once again, what information, or knowledge, should we stipulate that, in theory, an ideal chooser has for basing the relevant probabilities upon?

I do not know exactly what the answer to this question should be. My tentative suggestion is that we attribute to him something like complete knowledge of all particular facts about the universe, past and present, along with knowledge not of all possible sound laws of nature, but only of those laws *currently* known to humanity. Such information as this would be far from perfect, yet it would not be anywhere nearly so limited as the information at the disposal of any actual individual or group of individuals. Probabilities relative to such information would, therefore, not collapse into certainties, yet still would, I assume, be worthy of a standpoint said to be ideal.

But if, for purposes of his probability calculations, we attribute to the ideal chooser something like complete knowledge of all past and present particular facts about the universe, this creates a rather subtle problem of theory. When we find ourselves in some predicament requiring a difficult decision about what it is in our best interests to do, the reason for the predicament is typically not just that we lack information about the future, but that we lack certain crucial information about the present or past as well. Consider, for example, Jane's predicament in which she must decide whether or not to ask John for a kiss. We assumed earlier that the first possible effect of asking for the kiss—receiving it—has a .8 probability of occurring, and the second possible effect—a rejection—has a .2 probability of occurring. We may also assume that, all the while, John himself *knows* whether or not, if asked by Jane, he will consent. If, however, the ideal chooser is supposed to know all past and present particular facts about the universe for purposes of probability calculations, then he presumably knows what John knows, and if he knows what John knows, then, for the ideal chooser, the probabilities in question would obviously be either 0 or 1 (or extremely close to it) instead of being .8 and .2. That is to say, if the ideal chooser had this crucial information about John's present state of mind, then he would know with virtual certainty whether, upon asking John, Jane would get a kiss or be rejected. Thus, by stipulating that the ideal chooser's knowledge is to be so complete that it includes even this information about John's current state of mind, this seems to make it impossible in theory for the personal welfare norm set out above to be applicable to Jane's particular predicament; it is, after all, only because Jane *lacks* this crucial information that she is in the predicament in the first place. What, for all practical purposes, Jane needs to determine is what it is in her best interests to do, given that the crucial information about John's current state of mind is *unknown;* but if it is stipulated that the ideal chooser knows all present facts, the only thing the personal welfare norm can, in theory, be used to tell her is what it is in her best interests to do given that this crucial information *is* known. Thus we are faced with the problem of how to make the personal welfare norm applicable, in theory, to real-life predicaments such as Jane's.

The solution to this problem is simple enough; if we need to determine what is in our best interests given that we lack some crucial knowledge X (such as, in the case of Jane, John's present state of mind), then we simply attribute to the ideal chooser not complete knowledge of the past and present, but complete knowledge *except* for X. If knowledge of X is "withheld" from the ideal chooser, then (in his making a choice from the perspective of our best interests) he will not, so to speak, be choosing what is in our *unqualified* best interests. The ideal chooser will instead be choosing what is in our *qualified* best interests—that is, our best interests given that X is unknown. In short: our being able to use the personal welfare norm for prescribing what is in our "qualified" best interests makes it applicable to real-life predicaments resulting from any lack of knowledge whatever.

And, before concluding, let me say a word about the *utilitarian* norm to be introduced in the next chapter. This norm likewise is applicable to any real-life predicaments resulting from a lack of knowledge. In such cases, we need only to use it for prescribing not what maximizes expected utility *without qualification,* but what maximizes it *given* the absence of the knowledge we lack.

3
Equal Consideration of Everyone's Interests

3.1 THE UTILITARIAN NORM

So far we have determined what is to count as an ideal choice from the standpoint of one's personal welfare, a standpoint where one considers only one's own interests. We must now determine what is to count as an ideal choice from an *impartial* standpoint, a standpoint where one gives *equal* consideration to *everyone's* interests. Since we have already determined what is to count as a person's "interests," the problem now is to determine what is to count as "equal consideration." This problem, as I mentioned earlier, cannot be solved merely by an appeal to the way in which the phrase "equal consideration" is ordinarily used in everyday conversation, since this phrase may legitimately be given any number of different meanings, each equally consistent with ordinary usage. For example, everyone's interests might legitimately be said to have been given "equal consideration" where everyone's interests had been considered an exactly equal amount of *time*—say, sixty seconds—before making a decision. So I shall adopt one from among the innumerable possible criteria of "equal consideration" that are consistent with ordinary usage and defend it by other than linguistic means.

The criterion of equal consideration to be adopted and defended here is a variant of an ancient norm, some version of which is honored by every major religion of the world. This ancient norm is usually given the role of the fundamental norm of morality; however, that variant of this norm that I put forth as the criterion of equal consideration is not given this role in the moral theory defended here. Yet the role of equal consideration in this theory is, as we shall see, crucial. The ancient norm to which I refer is known as the golden rule: "Do unto others as you would have them do unto you." The criterion of equal consideration put forth here is a variant of the golden rule because it tells us to treat others as we would have them treat us, if we, not they, had to experience all the results of the treatment. In other words, choosing as you would were you to give equal consideration to the interests of everyone is choosing as if the interests of everyone to be affected by your choice were your own. If, as argued in chapter 2, interests (i.e., self-

Equal Consideration of Everyone's Interests 41

interest) can be analyzed in terms of experiences, what this comes down to is choosing as if the *experiences* of everyone to be affected by your choice were to be your own.

Say, for example, you were deciding whether to punch Archibald in the nose, which you no doubt would enjoy, but which would cause Archibald great pain. In order to give everyone's interests equal consideration in making your decision, you would have to place yourself in the shoes of all those who would be affected by your choice and ask yourself: If *I* had to experience the effects of my choice exactly as will all those who in reality will be affected by it, what would I choose to do? In this case, since (we may assume) the only two individuals affected by your choosing to punch Archibald in the nose would be you and Archibald, you are to ask yourself: If *I* had to experience the enjoyment I would derive from punching Archibald (which in reality I *would* experience) and also the pain Archibald would suffer (which in reality I would not experience, but am to assume I would experience nevertheless), then what would I choose to do? In imagining yourself experiencing Archibald's pain you must, of course, think of it as being not Archibald's pain itself, but an *exact reproduction* of his pain, since, technically speaking, you can only experience that which is qualitatively, rather than numerically, identical to the experience of another. And, although in reality your enjoyment and Archibald's pain might occur simultaneously, in asking yourself what you would choose to do if both experiences were to be yours, you are not to think of *yourself* as experiencing them simultaneously; to make sense of both experiences as being yours, obviously you must imagine yourself as having them at different times.

This placing of yourself in the shoes of everyone to be affected by your choice, and choosing as if all their experiences were to be your own, is, roughly, what will be meant here by *giving everyone's interests equal consideration*. Of course an *ideal* choice from a perspective of equal consideration for everyone would have to be made from a standpoint of perfect knowledge, and also would have to confront differing probabilities. If we assume that differing probabilities are (ideally) to be handled in exactly the same way as in choosing what is in our best interests—that is, in the way prescribed by the norm of personal welfare set out in the last chapter—then an ideal choice from a perspective of equal consideration for everyone would be one made according to the following norm.

Choose that alternative which you would choose if:
(1) you knew, for each alternative, exactly what all of its possible sets of effects were upon the future experience of everyone, along with each set's probability of occurring;
(2) you assumed that, for whichever alternative you chose, each of its possible sets of effects upon anyone's future experience would be experi-

enced by yourself *n* times, where *n* is the numerator of a fraction that represents the set's probability of occurring; and

(3) you were influenced by, and only by, this knowledge, and this assumption.

As with the norm of personal welfare (sec. 2.2), we are to assume that, for purposes of experiencing each of the possible sets of effects *n* times, the fraction representing the set's probability of occurring has, for each of the sets, been given a common denominator. And, also as with the norm of personal welfare, we are to assume that, in experiencing these possible sets, we do so without any "diminishing returns." In fact, this norm *is* the norm of personal welfare, except that you are to know, and assume that you will experience, not only the possible effects upon your own future experience, but also the possible effects upon the future experience of everyone else; and you are to assume you will experience these possible effects exactly as the effects, if they occurred, would be experienced by these others themselves.

Given this assumption, the best choice for you becomes not necessarily the one that can be expected to result in the best sentient states for yourself, but the one that can be expected to result in the best sentient states generally, no matter whose they might be. So if, for convenience, we refer to positive sentient states simply as *utility*, what the above norm prescribes is that expected utility be maximized throughout the universe, and as such it qualifies as being one version of what is typically called "the principle of utility." Thus the above norm—the one that delineates for us what an ideal choice from a perspective of equal consideration for everyone is—will be referred to here as the *utilitarian* norm. And that alternative one would choose from the ideal standpoint specified by this norm will be referred to here as that alternative which maximizes *expected utility*. To be more precise, the alternative will be referred to as the one that maximizes expected utility if, from this ideal standpoint, knowledge was limited to that of what each alternative's *possible* sets of effects and their probabilities of occurring were. If, from this ideal standpoint, we knew instead what each alternative's *actual* effects would be (if, in other words, all probabilities were 100%), then the alternative that would be chosen will be referred to here as the one that maximizes, not *expected utility*, but *actual utility* or (simply) *utility*.

The utilitarian norm, as it has been formulated here, is cumbersome to state in full; therefore, throughout this discussion I shall adhere to the following shorthand terminology. Since choosing from the ideal standpoint specified by this norm is what is to be meant here by choosing in such a way that "equal consideration is given to the interests of everyone," I shall state the utilitarian norm simply as: "Choose that alternative which you would choose if you were to give equal consideration to the interests of everyone." In general, anything of the form "that X which you would choose if you were to give equal consideration to the interests of each individual in group D" is to be taken as short for "that X which you would choose if: (1) you knew, for each alternative, exactly what all of its possible sets of effects were upon the future experience of each individual in group D, along with each set's probability of occurring; (2) you assumed that, for whichever alternative you chose, each of its possible sets of effects upon the future experience of any individual in group D would be experienced by yourself exactly n times, where n is the numerator of a fraction that represents the set's probability of occurring; and (3) you were influenced by, and only by, this knowledge, and this assumption." Group D may, of course, be any group whatever, such as the group consisting of those in a certain family, or of those at present in a certain nation, or even (in Rawls-like fashion) of those at present who are the worst-off within a certain nation. I shall refer to the group consisting of those individuals to which some norm (or standard) requires that equal consideration be given as the *domain* of that norm (or standard). Accordingly, the domain of the utilitarian norm ("Choose that alternative you would choose if you were to give equal consideration to the interests of everyone") is the "universal" domain of every being, anytime, anywhere. On the other hand, the norm "Choose that alternative you would choose if you were to give equal consideration to the interests of everyone who is at present a citizen of your country" is considerably more limited in its scope; its domain includes only current citizens of one's country.

I shall contend that, morally speaking, often it is not the utilitarian norm with its universal domain, but one of its many variations with a more limited domain, that we should follow; and, more often still, we should follow neither the utilitarian norm nor any of its variations, but some different sort of moral norm altogether. These contentions will be argued for in due course; now, however, I am interested only in having made clear exactly what is to be meant here by a norm's "domain," and what phrases of the form "that X which you would choose if you were to give equal consideration to the interests of each individual in D" are to be taken as short for.

3.2 THREE TYPES OF OBJECTIONS

Three types of objections are traditionally made against all versions of the utilitarian norm: objections on practical grounds, objections on moral grounds, and objections on conceptual grounds or grounds of logical coherence.

Objections on practical grounds arise from the absolutely enormous amount of factual information that a person would have to have in order to be certain of conforming to the utilitarian norm. As I have formulated this norm, a person would in principle need to know all the possible effects of each alternative upon the lives of everyone throughout all eternity, along with all the relevant probabilities—a mind-boggling amount of information indeed. Of course, most possible effects upon the lives of individuals far removed temporally or spatially would either be of only minute importance or have only a minute probability of occurring, and thus for all practical purposes could be disregarded. But even so, the amount of information necessary for knowing what the utilitarian norm prescribes would usually be overwhelming, an amount of information far beyond the reach of any ordinary mortal. The practical objection arising from these considerations is that, because our information is so incomplete and because we are all so subject to rationalizing, we might well *think* we are doing what the utilitarian norm prescribes, yet all the while really be doing great harm. In short: the difficulty there is in gathering enough information for compliance with the utilitarian norm leaves it forever subject to dangerous misapplication. Not only that, but interpretations of what the utilitarian norm prescribes would inevitably differ greatly from person to person, and these differing interpretations would, so it is further objected, generate a disastrous lack of uniformity in people's behavior. Clearly, much can be said in support of these practical objections, and much of the argument throughout this book will be directed toward determining to what extent objections of this type do, and to what extent they do not, justify constraints upon the use of the utilitarian norm and norms closely related to it.

Objections against the utilitarian norm on grounds of *morality* are based on claims that this norm contravenes what we know "intuitively" to be the requirements of justice, or contravenes other "intuitively" known requirements of morality. Those making this type of objection argue that we just "know" certain things to be morally wrong—things like slavery, punishing innocent people, breaking promises, and killing innocent people—yet with a little imagination we can easily envisage cases where doing just these things would in fact maximize expected utility and thus be prescribed by the utilitarian norm; therefore, it is concluded, use of the utilitarian norm in these and numerous other such cases is morally objectionable. Another way of stating essentially the same objection is as follows. Utilitarianism tells us to choose as if we were one single individual—namely, the "ideal chooser"—while, in reality, we are separate, distinct individuals; for this reason, a utilitarian code of morality sanctions any sacrifice at all of the individual for the sake of the group (as represented by this ideal chooser), no matter how "outrageous" this sacrifice might be (see, e.g., Rawls 1971, secs. 29–30; Norton 1976, 280). Whether the code of morality defended *here* is subject to this type of objection remains to be seen.

Objections of the third type—those on grounds of logical coherence or conceptual grounds—are often among the most difficult of all to answer satisfactorily, since answering them often requires a prior resolution of some of the more difficult issues in the philosophy of mind, metaphysics, or epistemology—issues far beyond the scope of this inquiry. This is one reason why I shall not pursue any such objections beyond the following section. (For the latest conceptual challenge to the utilitarian norm, or rather to the view of the self and self-interest that underlies it, see Parfit 1984. Parfit's arguments are far too complex for me to attempt any quick rebuttal, and with a lengthier treatment we would quickly become mired in metaphysical issues well beyond the scope of this inquiry.) The other reason I shall not pursue conceptual objections beyond the next section is that, although these objections are often among the most difficult to answer satisfactorily, they also, fortunately, often pose the least threat to the utilitarian norm; of the two versions of this type of objection commented upon in the next section, the first is so contrary to common sense that it is difficult to take seriously, while the second is such that, even if one of its many variations is sound, it would not be fatal.

3.3 TWO CONCEPTUAL OBJECTIONS

The first of the two conceptual objections I want to comment upon here takes the form of denying that we can ever know anything at all about the "inner" mental states or experiences of others. Since the utilitarian norm as formulated here requires us to choose as if we personally were to experience the effects of our choice upon the experiences of others, if we could never know anything at all about these experiences we would never have any basis for making this choice—a serious objection indeed. The common-sense way of justifying beliefs about the inner mental states of others is by an appeal to some version of the argument from analogy, an argument that proceeds essentially as follows. Since other people's physical behavior is strikingly similar to my own, and since my own behavior is (I know) always correlated with certain inner mental states, it is probable that other people's behavior is also correlated with certain inner mental states, ones strikingly similar to my own. When other people touch a hot stove, for example, they behave in a way strikingly similar to the way I behave when I touch a hot stove. I know that in such cases my own behavior is always correlated with pain; therefore (by analogy with my own case) it is probable that other people's behavior in such cases is always correlated with pain too. Yet, as perfectly reasonable as the argument from analogy might seem, this argument is said by certain philosophers to contain a fatal flaw of logic (e.g., Strawson 1959, chap. 3). Because of this allegedly fatal flaw we are left, some have concluded, with no knowledge at all about the "inner" mental states of others.

But surely such an extreme conclusion—and thus any objections to the utilitarian norm based on it—cannot be taken very seriously. I am certainly prepared to take seriously the conclusion that our beliefs about other minds can be only highly probable at best, but not the conclusion that we can have no knowledge about other minds at all. If we had no knowledge at all about other minds, this would entail its being just as probable as not that other minds do not even exist. Such a complete skepticism not only borders on the psychotic (if taken seriously), but would have truly shocking ramifications concerning how one should treat others. Admittedly, the solution to the philosophical problem of how we are able to know anything about other minds still, to some extent, eludes us, as does, for that matter, the solution to the problem of how we are able to know anything about anything at all. But it has been said that we need not await the final solution to the philosophical problem about perception in order to perceive; similarly, we need not await the final solution to the philosophical problem about knowledge of other minds in order to have such knowledge.

The second conceptual objection I want to comment upon here challenges the logical coherence of our being able to "put ourselves in the shoes of others"—that is, of our being able to assume, as the version of the utilitarian norm formulated here requires us to do, that we shall experience exact reproductions or duplicates of certain experiences of others (namely, those experiences of others resulting from whichever alternative we choose). This challenge is weaker, and therefore more credible, than the challenge of the complete skeptic just discussed. The claim is not that it is logically impossible for us to know anything at all about, or experience anything at all similar to, the experiences of others; the claim is only that it is logically impossible to know or experience genuine *duplicates* of other's experiences, even though we might know or experience what comes very close to being a duplicate.

This claim can be argued for in a number of ways, one of these being as follows. The utilitarian norm asks us to choose by assuming that we shall have to experience duplicates of the experiences of all those affected by our choice. But if, while we were supposedly experiencing these duplicates of other people's experiences, we retained the memory of our own prior experiences, then what we would be experiencing could not be genuine duplicates after all; what we would be experiencing could not be genuine duplicates since in reality other people's experiences do not occur against this background of our own personal memories—a background that has to affect or color all of our experiences somewhat. What we would be experiencing might be very *similar* to these other people's experiences but, as long as we retained our personal memories, could not possibly be *exact* reproductions of these experiences. On the other hand, if while supposedly experiencing these duplicates of other people's experiences we did not retain any personal memories from the duplicate of one person's experiences to the duplicate of another person's experiences, then there would be no basis for saying that "we" remained one and the same person all the while. All there would be is these duplicates of different people's experiences popping in and out of existence, with nothing at all to relate them either to us or to one another. The essence of personal identity would be lost. So if we interpret the assumption about our having to experience duplicates of other people's experiences as allowing us to retain our personal memories from one set of duplicate experiences to another, then we would not really duplicate the experiences of others exactly. If, on the other hand, we interpret it as forbidding us from retaining any memories from one set of duplicate experiences to another, then it could not be us, or indeed any person, who was experiencing the experiences, since any personal identity transcending the individual sets of duplicate experiences would necessarily be absent. Either way, so it would be argued, the assumption calls for something that is logically impossible.

It seems to me that one of the weaker points in this argument is the crucial presupposition that background memory is necessary for personal identity. Most of us would say that a person with severe amnesia, for example, has not changed in such a way as to make him a (numerically) different person from what he was before the amnesia, even though he has lost all his personal memories. Similarly, if we knew for certain that we were, sometime in the future, going to have to suffer the excruciating torture of, say, being dipped into boiling oil up to our waists, I do not think that most of us would find it any consolation to know also that just before being dipped we were going to fall victim to total amnesia; it seems that, in some deep sense that goes beyond mere bodily identity and is very hard to verbalize, *we* would still be the persons who were going to experience the pain. Accordingly, if the assumption about our having to experience duplicates of other people's experiences included the further assumption that we would always fall victim to total amnesia immediately before switching from one person's experiences to another's, then it seems that, in spite of these complete memory losses, our personal identity would not be lost. Equally important, the fact that we were gong to have to experience these duplicates of the pleasures and pains of other people would (and should) *matter* to us, even though we knew that we were also going to suffer this amnesia, just as the prospect of our being dipped into boiling oil would (and should) still matter to us, even though we knew that amnesia would immediately precede it. And, owing to the successive obliterations of personal memories, the exactness of the duplications would, of course, be preserved. So I suggest that the assumption in question, viewed in this way, is logically coherent after all. (For further elaboration of some of the logical questions that lurk in the background for a proponent of this utilitarian norm, but will I believe prove manageable [although, to be sure, not without a struggle], see Heyd 1983. Heyd focuses upon the logical coherence not of living part of the life of another, but of the closely related idea of reliving part of our own life, an idea the logical coherence of which [as distinct, of course, from the empirical possibility of which] is also presupposed by the utilitarian norm. Heyd concludes, incidentally, that this idea *is* logically coherent, although I find his "intuitions" about other matters, such as self-realization, to be rather off the mark.)

But let us now assume that my preceding line of argument proved unsuccessful, and thus it did become necessary to admit that experiencing duplicates of another's experiences is logically impossible. By no means would all be lost, even then. For one thing, it might be logically possible to experience duplicates of at least those *aspects* of another's experiences which are of intrinsic value and disvalue to him. That is, if we could not have experiences that were comparable to those of another in *all* respects, perhaps we could at least have experiences that were comparable in all *relevant* respects. Say, for example, it turns out that those aspects of our experiences which are of intrinsic value and disvalue are certain "hedonic tones" that are integrated into all experiences—hedonic tones roughly describable as, say, feelings of happiness and unhappiness; and say that these hedonic tones could be abstracted from the other aspects of our experiences. If so, then, for the utilitarian norm to work, it would not be necessary to be able to experience duplicates of *all* aspects of another's experiences; all that would be necessary is being able to experience duplicates of the hedonic tones of another's experiences. I see no reason why this would not be logically possible even if duplicates of all aspects of the experiences were not.

But we need not resort to such a controversial and currently unpopular thesis as that of "hedonic tones" in order to rescue the utilitarian norm—if indeed any rescue operation should become necessary. Even if it were logically impossible to know or experience an *exact* duplicate of another's experience, it is, I submit, logically possible to know or experience that which comes *close enough* to being an exact duplicate so that, for all practical purposes, it would do perfectly well. In trying to follow the utilitarian norm we can never aspire to any more than a high *probability* of success anyway, since there will always be practical, even if not logical, barriers to accumulating enough factual information for absolute certainty. If then it turns out that we must add to these practical barriers a logical barrier in the form of our not being able to know about or duplicate other people's experiences *exactly,* this by itself would not make enough difference to really make a difference, provided only that it is logically possible for us to know and have experiences that are *very similar* to those of others. In short: even if duplication were not logically possible, surely a high degree of similarity is, a high enough degree so that the above objection to the utilitarian norm would not prove to be fatal, even if it did prove to be sound.

3.4 PREFERENCE UTILITARIANISM

Although the version of the utilitarian norm formulated here—the "golden rule" version—is only one among many versions of the utilitarian norm that have been proposed, it is, I claim, the most satisfactory version. Its chief competitor—one especially popular with economists and political scientists—is that version of the utilitarian norm associated with "preference" utilitarianism. According to this version of the utilitarian norm, the alternative that maximizes utility is not, as with the golden rule version, the one that would be chosen from an ideal standpoint. Instead, the alternative that maximizes utility is the one that would satisfy on balance the most preferences, where equal weight is given to equally intense preferences no matter whose they might be. (I do not find it natural to speak, as does the preference utilitarian, in terms of "satisfying" preferences. Desires, not preferences, are the sort of thing we "satisfy." Preferences are "complied with." But I shall go along with the preference utilitarian's way of speaking, nevertheless.) And, once again, the preferences upon which the preference utilitarian concentrates are people's *actual* preferences, not what they *would* prefer under ideal conditions of perfect knowledge, and so on. (Thus R. M. Hare's version of utilitarianism [1981], even though formulated in terms of preferences, is not preference utilitarianism, since the preferences upon which Hare focuses are ideal ones.)

Why preference utilitarianism should be so popular, particularly among social scientists, I do not know, but I suspect its popularity has something to do with the ease of determining exactly what people's actual preferences are; all we need do is ask them, or observe the choices they make. We thereby avoid having to determine what people *would* prefer under ideal conditions. But any simplicity achieved by this version of utilitarianism is purchased at the price of a number of serious difficulties to which it, and thus that version of the utilitarian norm associated with it, are subject. So as to provide at least a rough idea of why I think the version of the utilitarian norm adopted here is more satisfactory, let me simply list, without comment, some of these difficulties. ("Desire" utilitarianism, which is the same as preference utilitarianism except that it is formulated in terms of actual desires rather than actual preferences, is subject to exactly the same difficulties.)

(1) According to preference utilitarianism, in deciding which alternative to choose we must take into account not only the *number* of preferences that each alternative satisfies, but also the *intensity* of each preference; yet we are given no satisfactory answer to the question: Which alternative are we to choose as between one that satisfies the greatest number of preferences, and one that satisfies preferences that are more intense?

(2) Since with preference utilitarianism we do, in making our calcula-

tions, need to take into account the intensity of people's preferences, we thus need a way of adding together *intersubjectively* valid units of preference intensity, something no one has found a satisfactory way of doing.

(3) Any serious attempt at applying preference utilitarianism would soon encounter the well-known paradox of which alternative should be chosen where A is preferred to B, B to C, and C to A.

(4) Preference satisfaction might be capable of being maximized only by manipulating people's minds so as to allow them only those sorts of preferences which *can* readily be satisfied, thus raising the specter of using preference utilitarianism to justify various forms of "brainwashing."

(5) People's preferences are notoriously subject to change; what a person prefers at one time of day, or at one age in life, might well be entirely different from what he prefers at another time of day, or at another age in life. For purposes of preference utilitarian calculations, which of people's always-changing preferences are to be taken as the relevant ones? The most natural answer to this question has to be that the relevant ones are the ones people have at precisely the time at which the utilitarian decision in question is to be made. But then what about those people who, at this time (or at whatever other time might be chosen as the relevant one), are depressed and who, as a result, temporarily prefer to be dead than alive; what about those who at this time are children with very immature preferences; what about those who at this time, being mentally ill, are plagued with irrational preferences; what about all those who at this time, due to a mistake of fact, have preferences they otherwise would never have had? It is outrageous for the preference utilitarian to hold these people committed to the satisfaction of these preferences just because they happen to have them at whatever time is chosen as the relevant one.

One way to avoid this last difficulty is to hold that the relevant preferences are not those a person *does* have at some given time, but those the person *would* have if fully rational, in a normal state of mind, aware of all relevant facts, and so on. But then the utilitarian norm resulting from a move to ideal preferences such as these would no longer be the one associated with preference utilitarianism, since preference utilitarianism focuses only on actual preferences. This norm would instead be similar or identical to that version of the utilitarian norm adopted here, a version that avoids all the above difficulties. It is therefore, I submit, the more satisfactory version.

3.5 THE UTILITARIAN STANDARD

So far I have been focusing upon the utilitarian *norm,* as most discussions of utilitarianism do. Recall, however, how criteria are being classified for purposes of this inquiry. According to this classificatory scheme, as set out in Section 1.2, criteria can be in the form not just of norms, but of values as well. What is of fundamental value from a utilitarian perspective is, of course, expected utility.

As explained in Section 1.2, expected utility, as does any value, forms the basis for a standard in terms of which alternatives may be evaluated. According to this standard—which we may call the *utilitarian* standard—some alternative A is "better," or "more justified" than some other alternative B if and only if A has more expected utility than B. What is meant here by A's having *more expected utility* than B is that we would choose A over B, were we choosing from that ideal standpoint implicit in the utilitarian norm. Or, in terms of our "shorthand" terminology (sec. 3.1), A is "better" than B if and only if we would choose A over B, were we to give everyone's interests equal consideration. And notice, incidentally, that A and B most certainly need not be alternative acts; they may be, for example, alternative events, or alternative states of affairs.

Although some version of the utilitarian norm (usually called the "principle of utility") is that around which most utilitarian theories revolve, a utilitarian criterion in the form of a *standard* is actually more plausible. As I shall argue in the next chapter, the most plausible way to use a utilitarian criterion is for purposes of evaluation. To be more precise, I shall argue that its most plausible use is for evaluating what I shall call *social-pressure systems.* And since the existence of a social-pressure system is a "state of affairs," this amounts to using the criterion for evaluating certain states of affairs. But a utilitarian criterion used for purposes of evaluating alternatives must be in the form of a standard, not a norm, since, strictly speaking, evaluations are made in terms of standards (see again sec. 1.2). So, if I am right, the most plausible way to use a utilitarian criterion is as a standard and, accordingly, it is the utilitarian *standard*, not the utilitarian *norm*, around which the utilitarian theory proposed here revolves. Contrary to most utilitarian theories, the role (as set out in sec. 6.7) played by the utilitarian *norm* in this theory is relatively small.

4
Social-Pressure Systems

4.1 THE STANDARD OF EVALUATION

Moral controversy will always be with us. Current controversies rage between supporters and opponents of abortion, of euthanasia, of "reverse discrimination," and so on. How should we go about trying to determine who is right in such controversies? How, that is, should we go about trying to determine which of alternative moral norms being advocated is most justified? According to what *standard* should moral norms be evaluated?

I propose that moral norms be evaluated in terms of the utilitarian, or equal consideration, standard set out in the last chapter. In other words, I propose that moral norms be evaluated in terms of that standard according to which an alternative is justified to the extent that it would be chosen over other alternatives if, in choosing, everyone's interests had been given equal consideration. According to this standard, the alternative that would be *most* justified would be the one that, from this ideal standpoint, would be chosen over *all* alternatives. Such an alternative would exemplify the ideal of equal consideration.

I am not proposing that the utilitarian standard be the only criterion we use for evaluating moral norms. I shall myself make use of other criteria here, such as, for example, that of being relatively easy to comply with (see chap. 5). Rather than the utilitarian standard being our *only* criterion, I am proposing that it be our *ultimate* criterion, the one to which we turn whenever appeal to other, less abstract values and standards fails to settle the issue to everyone's satisfaction. And, as our ultimate standard, any other, less abstract values and standards to which we may appeal must of course be justifiable, ultimately, in terms of it as well.

Evaluating moral norms in terms of the utilitarian standard is (roughly speaking) to evaluate them in terms of their consequences; if their consequences are "good," the norms should be given a high evaluation; if their consequences are "bad," a low evaluation. So far, so good. But now we are faced with a question. Strictly speaking, norms *per se* do not have consequences; strictly speaking, the sorts of things that have consequences are, instead, acts, courses of action, states of affairs, events, and so on. Of course an act, one sort of thing that may be said to have consequences, can be *in compliance with* a norm but, even so, it is the act in compliance with the norm, not the norm *per se* that is the bearer of the consequences. The question we are faced with then is: How can norms be evaluated in terms of their consequences if norms themselves, viewed in isolation from any acts that may be in compliance with them, do not, strictly speaking, *have* consequences?

The most natural answer to this question, the answer given most often by those who propose evaluating norms in terms of their consequences, is that our evaluation of norms should focus on the consequences of *acts* that are in compliance with them. If the consequences of such acts are good, then the norms themselves should be viewed as good. Notice, however, that if we evaluate norms by focusing on the consequences of complying with them, we are not, strictly speaking, evaluating the norms directly, but only indirectly; what we are evaluating directly are acts, acts *in compliance with* these norms.

This may appear to be mere quibbling; norms are so closely associated with those acts which are in compliance with them that it seems only natural that the consequences of those acts be attributed to the norms themselves, and that the norms be evaluated in terms of these consequences. It is, however, precisely this—evaluating norms by focusing merely upon the consequences of complying with them—that is the key mistake of most utilitarian approaches, the mistake that makes most standard objections against utilitarianism possible. But if, in evaluating norms, we should not focus our evaluation upon the consequences of compliance with them, then upon what exactly *should* the evaluation focus? The answer to this question, and the rationale behind it, are crucial for understanding the theory of morality being proposed here and, ultimately, for understanding why this theory avoids the standard objections against utilitarianism.

The best way to explain my answer to this question, I think, is to begin by noting a few elementary things about the relationship between *moral norms* and *social pressure*. Moral norms—those of personal and political morality—are not, as are legal norms, brought about by the authoritative "decrees" of some group of people who are specifically authorized to bring them about. Rather, moral norms are brought about and maintained informally through the combined efforts of ordinary people throughout the society who, each on his or her own initiative, and in his or her own way, exert social pressure for compliance with the norms. The most common kind of social pressure is simply criticizing those who do not comply with the norms, and praising those who do. But social pressure can and does take many other forms as well. We could, for example, spank those who do not conform and give lollipops to those who do. These are not, of course, forms of social pressure widely used upon adults, but are used upon children. Other kinds of social pressure include ostracism (having nothing to do with those who do not comply), reciprocal treatment (giving those who do not conform a "dose of their own medicine"), and ridicule. This last kind of social pressure—making an object of ridicule of the noncomplier—is typically used for social norms, such as norms of etiquette, which we take less seriously than norms of morality. Notice, finally, that (the "state of affairs" of) some moral norms X rather than other moral norms Y being backed with social pressure has *consequences,* just as complying with X rather than Y has.

Let us now return to the crucial question posed above: If, in evaluating moral norms in terms of consequences, we should not focus upon the consequences of complying with them, then upon what exactly *should* we focus? My preliminary answer is, quite simply, that, rather than focusing upon the consequences of *complying* with the norms, we should instead focus upon the consequences of *their being backed by social pressure*.

4.2 SOCIAL-PRESSURE COMBINATIONS

Before I explain the rationale behind evaluating moral norms by focusing upon the consequences of their being backed by social pressure, we must first attend to one complication: which moral norms it would have the best consequences to back with social pressure would depend in part upon the *amount* and *form* of social pressure there was to be. If, for example, the amount of social pressure there was to be were enormous, then probably those moral norms it would have the best consequences to back with *this* social pressure would be ones that were not especially demanding in what they required of us; enormous social pressure for compliance with moral norms that *were* especially demanding would probably be disastrous, resulting in a dramatic increase in anxiety-related psychological disorders, and the like. On the other hand, if the amount of social pressure there was to be were unusually light, then especially demanding moral norms, which served to offset this unusually light social pressure, might be just the right thing. And which *form* of social pressure there was to be as between, say, the alternatives of criticism, ridicule, and physical force might well affect which moral norms would be optimal also. In short, for different amounts and forms of social pressure, different moral norms would be optimal. The problem this poses is: For purposes of determining which moral norms it would have the best consequences to have backed with social pressure, exactly what amount and form of social pressure are we to assume there would be? No matter what we assumed, it seems we would thereby be stacking the deck in favor of some norms and against others.

Let me try to state this problem with the help of some new but, I think, useful terminology. Let us call that norm which some amount and form of social pressure are directed toward achieving compliance with, or that value it is directed toward having exemplified, the *object* of the social pressure. Compliance with the norms and the exemplification of values results from people having "dispositions" or "inclinations" to behave in appropriate ways. So we *could* perhaps take the objects of social pressure to be these dispositions or inclinations. But it is, I think, simpler and more straightforward just to take the objects to be the norms and values that the social pressure is directed toward achieving compliance with, or having exemplified. In this way, with social pressure directed toward achieving compliance with the norm "Pay your debts," or toward having the virtue of courage exemplified, the norm "Pay your debts," or the virtue of courage, would then be the "object" of this social pressure. Using this terminology, the problem before us can now be stated as follows: we cannot determine which moral norms would make the best *objects* of social pressure without knowing something about what *amounts* and *forms* of social pressure there are to be.

And, to complicate the problem further, in determining which objects of social pressure there should be, we might well need to know also something about the *scope* of the social pressure there is to be. By the *scope* of some social pressure, I mean the places or, to be more exact, the societies (and groups within societies) throughout the world where the social pressure is found.

What then is the solution to this problem? It is, I submit, simply to broaden the range of our evaluations somewhat; instead of asking which moral norms it would be best to have as the objects of social pressure, let us ask instead which *combinations* of (1) object, (2) amount, (3) form, and (4) scope of social pressure it would be best for there to be. Such combinations of object, amount, form, and scope I shall, for convenience, refer to as *social-pressure combinations*. Evaluating moral norms by focusing upon social-pressure combinations that have the norms as their objects has this advantage. It allows us to combine each norm with that amount and form of social pressure most appropriate for it, thereby giving none an advantage for purposes of the evaluation.

One final note. Alternative social-pressure combinations may differ altogether in the object, amount, and form of social pressure that go to make them up but, in order for them to be said to be "alternatives," their *scopes* would have to overlap, at least to some extent. In any case, whenever alternative social-pressure combinations are evaluated here, let us, unless I state otherwise, simply assume that their scopes are identical, the scope of each being contemporary Western society.

I began this chapter by saying that moral norms should be evaluated not in terms of the consequences of complying with them, but, roughly speaking, in terms of the consequences of having them backed with social pressure. Now I can be more precise. What I am really saying is that moral norms should be evaluated in terms of the consequences of the social-pressure combinations of which they happen to be the objects—that is, in terms of what it would be like for these combinations to exist. Or, stated more fully, they should be evaluated according to whether the social-pressure combinations of which they are the objects are ones we would choose that there be, were we to give equal consideration to the interests of everyone.

4.3 THREE-DIMENSIONAL EVALUATION

As I also said at the beginning of this chapter, it is crucial that we understand exactly *why* moral norms should be evaluated from this rather unorthodox perspective, a perspective that focuses not upon the consequences of compliance with the norms, but upon the consequences of the social-pressure combinations of which they are the objects. Now that this perspective is clear, let us concentrate on the reason for it. The reason, in short, is this: to focus upon the consequences of social-pressure combinations is to undertake an evaluation along not just the one or, at most, two dimensions along which moral norms are normally evaluated; it is to undertake an evaluation along three different—and equally relevant—dimensions. So only by an evaluation from this rather unorthodox perspective do we get the *complete* picture.

Let me explain. Take any given social-pressure combination C, which has as its object some moral norm N. To determine the consequences of C's existence, we need to take into account, first, the consequences of people *complying* with N. That is, we need to take into account the consequences of *successful* compliance. The need for evaluation along this dimension—that of compliance—is of course widely recognized. It is, indeed, the one and only dimension along which moral norms are normally evaluated. For a complete picture, however, we need to take into account also how many people who try to comply are likely not to succeed, how many people are likely not even to try, and what the consequences are of these *failures* to comply. The need for evaluation along this dimension—that of *non*compliance—is not widely recognized, and thus evaluation along this dimension is rarely undertaken. But, in order to determine the desirability of C's existence relative to the existence of alternatives, we obviously *do* have to undertake an evaluation along this dimension. Finally, to determine the desirability of C's existence, we need also to take into account the costs of *maintaining* C's existence. These would be costs in the form of the time and energy that must be expended in order for the social pressure called for by C to continue to exist, and costs in the form of any anxiety, guilt, and so on, that this social pressure would generate—costs that may be referred to as the *social-pressure* costs of C. The more complex the norm that is the object of C, or the greater the self-sacrifice demanded by this norm, the higher these costs will tend to be. The need for evaluation along this dimension—that of social-pressure costs—is recognized in the literature least of all and, therefore, evaluation along this dimension is virtually never undertaken. Evaluation from the perspective being advocated here, on the other hand, obviously does require evaluation along this dimension; it obviously does require that we take social-pressure costs fully into account. (Aside from one exception, I am not aware of *any* other moral theory explicitly designed to take social-pressure costs fully into account. The one exception is the theory set out by Richard B. Brandt (1979), and I question whether even Brandt, with his focus upon what he calls "moral systems," accomplishes this as straightforwardly or as thoroughly as does a focus upon social-pressure combinations.)

The terminology of "social-pressure combinations" is unfamiliar and somewhat cumbersome. Actually, however, in evaluating moral norms here, I shall have little need to resort to this terminology. Those who evaluate moral norms by focusing upon the consequences of acts in compliance with them do not talk as if they were really evaluating acts, and norms only indirectly. Rather, they talk simply in terms of evaluating norms. Likewise, although I propose here to evaluate norms by focusing upon the consequences of there being social-pressure combinations with the norms as objects, I shall not talk as if I were really evaluating social-pressure combinations, and norms only indirectly. Rather, I also shall talk simply in terms of evaluating norms. So, in evaluating moral norms (or *codes* of moral norms) here, the term "social-pressure combination" will be used only rarely. Nevertheless, we must remember that the norms (or codes) *are* being evaluated not by focusing merely upon the consequences of compliance with them, but by focusing instead upon the consequences of social-pressure combinations (or entire "systems," as explained in sec. 4.5) with them as objects. For, as we have seen, it is only by means of this somewhat unorthodox focus that our evaluation will provide us with a complete, "three-dimensional" picture.

4.4 PRACTICAL APPLICATIONS

The reason we evaluate things is, of course, to aid us in deciding what to *do*, to help us in choosing how to *act*. Evaluation, in other words, is a practical activity, done not for its own sake, but for the sake of guiding behavior. But then exactly what sort of behavior are evaluations of *moral norms* supposed to guide? Here again our first impulse, the most natural impulse, is to think in terms of compliance. Just as we tend naturally to think that the *focus* of our evaluations should be the consequences of compliance (see above), we tend also to think that the *practical application* of these evaluations should be that of indicating to us which norms to comply with.

But here again what we tend naturally to think is wrong. The most *direct* practical application of our norm evaluations usually is not, and should not be, that of telling us with which norms to comply. Our evaluations *may* serve this purpose, but the connection between our evaluations and our compliance decisions is usually not simple and direct. That is because there is a factor other than how justified the norms are that must be taken into account in deciding which ones to comply with: this other factor is social pressure or, in other words, how society "punishes" or "rewards" us for our compliance or noncompliance. The very purpose of social pressure is that of making it normally in our best interests to comply with those norms which are the objects of the social pressure, even though compliance with these norms may not otherwise have been in our best interests *and* even though they may not be the norms we happen to have evaluated most highly (i.e., think most justified). So even though we may not think the norms that our society backs with social pressure are the ones that are most justified, because of this social pressure, it normally is in our best interests to comply anyway. And if it is in our best interests to comply anyway, most of us will, most of the time, do so. Take, for example, the person who believes that moral norms prescribing that he commit acts of terrorism are more justified than the norms, backed by social pressure in his society, that prohibit terrorism; he probably will, because of this social pressure, comply with society's norms in spite of this belief. And the fact that most of us will, most of the time, comply even when we consider other norms to be more justified is, as this example suggests, a very good thing. If social pressure were not successful in generally persuading people to comply with society's norms, then not only would we be constantly harassed by fanatics of all sorts, but the very uniformity and predictability in people's moral behavior that a moral code must generate would be impossible (see chap. 5). In sum, normally people's evaluations of moral norms *are* not and (for the good of society) *should* not be the main factor to which they appeal for determining which moral norms to comply with; the main factor is and, in most cases, should be social pressure. (On the other hand, social pressure should not, ideally, be so intense as to stifle *all* deviations for reasons of conscience from society's morality; social pressure this intense would stifle any change in morality for the better. But I shall not pursue this matter further here, since it is discussed in detail in chapter 11.)

If we normally do not, and probably should not, evaluate moral norms primarily to determine which ones to comply with, then we have come back to my original question: What practical application do these evaluations serve? What sort of behavior do they serve to guide? The correct answer, I think, is that these evaluations do, and should, serve mainly to guide us not in our own "compliance" decisions, but in our decisions as to which moral norms to help bring about and maintain *social pressure* for compliance with.

So as to distinguish these decisions—that is, ones concerning which norms to help support—from our compliance decisions, let us call them *support* decisions. We support a norm, or value, in doing something that, in one way or another, contributes to *social pressure* in support of the norm, or value. The most common means of support include praise, blame, moral persuasion, and criticism. In deciding to criticize, or publicly blame, a person for not complying with some norm N, we are, in effect, deciding to "support" N. (Deciding to comply with N ourselves *may* be one thing that contributes somehow to social pressure in support of N. So perhaps we *could* think of the category of support decisions as including, but by no means being limited to, compliance decisions. My inclination, however, is [somewhat arbitrarily] to exclude compliance decisions from the category of support decisions, since this way of talking is the most convenient way for purposes of this theory. So, as I shall be using these terms, it is possible for a person to *comply* with some moral norm N, while actually *supporting* some alternative moral norm N'. Compliance without support is common practice with legal norms, where we may, for example, comply with current tax laws, while actively supporting extensive changes in these laws.)

Which norms and values to thus support, in *what* way, and to what *extent* are decisions all of us must constantly be making for ourselves. It is, I am claiming, in guiding *these* decisions—our support decisions—that our evaluations of moral norms have their main practical application. This is their main practical application because in deciding which moral norms to help support with social pressure, but not in deciding which moral norms to comply with, our choice is not seriously constrained by existing social pressure. Although there normally is, and should be, fairly intense social pressure for *compliance* with certain moral norms, there is relatively little social pressure for *supporting* these norms. In other words, in choosing which norms to help support through praise, blame, persuasion, and, in general, our own social pressure, society gives us far more freedom than in choosing which norms to comply with, therefore people can, and sometimes do support, through argumentation as well as through praise and blame, moral norms that are outrageous; as long as they merely "advocate" these norms rather than comply with them, any social reprisal will normally be relatively mild. Compare with this the freedom our society allows people in their criticism of the law; people are generally free to be as outspoken as they please in their criticism of existing law, a freedom that does not, however, extend to their failing to comply with it. All this is of course exactly what we should expect from a society that values freedom of speech and conscience, as our society does and should (see sec. 7.3). In short: we are not, and should not be, in jeopardy of being "punished" socially nearly as much for what we say as for what we do—otherwise being a moral philosopher would be a rather dangerous occupation. Therefore, with relatively little social constraint upon our freedom to personally help bring about and maintain social pressure in support of whichever moral norms we think most justified, the main practical application of our moral evaluations is that of guiding our support decisions, not our compliance decisions. Since, however, this practical application of our evaluations, as well as the main rationale for the standard being proposed here for making these evaluations, are discussed in detail in Part IV, I shall not pursue this topic further now.

In sum, the purpose of this chapter so far has been to suggest no less than a fundamental change in the perspective from which we philosophize about moral norms. We usually do so from the general perspective of compliance. We usually evaluate norms by focusing upon the consequences of people's compliance, and we usually take the practical application of these evaluations to be mainly that of guiding decisions about our own compliance. But for the reasons I have been discussing, this general perspective is misguided. I suggest instead that we philosophize about moral norms from the general perspective of support for them through social pressure; that we evaluate them by focusing upon the consequences of there being social-pressure combinations with the norms as objects, and that we take the practical application of these evaluations to be mainly that of guiding our decisions about which norms personally to help support with social pressure. As I hope to show throughout the remainder of this book, such a shift in perspective has wide-ranging ramifications. As will become apparent as we proceed, if we focus upon social-pressure combinations, a utilitarian approach to the evaluation and justification of moral norms becomes far more plausible than otherwise. (Notice, for example, that this shift in perspective leaves recent objections against indirect utilitarianism, such as those by Bernard Williams 1985, chap. 6, inapplicable to this theory.) And (as we shall see in Part IV), only by our focusing upon social pressure combinations—or even better, upon entire social-pressure systems—does the connection between giving equal consideration to everyone's interests and our own self-interest become clear.

4.5 THE EQUAL CONSIDERATION SYSTEM

So far I have been discussing the use of the utilitarian, or equal consideration, standard only in connection with the evaluation of moral norms. Of course, I have not yet shown why we *should,* in evaluating moral norms, give equal consideration to the interests of everyone; I shall attempt to justify this in Part IV. But assuming now, for the sake of argument, that we should, then I see no reason why we should not give equal consideration to the interests of everyone in evaluating other kinds of social norms, and even social values, as well. In short, I view the utilitarian standard as one for evaluating not just moral norms, but any kind of social norms and values characterizable as informal.

A *social* norm or value is, as I understand it, simply a norm or value in support of which there is, or is supposed to be, some degree of social pressure. This social pressure may, as we have seen, take many different forms, and typically takes the form of criticism and praise. An *informal,* as opposed to a formal social norm or value is, roughly, one that does not come about through the decision of some recognized authority, as does law, but simply "evolves," as does morality, through the decisions of numerous people, none of whom are acting in any official capacity. The key to the difference between formal and informal social norms and values is that formal social norms and values, but not informal ones, come about through the decision of a person, or persons, fulfilling a certain *role* within some organization, group, or institution, a role that could have been fulfilled by some person, or persons, other than the ones who did fulfill it. Thus with formal social norms, but not with informal ones, it always makes sense to speak of them as emanating from an anonymous occupant, or occupants, of a role such as, for example, that of legislator for legal norms, corporation president or "boss" for company norms, coach or manager for team norms, and club president for club norms.

According to the theory being proposed here, the utilitarian standard is not directly applicable to the evaluation of any social norms and values that are formal, but is applicable to the evaluation of all that are informal. Informal social norms include not only norms of morality, but also norms that sociologists call folkways—that is, norms of etiquette, good taste, and so on—and even linguistic norms. In addition, informal social norms and values include those which are used for promulgating and evaluating formal ones; thus, by being directly applicable to the evaluation of *these* informal social norms and values, the utilitarian standard is therefore at least *indirectly* applicable to the evaluation of those which are formal (see, in particular, chap. 8).

This discussion has proceeded thus far as if we were assuming that norms and values could be evaluated fully in isolation, without taking into account their relationships with other norms and values. It is time to recognize that this assumption is unsound in principle, even though we shall be able to, indeed must, retain it in practice. But, in principle, norms and values are not independent; rather they are interrelated and mutually supporting.

Take, for example, a moral norm forbidding all racial discrimination. What would we have to take into account in deciding whether to recognize an exception to it for "reverse" discrimination, discrimination *in favor* of groups previously discriminated against? The purpose of such an exception would be that of allowing us to mitigate (through reverse discrimination) the unfair disadvantage at which prior discrimination had put these groups. One thing we would have to take into account would be whether the unfair disadvantage could be just as successfully mitigated without our having to recognize this exception. But then whether or not it could be would depend in part upon how it is best to construe *other* norms of morality—in particular, upon how it is best to construe moral norms requiring compensation for past wrongs. For, depending upon how it is best to construe these norms, a practice that amounted to reverse discrimination might be justified as compensation for a past wrong, thereby making any exception to the norm prohibiting racial discrimination unnecessary (since then the practice would not be "discrimination," but "compensation"). And how it is best to construe moral norms requiring compensation for past wrongs might, in turn, depend upon how it is best to construe still other moral norms, and so on. What I am trying to suggest is simply this: any adequate code of morality is made up of interrelated, mutually supporting norms that stand or fall, not independently, but as a whole.

But let us now take this matter yet a few steps farther. What sort of *moral* code is best for some society no doubt depends, in part, upon what norms of *etiquette, aesthetic* norms, *linguistic* norms, and so on, are best for that society, and vice versa. Moreover, notice the close relationship between informal social *norms* of all sorts, and informal social *values*. Values often serve to guide us in our attempts at complying with norms, especially those which are broadest in their scope, such as the general welfare norm to be discussed below (chap. 8). And, on the other hand, compliance with certain norms is a necessary condition for certain values being exemplified; for example, a person must generally comply with the sort of norms that prohibit falsehoods, cheating, and the like, in order to exemplify the virtue of honesty. Finally, given the vast amount of interaction between societies today, which informal social norms and values are best for any one society no doubt depends, in part, upon the norms and values of other societies. For, in deciding which norms and values are best for any one society, we must take such matters into account as their consistency with the norms and values of other societies, and what the advantages and disadvantages of this consistency are.

The conclusion to which this all leads is that, probably, the informal social norms and values of any sort, throughout the world, are, to a greater or lesser extent, interrelated and mutually supporting. So, in principle at least, the most appropriate units to focus upon in evaluating norms and values are probably not *individual* norms and values, but whole *systems* of norms and values. And since, in evaluating norms and values here, we are focusing upon the consequences of there being social-pressure combinations that have them as objects, for our purposes a "system" of norms and values amounts to a system of social-pressure combinations that have these norms and values as objects. (Or, as I shall be putting it, the norms and values are "part" of the system.) Let us call such a system a *social-pressure system*. The world's *current* social pressure system consists of all the informal social norms and values that, everywhere in the world, currently *are* supported by social pressure and, for each of them, the amount, form, and scope of social pressure there *is* in support of it. The *ideal* social-pressure system for the world consists of all the informal social norms and values that, anywhere in the world, it would be *best* to have supported by social pressure and, for each of them, the amount, form, and scope of social pressure it would be *best* to have in support of it. Both the world's current social-pressure system and its ideal system are "complete" systems because they are ones that include all social-pressure combinations for anywhere in the world. Because of the interrelationship of norms and values everywhere, we may perhaps think of a complete social-pressure system as we are sometimes told to think of the law—namely, as a "seamless web." And, because of these interrelations, in principle the most appropriate units upon which to focus our evaluations are probably not individual norms and values, but nothing less than complete social-pressure systems.

But I hasten to emphasize that this is the case only *in principle*. In practice complete social-pressure systems are obviously far too large and complex for any ordinary mortal to focus upon as a whole. Thus, in practice, we must be content with continuing to focus upon only one small part of such a system at a time (i.e., upon only, say, one moral norm, a relatively small set of moral norms, one value, or a relatively small set of values at a time).

On the other hand, we must not forget that the ideal result of any such piecemeal evaluation, the result we should try to approximate as closely as possible, is the result we *would* reach, if we *were* able to focus upon complete systems. Compare here the ideal judicial decision that, according to Ronald Dworkin, can, in principle, be reached only by a hypothetical judge (whom Dworkin calls "Hercules") who is able to focus upon complete legal systems (which Dworkin calls "theories of law"). (Dworkin 1977; see also chap. 9 below.)

Although, in practice, our evaluations can focus only upon minute parts of complete social-pressure systems—in this book my focus is upon moral norms for our society—it nevertheless does make perfectly good sense to examine what the best (i.e., most justified) social-pressure system is probably like in general. And this is what I shall conclude this section by briefly attempting to do. According to the theory being proposed here, the best social-pressure system is, of course, the one we would choose that there be were we to give equal consideration to the interests of everyone. Let us, for convenience, call this social-pressure system the *equal consideration* system. I shall conclude this section by examining very briefly what, in general, the equal consideration system is like.

I shall, in particular, concentrate upon whether the equal consideration system contains norms that manifestly contradict one another. What I mean by norms that *manifestly* contradict one another is ones that conflict *per se* (as opposed to *per accidens*) in that their conjunction is self-contradictory. It is at least arguable, I think, that all *moral* norms within the equal consideration system are consistent with one another; that, in other words, for there to be, everywhere in the world, social pressure for compliance with the same set of moral norms maximizes expected utility. This is arguable, since what a moral norm's content is, matters. Let me explain. There are certain kinds of informal social norms whose content is not important; what is important is that there be a certain degree of uniformity in complying with them. Take the linguistic norms that delineate what verbal and written "symbols," within a society's language, are to express what: it makes little, or no difference, for example, whether a society uses the symbol "hello," or "bonjour," or "guten tag" to express a greeting; what is important is that there be, within the society, a certain degree of uniformity in what linguistic symbols are used—enough uniformity so as to make communication easy. Now consider moral norms. Of course uniformity is important in morality also, especially uniformity within a society as opposed to uniformity between societies. But clearly with moral norms it is not only uniformity that is important, but also content. It is important, for example, whether people uniformly comply with the moral norm "Do not kill human beings, except in self-defense," or instead uniformly comply with the moral norm "Do not kill human beings, except in self-defense *and* except for euthanasia." Since with moral norms content as well as uniformity is important, it may well be that the moral norms of the equal consideration system are the same for all societies—these moral norms being the ones that have the "best" content. The moral norms of the equal consideration system would not, of course, be the same for all societies unless conditions in each were similar enough so that what was "best" would be very much the same in each. But it may well be that conditions in each *are* similar enough, or at least soon will be as modern transportation and mass communication continue to bring societies closer and closer together.

But now let us turn from norms of morality to norms of etiquette, good taste, and so on; in other words, to folkways. With respect to whether their content matters, folkways generally seem to be somewhat closer to norms delineating linguistic symbols than they are to norms of morality. It does not, for example, matter much whether it is held to be in good taste to eat with a fork or with chopsticks as long as, in what is held to be in good taste, there is a certain degree of uniformity. Content does matter with folkways sometimes, however. Take, for example, the ancient norms of good taste that required Chinese women to deform themselves by binding their feet. Because of the misery it caused women, this norm of good taste clearly was not one that was just as good as any other. Nevertheless, there clearly is no one best code of folkways that, because of its superiority over all alternatives, should exist everywhere. On the contrary, I should think it best that folkways not be the same everywhere if for no other reason than that this would be intolerably dull; variety, it is said, is the spice of life; so owing to our taste for spice, if nothing else, I should think it is variety from place to place in folkways that maximizes expected utility. Accordingly, I suggest that the equal consideration system does contain norms that blatantly contradict one another. It probably, for example, includes the norm "Eat with a fork" and at the same time includes the contradictory norm "Eat with chopsticks." It no doubt fails to maximize expected utility for there to be social pressure for compliance with each of these norms at the same time and place, but it probably does maximize expected utility for there to be social pressure for compliance with the former norm at some places while at the same time there is social pressure for compliance with the latter norm at other places, in which case the equal consideration system would include them both. And, although at one point in time it probably did not matter which places had which norm, once one of the norms *had* achieved predominance at a certain place, the mere fact of its predominance might then be the reason it would be best that it remain predominant; at *that* point change might well be more trouble than it was worth. So, in sum, the equal consideration system does no doubt contain norms that are inconsistent with one another; but with *moral* norms it probably tolerates much less inconsistency, if any at all, than with other types of norms, since with moral norms content, as opposed to mere uniformity, matters more than with other types of norms.

4.6 WHY PHILOSOPHY YIELDS NO FINAL ANSWERS

A very curious thing distinguishes philosophy from other disciplines: in philosophy there seems to be nothing of importance about which professional philosophers can *agree*—everything in philosophy seems to be chronically controversial. While impressive bodies of knowledge grow in other disciplines, philosophers seem forever unable to establish anything. This has led many to conclude that, therefore, all philosophic conclusions must be "relative" (or "subjective") where what is meant is that, in the final analysis, there is no way of showing any philosophic conclusions to be more justified than any others.

But this chronic disagreement has, I believe, a better explanation. Philosophy is, I suggest, essentially the study of what informal social norms and values (or standards) there should be. Philosophy, in other words, is concerned with social criteria—not so much with those which currently prevail (which are primarily the concern of the social scientist) as with those that *should* currently prevail, and why. In my view, there is little difference between what is being done by, for example, (1) the "ordinary language" philosopher engaged in conceptual analysis, (2) the traditional epistemologist (including the philosopher of science, of law, of history, of religion, and so on, to the extent that he or she is investigating criteria for justified knowledge claims), and (3) the moral philosopher working in the area of contemporary moral problems. They are all, I suggest, attempting to work out a "theory" about which, from among alternative informal social norms and values, should be generally accepted, or about how those which are already generally accepted should be understood. And attempting to work out how a norm or value should be understood goes, I suggest, beyond simply pointing out what its "core area" of application is (as do dictionary writers for linguistic norms); it includes attempting to work out, in part at least, how, *given* this core area, the norm's or value's borderline area should be "filled in." So, if I am right, "ordinary language" philosophers, traditional epistemologists, and moral philosophers have more in common than is, perhaps, generally recognized: they all focus on informal, social norms and values. The main difference between them is simply that the "ordinary language" philosopher focuses on those informal, social norms that delineate concepts such as *truth, mind,* and *justice,* (these being linguistic norms); the epistemologist focuses, in part, on those which delineate justified knowledge claims (which include, for example, any norms that delineate sound inductive or deductive reasoning); and the moral philosopher focuses on those which delineate morally right conduct (which include nonlinguistic norms such as those prohibiting murder, theft, etc.). But as legislators know from their experience with creating legal norms, because of changing conditions and new knowledge, norms and values are forever subject to revision. And as judges know from their experience with interpreting legal norms, because new and unexpected borderline cases are forever arising, the job of filling in the borderline areas of norms and values is never complete. Thus the philosopher's task of working out the best system of informal social norms and values—be these moral, linguistic, or epistemological—never comes to an end, any more than does the legislator's and judge's task of working out the best legal system. Their conclusions must always remain very much subject to revision in the light of changing circumstances, new knowledge, the discovery of hidden inconsistencies, and unexpected borderline cases. It is for this reason, and not at all because philosophic conclusions are "relative," that a body of settled knowledge fails to take root in philosophy as it does in other disciplines. So, although there may be no final answers in philosophy, there is progress.

But, it might be asked, are not conclusions about which informal social norms and values there should be just the sort of conclusions that *are* relative? I do not think so. As do scholars in other disciplines, philosophers possess a methodology—a "bag of tools"—that helps them distinguish conclusions that are justified form ones that are not. Among the more widely used of these tools are the "testing" of tentative conclusions by means of hypothetical examples, the rejection of useless complications by appeal (for instance) to Occam's razor, and the working-out of a "reflective equilibrium" (as described in chap. 9). But the ultimate criterion in terms of which informal social norms and values should be evaluated—that which more than anything else would rescue philosophic conclusions from relativity—is, I am arguing, the utilitarian, or equal consideration, standard.

Yet this criterion is not one to be appealed to *explicitly* very often; just like the general welfare norm in legislative and judicial reasoning (see chap. 9), it is to remain in the background, while most issues are decided by appeal to that which is less abstract.

4.7 IF EVERYONE ADOPTED THE UTILITARIAN STANDARD

In this chapter I have introduced what I take to be the method in terms of which informal social criteria should be evaluated, or justified. This method, which makes use of the utilitarian standard—tells us that informal social criteria are fully justified if and only if they are part of the social-pressure system we would choose that there be, were we to give everyone's interests equal consideration. Although this method is put forth as a way to justify informal social criteria of any sort, I shall, in the remainder of this book, concentrate upon its use only for *moral* justification—that is, the justification of moral norms, or entire codes of morality. A crucial aspect of this method is that of evaluating norms, or codes, by focusing upon the consequences of the *social-pressure system* of which they are a part, rather than upon the consequences of *complying* with them. As we saw, only by thus focusing upon social pressure, not merely compliance, can we get a complete, three-dimensional evaluation, one that gives us the whole picture, not just part of the picture.

I have been referring to the social pressure system that is most justified, in terms of this method, as the "equal consideration" system (sec. 4.5). For convenience, I shall refer to any codes of morality that are part of this system as *equal consideration,* or *EC* codes. A code of morality may be designed either for governing the behavior of individuals, or governing the behavior of governments. A code for governing the behavior of individuals—one that might contain norms prohibiting such things as stealing, lying, and cheating—I shall call a code of *personal* morality. A code for governing the behavior of governments—one that would contain norms such as those pertaining to the use of force against other countries—I shall call a code of *political* morality. For any society there is both an EC code of personal morality and an EC code of political morality, each of which is part of the equal consideration system.

With this terminology in mind, the overall structure of the theory being proposed here can be roughly diagramed as follows.

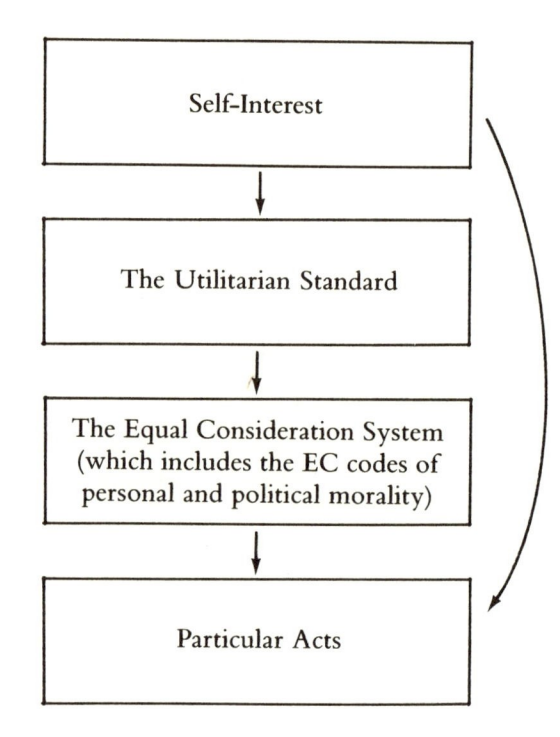

```
┌─────────────────────────┐
│      Self-Interest      │
└─────────────────────────┘
             │
             ▼
┌─────────────────────────┐
│ The Utilitarian Standard│
└─────────────────────────┘
             │
             ▼
┌─────────────────────────┐
│ The Equal Consideration │
│ System (which includes  │
│ the EC codes of         │
│ personal and political  │
│ morality)               │
└─────────────────────────┘
             │
             ▼
┌─────────────────────────┐
│    Particular Acts      │
└─────────────────────────┘
```

In this diagram an arrow from any one box A to any other box B means that B is justified in terms of A. The method proposed here for justifying a moral code is represented by the box with the utilitarian standard in it. And, for convenience, we may speak of this method as being that of evaluating moral codes in terms of the utilitarian standard. This convenient way of speaking should do no harm as long as we remember that there is more to this method than merely using the utilitarian standard; as we have seen, it also involves evaluating moral codes not solely from the perspective of compliance with them, but as parts of social-pressure systems.

Let me conclude this chapter with a brief look at what a society would be like where everyone adopted this method of moral justification. In such a society, rather than there being, as in our society, all sorts of differing fundamental criteria to which people appeal for justifying their norm conceptions—criteria ranging from intuition to papal interpretation of divine command—there would be only one: the utilitarian standard. And by a person's *norm conceptions,* I mean those norms which the person thinks should be backed by social pressure.

The first thing to notice about such a society is that the utilitarian standard, although fundamental, would by no means be the only criterion people in this society used for justifying their norm conceptions. Numerous other, less abstract norms and values would be relevant as well, criteria of the very sort to which people in our own society might well appeal (i.e., freedom, efficiency, equality, various moral norms, rights, etc.). Of course, in this hypothetical society each of these less abstract criteria would itself be justifiable ultimately only in terms of the utilitarian standard. And in principle, although not in practice, these less abstract criteria would not answer to the utilitarian standard individually, but as an entire system of interrelated, mutually supporting norms and values (sec. 4.5). The utilitarian standard, therefore, often would not be appealed to immediately by these people, but would remain in the background as the ultimate "court of appeal," while much of their everyday moral justification proceeded, as in our own society, in terms of these less abstract criteria.

Naturally, in this hypothetical society people would have differing views about exactly which less abstract criteria the utilitarian standard justified, and exactly how much weight each criterion should be given, all of which would contribute to differences among people in their norm conceptions. This brings us to the second thing to notice about this hypothetical society: in spite of everyone's using the same general method of justification, people's norm conceptions would still differ from person to person, especially in details, just as they do in our own society. In short, their final criterion—the utilitarian standard—would likely be interpreted in many different ways.

But is not the likelihood of many differing interpretations of the utilitarian standard, it might now be objected, good grounds for rejecting this method of justification? In section 5.1, I shall myself reject using the utilitarian *norm* as the fundamental *norm of morality* largely on just these same grounds—that is, on the grounds that this norm is always subject to many differing interpretations. The utilitarian standard, it might be said, is hardly any less likely than the utilitarian norm to generate differing interpretations; therefore ought it not to be rejected also?

I do not think so. It is true that, as I shall argue in section 5.1, for a *norm of morality* to be subject to many differing interpretations is indeed objectionable, and usually good grounds for rejecting it. Norms of morality are the sort of criteria that must be supported by social pressure, and successful support of a norm is unlikely unless, most of the time, there is substantial agreement about its interpretation. The utilitarian standard, however, *is not meant to be a norm of morality;* it is not even a norm, but a standard, a standard for evaluating informal social norms (and values). As such, it is not the sort of criterion that itself is supposed to be supported by social pressure. Society, partly from respect for freedom of conscience, can and should tolerate much greater differences in people's opinions about what norms *should* be supported by social pressure than it can in people's opinions about what sort of acts those norms that *are* supported by social pressure prescribe (see sec. 4.4 and chap. 11). Moreover, I am not aware of any reasonable criteria that have been proposed for evaluating moral norms that are any less subject to differing interpretations than the utilitarian standard. Criteria other than the utilitarian standard that have been proposed for evaluating moral norms include, for example, intuition, revelation, and Rawls's "original position" (which is compared with the utilitarian standard in chap. 12). For each of these criteria, opinions about what follows from it are not less controversial than would be opinions about what follows from the utilitarian standard. As Aristotle says: it is the mark of an educated man to look for precision in each class of things just as much as the nature of the subject admits.

But let me continue the examination of the hypothetical society where everyone adopted the method of moral justification proposed here. In this society, in spite of many differing interpretations of the utilitarian standard, a tolerably clear majority view would, through social pressure, eventually emerge on most (but probably not all) matters of morality. In our own society we have not just one standard of evaluation that admits of many differing interpretations, but many differing standards that admit of many differing interpretations. So if, in our own society, we manage, through social pressure, to nevertheless achieve a workable consensus on most matters of morality, we may assume the people in our hypothetical society would also. This underscores the point I tried to make above: society does not need nearly as much uniformity in people's opinions about what moral norms should be backed by social pressure as it does in their opinions about what those which *are* backed by social pressure prescribe.

In any case, we see that, with respect to people appealing to criteria much less abstract than the utilitarian standard for most everyday evaluations, and with respect to their having many differing norm conceptions yet nevertheless achieving, through social pressure, a workable consensus on most matters, this hypothetical society would not differ much from our own society today. But then if, in these respects, this hypothetical society did not differ very much from our own society, why, it might be asked, work toward uniformity in people's methods of moral justification anyway? What, in other words, would be the advantage of everyone's using the method of justification proposed here, rather than there being the hodge-podge of differing methods used now?

First of all, by everyone's using this method it is to be expected that people's differing norm conceptions, and hence society's prevailing moral norms, would, as time goes by, come to resemble the moral norms of the EC code to an ever greater extent, more so than would be likely without this uniformity in people's methods. Assuming that this method of moral justification is itself justified, as I argue it is (Part IV), and that therefore the EC code *is* the most justified one, this gradual trend would, of course, be all to the good. And a society in which everyone appealed to the utilitarian standard would, I suspect, be less likely than ours to produce people with norm conceptions as obviously incompatible with the norms of the EC code as those of a Hitler, or of a Reverend Jim Jones. Finally, although moral disagreements would be far from absent altogether, a common method of justification probably would not generate quite the degree of moral divisiveness that we find in our current society, a divisiveness that perhaps contributes more than we realize to the stress and insecurity of our times. With a common method people would know that, in principle at least, there always is a single, right answer—that which is justifiable in terms of the one standard everyone accepts as final. Thus they would always have a good reason for persevering in their attempts to resolve their disagreements by means of rational discussion, rather than resorting to the use of force to which those for whom there is no single, right answer are all too often driven.

Part II

PERSONAL MORALITY

5
The Direct Utilitarian Code

5.1 WHAT THE UTILITARIAN STANDARD DOES *NOT* JUSTIFY

With the completion of chapter 4, we now have before us the method of moral justification being proposed here. As we have seen, this method has two aspects. One is focusing our evaluations of moral norms, or codes, not merely upon the consequences of *compliance* with them, but instead upon the consequences of *social pressure* in support of them. As we saw, what this comes down to is an evaluation of them in terms of the consequences of the "social pressure" system of which they are a part. We also saw what the justification, or rationale, for this somewhat unorthodox focus is. Only by means of it will our evaluations be three-, not merely one- or two-dimensional; in other words, only by means of this somewhat unorthodox focus will everything be taken into account that should be taken into account. The second aspect of the method being proposed here is that of using the *utilitarian standard* for making these three-dimensional evaluations. But we have not yet seen what the justification for this aspect of the method is. The argument for justifying this aspect of the method—that is, the argument for justifying the utilitarian standard—I am postponing until Part IV of this inquiry. Let me explain why.

Part of the argument in Part IV will turn upon the relative merits (from a perspective of self-interest) of two social pressure systems. The first of these two systems is the one "derivable" from the utilitarian standard, from, in other words, giving *equal* consideration to everyone's interests—the social pressure system I have been referring to as the *equal consideration* system. The second is a system "derivable" from giving *special* consideration to the interests of some group, say whites as opposed to blacks. I refer to such a system as a *biased* one. Now for purposes of comparing the relative merits of these two systems we already have, I would think, a good enough understanding of what a biased system is like. But merely from what I have said so far about the equal consideration system, I doubt if we have a good enough understanding of it. Postponing the argument for justifying the utilitarian standard will allow us to examine the equal consideration system

75

in more detail first, so as to gain the understanding necessary for fully appreciating this argument.

An understanding of the equal consideration system appropriate for our purposes is gained by examining what codes of morality are inherent in it; in other words, by examining what codes are justifiable in terms of the utilitarian standard. In Part II of this inquiry, I shall focus on *personal* morality; in Part III, on *political* morality. Having examined these codes, the stage will then be set for arguing in Part IV that to justify codes of morality in terms of the utilitarian standard (as called for by the method of moral justification being proposed here) is *itself* justified, and with this argument the rationale for this method will be complete.

I propose that we begin our examination of what code of personal morality the utilitarian standard justifies with basics: Why should a society have a code of morality anyway? At least part of the answer is that a decent code of morality enables there to be the degree of security, and of trust in others, that is necessary in order for there to be mutually beneficial interaction among people. It makes this security and trust possible, in large part, by making possible a much greater degree of uniformity, and thus predictability, in people's behavior than there would otherwise be. In a society with a decent code of morality people will, because of this code, pay their debts, keep their promises, refrain from violence, tell the truth, and so on. Not all of the time, of course, but most of the time. Therefore, to this extent, there will be a certain uniformity, and thus predictability, in people's behavior, the kind of uniformity and predictability upon which security and trust depend. Making this uniformity, and thus predictability, possible is the job, or one of the main jobs, of a code of morality.

As a matter of fact, sometimes it might not make much difference if two societies differ in *what* their morality prescribes, as long as the morality of both generates an equal degree of uniformity. Say, for example, that the morality of society A is such that it motivates most people in that society to refrain from unprovoked violence against another no matter what, whereas the morality of society B, having a different norm with respect to physical violence, motivates most people to refrain from unprovoked violence against another only if he is not wearing a green hat. Although these societies differ in *what* their moralities prescribe with respect to physical violence, provided only that each society's moral norms are observed with an equal degree of uniformity, one can be equally secure against physical violence in either of them; to be just as secure in society B as in society A one need only, while in society B, refrain from wearing a green hat. To be sure, the fact that each of these moralities provides equal security against physical violence does not mean that, according to the utilitarian standard, they are equally justified; these moralities do not, for one thing, provide equal freedom to wear the hat of one's choice. Being able to generate uniformity does not by itself, as far as the utilitarian standard is concerned, make a morality acceptable. But if, with respect to certain kinds of behavior, the morality cannot generate a large degree of uniformity (and thus predictability), then clearly the morality is not acceptable. So, although not a sufficient condition for acceptability, being able to generate this uniformity is a necessary, or minimum, condition.

We cannot, from this minimum condition alone, come to any conclusion about exactly what moral norms the utilitarian standard justifies. But we can, I claim, come to one very important conclusion about what it does *not* justify. The utilitarian standard does not justify the utilitarian norm, even though both are utilitarian criteria. (Recall here the distinction between norms and standards—see secs. 1.2 and 3.6.) To be more exact, I am claiming that the utilitarian standard does not justify a moral code in which the utilitarian norm is *fundamental*—fundamental in the sense that doing what it prescribes has priority over everything else within the code. Such a code—one in which some version of the utilitarian norm has priority over everything else—is typically referred to as an "act" utilitarian code to distinguish it from a "rule" utilitarian code—one where the primary role of the utilitarian norm (or other utilitarian criterion) is not that of being a moral rule or norm *within* the code, but that of being the criterion to which we appeal for *justifying* moral rules. (For defenses of an act utilitarian code, see Sartorius 1975; Sidgwick 1907; Smart 1973.) I prefer to call a moral code in which the utilitarian norm is fundamental not an *act*, but a *direct* utilitarian code so as to distinguish it from an *indirect* utilitarian code such as is being advocated here—a code where the utilitarian standard is appealed to not merely for justifying the *rules* of the code, but for justifying the entire *social-pressure system* of which the code is a part. What I am claiming then is that an indirect utilitarian code justifiable in this way by appeal to the utilitarian standard is not also a direct utilitarian code—one where the utilitarian norm is fundamental.

A code in which the utilitarian norm is fundamental cannot be justified by appealing to the utilitarian standard simply because such a code would fail to meet the above minimum condition of acceptability for *any* moral code. A code in which the utilitarian norm is fundamental could not generate a minimally acceptable degree of uniformity in people's behavior. I mentioned earlier (sec. 3.2) how extraordinarily much information a person must have in order to be sure of complying with the utilitarian norm. A person must, in principle, know all the possible sets of effects of each of his alternatives upon people's experiences for all of eternity, as well as each set's probability of occurring. Not only that but, in principle, nothing else must influence the person's choice other than this knowledge and the assumption that he himself will have to experience all the possible sets of effects of whichever alternative he chooses. In reality, however, we all have vastly different stores of factual information, with none of us even coming close to having the huge amount of information which, in principle, is required by the utilitarian norm, and we all have different things influencing our choices other than just that which, according to this norm, should influence them. So it is extraordinarily unlikely that there would ever be much uniformity throughout any society in people's interpretations of what the utilitarian norm requires. Some people would conclude that under such and such circumstances it maximizes expected utility to assassinate the president, others would conclude just the opposite, and so on, so that if people took their duty to maximize expected utility seriously, they would be doing all sorts of strange and unpredictable things; we could never be sure but that someone might consider it utility maximizing to break his word to us or, worse yet, to stick a knife in our back. Obviously such a code would not generate the uniformity and predictability necessary for security and trust, and for mutually beneficial interaction among people. Consider, for example, the following picture G. J. Warnock (1971) paints of what life would be like in a society in which the utilitarian norm is fundamental. Suppose, he says, that I entrust the care of my health to a utilitarian doctor. Although I know this doctor's intentions must be *generally* beneficent, I can never be sure what his intentions regarding me in particular are. I can never be sure whether he intends to take excellent care of me, or intends perhaps to cleverly kill me off instead. I can never be sure because, as a utilitarian, he is committed to doing that and only that which maximizes expected utility and, for all I know, he might think killing me maximizes expected utility. For example, he might secretly think me to be a scoundrel—someone who causes more disutility than utility—and who therefore it would maximize utility to be rid of. Furthermore, how could my anxieties about his secret thoughts and intentions ever be alleviated? It would do no good to ask him to "promise" not to kill me, nor would it do any good to ask him to disclose his intentions. Although he might indeed, if I ask, make such a promise, he will of course keep this promise only if he thinks it maximizes expected utility to do so. And he knows that I know I can not rely upon his keeping his promise; therefore, he will know that it matters that much less if in fact he does not keep it; the result of all this being that any such "promise" will be perfectly idle. Similarly, if I ask him to disclose his intentions, he will answer truthfully only if he thinks it maximizes expected utility to do so. And, as Warnock (33) tells us: "knowing that, I will not unqualifiedly believe him; and knowing *that,* he will realize that, since I will not do so, it will matter that much less if he professes intentions that he does not actually have. And so on, until my asking and his answering become a pure waste of breath."

What this illustrates, of course, is how a direct utilitarian code, which could not generate sufficient uniformity or predictability in people's behavior, would undermine the basis for promise-making, and even for communication with one another; and why, therefore, such a code is not justifiable from the perspective of an *indirect* utilitarian. Direct and indirect utilitarianism are, in other words, incompatible.

So far I have argued that a direct utilitarian moral code is unacceptable because such a code would fail to generate the degree of uniformity in people's behavior that any acceptable moral code must generate. But I need not rest my case on the need for uniformity alone; such a code is unacceptable for other reasons as well. Such a code is, for one thing, too pervasive to be acceptable; it requires that everything we ever do be designed to maximize expected utility; in principle, even our choice each morning of what color underwear to put on would be governed by the utilitarian norm. Furthermore, the most saintly or heroic of self-sacrifices—sacrifices normally viewed as going far beyond the demands of ordinary duty, sacrifices such as giving virtually every penny of our wealth away to those who need it more—would no longer be morally optional; provided only that such self-sacrifices maximized expected utility, they would be mandatory. It is unlikely that the utilitarian standard justifies a code of morality that invades our private lives as much, demanding from us as much, as this. Too much morality, through allowing too little personal freedom, can exact just as great a toll as can too little morality, through allowing too much personal freedom.

And a code requiring that everyone always maximize expected utility might have certain disadvantages that one would not expect. Let me provide one example. I do not know if the supposition about human motivation upon which this example is based is true, but the supposition is not altogether implausible. Suppose that the requirement that we always do what maximizes expected utility entails that we always (1) work hard and use our talents as best we can to contribute to the total product of society and (2) give away any surplus wealth we earn through meeting this standard of work (i.e., any beyond what we absolutely need) to the unfortunate people of the world who genuinely need it more than we do; and suppose that this entailment is generally recognized. Suppose furthermore that human nature is such that, for us to have adequate incentive to meet the above standard of work, we must be allowed to *keep* a large proportion of the surplus wealth we earn through meeting the standard—that is, our keeping a large proportion of the surplus wealth we earn through working hard must be *socially tolerated*. Given these suppositions, the advocate of a moral code in which the utilitarian norm is fundamental is faced with the following dilemma; for us to have adequate incentive to work hard, conduct known to be inconsistent with the requirements of the utilitarian norm has to be socially tolerated, this conduct being that of keeping a large proportion of the surplus wealth we earn rather than giving it away to the more needy. But if conduct known to be inconsistent with the utilitarian norm were socially tolerated in some society then, in that society, the utilitarian norm could not be morally fundamental. It makes no sense to say that society S has a moral norm known not just to encourage, but to *require* Y; yet, in S, not doing Y is socially tolerated. So either the utilitarian norm could not be morally fundamental, or else the incentive for us to work hard and use our talents would have to be inadequate, which would indeed be an unexpected disadvantage.

What examples such as the above suggest is that, even if a code of morality where the utilitarian norm is fundamental were able to provide a tolerable degree of uniform behavior (which I have argued it could not), this code is unacceptable for still other reasons. Therefore, I conclude, this code is not part of the social-pressure system we would choose that there be, were we to give everyone's interests equal consideration; it is not, in other words, justifiable in terms of the utilitarian standard. Indirect utilitarianism is indeed incompatible with direct utilitarianism.

5.2 HARE'S TWO-LEVEL THEORY

R. M. Hare, however, has recently proposed a moral theory in which he claims to have *reconciled* the two forms of utilitarianism I have just concluded are incompatible. He claims to have reconciled direct and indirect utilitarianism or, as he prefers to call them, act and rule utilitarianism (Hare 1981; see also Hare 1976). I think Hare's moral theory is, in many respects, closer to the truth than any other. But with respect to the reconciliation of these two forms of utilitarianism, I shall argue in this section that he is mistaken. (Hare uses the terms "act" and "rule" utilitarianism much as I use the terms "direct" and indirect" utilitarianism and, in discussing his theory, I shall adhere to his terminology.)

At the heart of Hare's theory is an analysis of moral thinking into two levels, an analysis that he puts to use in answering traditional objections against utilitarianism, and that provides him with the means by which he attempts to reconcile act and rule utilitarianism. The first of Hare's two levels of moral thinking he calls the "intuitive" level. Moral thinking at the intuitive level is done by appeal to what he calls "prima facie moral principles." These principles (or, as I would call them, norms) are ones that are relatively simple, and resemble the sort of moral norms most of us are brought up to observe—norms forbidding such things as promise-breaking, theft, murder, and falsehoods. These are, Hare says, the *only* sort of moral principles the moral intuitionist recognizes, and therefore when faced with a conflict between them, or when confronted by someone with intuitions different from his, the intuitionist will be at a loss.

What the intuitionist fails to realize, Hare claims, is that there is another level of moral thinking, one that Hare calls the "critical" level. Moral thinking at the critical level is done by appeal to what is, in effect, a version of the utilitarian norm, a norm that prescribes that we choose that alternative which maximizes overall preference satisfaction, where equal preferences are to be given equal weight, regardless of whose preferences they might, in reality, happen to be. Hare himself does not speak of thinking at the critical level as proceeding by appeal to the utilitarian norm. Rather than referring to what he is proposing for use at the critical level as a "norm," or "principle," he refers to it as a "method." But he does tell us that the judgments this "method" yields are "the same as a careful act-utilitarian would make" (1981, 43) and, of course, we always speak of act utilitarians as proceeding by appeal to some version of the utilitarian norm. Therefore, I do not think it misrepresents Hare's view if, for convenience, we speak of what Hare is proposing as a version of the utilitarian norm, provided we keep in mind that we are not speaking of the classical version of this norm that prescribes that "happiness" be maximized, but a version that prescribes that preference satisfaction be maximized. Furthermore, Hare (for purposes of simplicity) limits what preferences are to be taken as the relevant ones to preferences for *experiences* (1981, 90–91). And, what is equally significant, only ideal preferences are to count; that is, only preferences as they would be had they been *fully exposed to facts and logic* (1981, 104–5). So Hare's version of the utilitarian norm is very similar to the one formulated here (sec. 3.1). It is at this critical level of thinking—that is, the level at which we are to appeal to the utilitarian norm—where those conflicts which arise between the prima facie principles we use at the intuitive level are to be resolved, and where these prima facie principles are to be chosen in the first place—chosen on the basis of their "acceptance-utility" (1981, 50).

What exactly it means to "accept" a moral principle is, unfortunately, left unclarified by Hare (a serious omission). But I assume that the "acceptance" of some principle P includes a certain willingness to try to comply with P, as well as a certain willingness to help bring about or maintain social pressure for the compliance of others with P. It should be noticed that the acts prescribed by prima facie principles with maximum acceptance-utility would not correspond exactly to those that it would maximize expected-utility to perform. For prima facie principles to have maximum acceptance-utility they must, for the most part, be ones that are relatively *simple* and *easy to comply with,* and their being relatively simple and easy to comply with is inconsistent with their always prescribing acts that it would maximize expected utility to perform (cf. sec. 6.1 above).

But it these prima facie principles do not always prescribe the act that maximizes expected-utility, this means that the act prescribed at the intuitive level of thinking does not always correspond to the act that would be prescribed, after full exposure to facts and logic, at the critical level of thinking. This then raises the question of which act, the one prescribed at the intuitive level, or the one prescribed, after full exposure to facts and logic, at the critical level, is definitive of (i.e., in the final analysis, delineates) the morally right act. Hare answers as follows: "[The prima facie principles] are not definitive of 'the right act'; but if we wish to act rightly we shall do well, all the same, to follow them" (1981, 38). So if the prima facie principles are not definitive of the right act, we may assume that, for Hare, the definitively right act is the one prescribed, after full exposure to facts and logic, at the critical level; in other words, the one prescribed by the utilitarian norm.

But if it is following the utilitarian norm, not the prima facie principles, that is definitive of the morally right act, then why, it may be asked, shall be do well, all the same, to follow the prima facie principles? The answer is that, ordinarily, we do not have the time or the facts necessary for determining reliably what the definitively right act is; the prima facie principles then tell us what our "best bet" is, given this lack of time and facts—that is, given human fallibility; they tell us, in other words, what we most likely would have chosen at the critical level if we *had* had sufficient time and facts (1981, 35–39). And since we lack sufficient time and facts for a reliable choice most of the time, the intuitive level of moral thinking, carried out in terms of these prima facie principles, is the level of moral thinking that is appropriate for most everyday moral decisions. But these prima facie principles are not, Hare insists, mere "rules of thumb." Owing to our upbringing, they are associated with "very firm and deep dispositions and feelings"; thus, unlike mere rules of thumb, a breach of them normally excites in us a feeling of compunction (1981, 38–39).

Having seen how Hare distinguishes between two levels of moral thinking, we can now see why he claims his position reconciles act and rule utilitarianism. According to Hare, both the act and the rule utilitarian are right about one level of moral thinking: the act utilitarian is right about the critical level; the rule utilitarian is right about the intuitive level (1981, 43). We can now also see how, in a delightful piece of philosophical writing that must be read to be fully appreciated (chap. 8), Hare counters the intuitionist's standard argument against utilitarianism. The intuitionist's standard argument is simple: he produces some example where what maximizes expected utility appears to contravene one of our deeply held moral principles; and since (the intuitionist assumes) contravening this deeply held moral principle is morally wrong, he concludes that utilitarianism must thus be rejected. In reply Hare, first of all, points out that if the example that the intuitionist produces is a realistic one, one that might well occur under ordinary circumstances, then he (Hare) has no significant disagreement with the intuitionist about what moral principles should be used to decide the case; intuitive-level prima facie moral principles should be used, principles that, for all practical purposes, correspond to the very ones the intuitionist is claiming should be used. Intuitive-level principles should be used—and used even though what they prescribe might not, in the case at hand, maximize expected utility—because, in ordinary cases of the sort in question, they are, given our normal lack of time and facts, our "best bet." In order to provide an example where, on Hare's view, we must resort to critical thinking, and thus to the utilitarian norm itself rather than these prima facie moral principles, the circumstances in which the example is couched would have to be so extraordinary, the case so fantastic, that even the intuitionist would have to doubt the appropriateness of using the prima facie principles to decide it, principles designed only for deciding ordinary, everyday cases. But then if we have doubts about the appropriateness of using these prima facie principles, the fact that the act that maximizes utility contravenes these principles is no longer a very compelling reason for rejecting utilitarianism.

But, if I am right, this ingenious reconciliation of act and rule utilitarianism by means of this two-level analysis does not quite succeed because, in the final analysis, the intuitive level of moral reasoning cannot be kept distinct from the critical level; it "collapses" into the critical level, leaving Hare not with a reconciliation between act and rule utilitarianism, but with just act utilitarianism. The problem is not that the prima facie principles to be used at the intuitive level end up prescribing exactly the same acts as the utilitarian norm to be used at the critical level; as we saw, they would not. Rather, the problem lies in determining, for whatever case is at hand, which level of moral thinking, the intuitive or the critical, we should be using—that is, in determining whether we are pressed enough for time, or whether the case before us is "ordinary" enough, for us to invoke the prima facie principles, or whether we should go directly to the utilitarian norm instead. There are only four alternative means of determining this: (1) by means of some third level of moral thinking more basic than either the critical or intuitive levels; (2) by means of the critical level; (3) by means of the intuitive level; and (4) by means of no standard at all—that is, arbitrarily. Hare does not provide us with any third level of moral thinking, and surely such decisions should not be made arbitrarily, which leaves only alternatives (2) and (3). Hare does say that, with any deep experience in moral thinking, a person will have acquired some *methodological* prima facie principles that will tell him when to use critical thinking and when to use intuitive thinking (p. 52); so perhaps the answer is that these decisions should be made at the intuitive level, by means of methodological prima facie principles. Methodological prima facie principles may help—depending upon how simple these methodological principles themselves are—but they cannot be the whole answer. For one thing, we are still left with the question: How are we to determine what these methodological prima facie principles should be, and when they should be invoked? Hare's answer is that we are to determine these matters by means of critical thinking (1981, 50). It is then critical thinking—that is, the utilitarian norm—that is the *final* arbiter for when we are to use critical thinking and when not; that is to say, it is the final arbiter as far as *morality itself* is concerned. Therefore, in every case when we do use intuitive thinking, we are, as far as morality is concerned, to do so only because this is how the utilitarian norm tells us to proceed. It is in this sense that the intuitive level collapses into the critical level, leaving us, I suggest, not with a reconciliation of act and rule utilitarianism, but with just act utilitarianism—a very sophisticated act utilitarianism to be sure, but act utilitarianism nevertheless. So it must be concluded that, in the final analysis, the code of morality that Hare supports is an act (or direct) utilitarian code after all, a code of morality in which the utilitarian norm is fundamental. It is true that Hare himself never says that he supports an act utilitarian *code of morality,* but if my arguments so far are sound, then what Hare does say commits him to supporting such a code nevertheless (if, in fact, the distinction between an act utilitarian "code of morality" and an act utilitarian "method of moral thinking" is a meaningful one to begin with).

Hare might reply that, although perhaps his view does, in this sense, collapse into act utilitarianism, he is not particularly bothered by this; he is not particularly bothered since his defense of utilitarianism against the intuitionist's argument remains sound. That is to say, a perfect practitioner of his method of moral thinking, or of his code of morality (whichever we may want to call it), would still always choose, at the critical level, to think at the intuitive level, unless confronted by a genuinely fantastic case, and so forth.

That may well be so. The only problem is that none of us is, or ever could be, perfect practitioners of this method, or even come close to being perfect practitioners. To be perfect practitioners of this method we would, among other things, have to be able to do perfect critical thinking about what our prima facie principles should be, and when they should be invoked. But, as Hare himself admits (1981, 45), perfect critical thinking—and I see no reason why this should not include critical thinking about what our prima facie principles should be, and when they should be involved—requires "superhuman powers of thought, superhuman knowledge, and no human weaknesses" (1981, 44). Critical thinking is, in other words, very difficult indeed. This raises an objection to Hare's utilitarian theory that is, I think, even more serious than the one raised by the intuitionist. Since critical thinking is so very difficult, people's *interpretations* of what is prescribed at the critical level are not likely to be very uniform. In particular, people's interpretations of what prima facie principles are prescribed, and when to invoke them, are not likely to be very uniform. After all, decisions at the critical level on these matters, just as on other matters, must sometimes be made quickly, must often be made with a scarcity of facts, and must always be made by us very fallible human beings. But if these interpretations were not very uniform, then people's moral behavior, stemming as it would from these interpretations, would not be very uniform either. And finally, without much uniformity, and thus predictability, in people's moral behavior, there would not be much security or mutual trust; there would, as concluded above (sec. 5.1), be an intolerable degree of chaos.

Hare might reply by pointing out that so far I am overlooking one very important point: the prima facie principles, as we saw, are not exactly mere rules of thumb, but are backed by social pressure, social pressure that creates in people deep feelings of attachment to these principles, feelings that generally give rise to remorse or guilt on the part of those violating them. Hare might then conclude that, because of this social pressure, and thus these deep feelings of attachment, the "chaos" referred to above would never materialize; this social pressure would be sufficient to maintain adequate uniformity in people's moral behavior in spite of differing interpretations of what is prescribed at the critical level, just as, in most societies, social pressure manages to maintain a tolerable degree of uniformity in the face of differing moral opinions.

This reply might well, once again, be good enough, except for one remaining problem: although social pressure is indeed sufficient for maintaining tolerable uniformity in most societies, in the moral code of most societies the utilitarian norm is not fundamental while, as we have seen, in the moral code that Hare supports, it is; and this is crucial. It is crucial because, with a moral code where the utilitarian norm is fundamental (i.e., where conformity to it, and it alone, is definitive of moral rightness) the requisite social pressure for compliance with subsidiary prima facie principles could never be generated. That is, it could never be generated, assuming only that the code recognized, as it should, excuses for innocent mistakes of fact. Let me explain. In every code of morality of which I am aware, people are excused from failing to adhere to the moral principles (i.e., norms) within the code if their failure is attributable not to improper motivation, but to an innocent mistake of fact, one that anyone might have made. Say, for example, you have no reason whatever to know that someone has by mistake put arsenic into your sugar bowl and that you, therefore, serve some unfortunate person poisoned tea, your innocent mistake of fact will excuse you from any blame for having poisoned him. The recognition of such an excuse is, I submit, crucial, if for no other reason than for people's peace of mind. Although it is unlikely we will ever mistakenly serve anyone poisoned tea, it is very likely that *sometime* during our lives we will make a serious, but innocent, mistake of *some* sort. So, were it not for the recognition of such an excuse, we would remain in constant jeopardy of severe moral condemnation for that over which we have virtually no control—namely, innocent mistakes of fact—a situation hardly conducive to the very peace of mind for which we have a morality in the first place. But it is precisely because of this excuse for innocent mistakes of fact that adequate social pressure for compliance with simple, prima facie moral principles could never materialize with a code in which the utilitarian norm was fundamental. People with false opinions about *which* prima facie principles the utilitarian norm required compliance with, and *when* exactly this compliance was required, could never legitimately be held morally blameworthy for behaving in accordance with these false opinions. They, as well as anyone else, would be doing their best to comply with the code's overriding moral duty to maximize expected utility; thus if, in adhering to the wrong prima facie principles, or in adhering to the right ones at the wrong times, they did not succeed in maximizing expected utility, their failure would have to be attributed not to improper motivation, but to a mistake of fact as to what the utilitarian norm required. And, given how extremely difficult it normally is to determine what the utilitarian norm requires, if any mistake of fact should excuse one from moral blameworthiness, then surely a mistake about this matter should. Yet it is (roughly speaking) only through holding people morally blameworthy for certain acts and not for others that adequate social pressure for compliance with moral norms can be generated. So if, because of their mistakes of fact, people could not normally be held morally blameworthy for failing to comply within the utilitarian norm, then adequate social pressure for compliance with it and, *a fortiori*, with prima facie principles adherence to which is said to be required by it, could never be generated. If adequate social pressure for compliance with any such moral principles could never be generated then, with a code in which the utilitarian norm was fundamental, adequate uniformity of behavior would never materialize. And if adequate social pressure for compliance with these principles could never be generated, then Hare's two-level analysis of moral thinking would indeed collapse into one level, that of critical thinking; in other words, that of appeal to the utilitarian norm. Thus, I conclude, instead of reconciliation between act and rule (or direct and indirect) utilitarianism, Hare is left with only act (or direct) utilitarianism.

So where, exactly, am I claiming that Hare has gone wrong? He is right, I think, in advocating that we justify moral principles or norms in terms of a utilitarian criterion (or "method"). Where I think he has gone wrong is in making this method of moral justification itself a requirement of morality. His theory would, I think, be stronger if, as in the theory proposed here, the justification of moral norms in terms of a utilitarian criterion *were not itself a requirement of morality*. This way, when someone failed to comply with the moral norms justifiable in terms of this criterion, and his failure was due merely to a mistake of fact about *how* to comply successfully, we could excuse him without thereby being committed to excusing as well the person whose failure was due instead to a mistake of fact about *which* moral norms the utilitarian criterion justifies. The key is that the mistake-of-fact excuse is applicable only to requirements of morality; so if justifying moral norms in terms of the utilitarian criterion is not a requirement of morality, we are thus not committed to excusing the person whose failure to comply with these norms is due to a mistake of fact about which norms the criterion justifies. Only then does it become possible for adequate social pressure for compliance with moral norms to take hold.

Making a utilitarian justification of moral norms itself a requirement of morality is not the only way in which I think Hare's theory goes wrong. I also disagree with the way in which Hare attempts to justify this method of justification. His attempt to justify this method has, in effect, two components: a logical component and an empirical component. The logical component is an appeal to "the logic of moral concepts" (Hare 1981, esp. chaps. 6 & 12). (Incidentally, it is, I think, because of this appeal that Hare insists upon making his method of justification a requirement of *morality;* if it were not he could not attempt to justify it by appealing to the logic of *moral* concepts.) The empirical component is an attempt to justify this method by an appeal to self-interest (Hare 1981 chap. 11). It is, however, the logical component—an appeal to the logic of moral concepts—that Hare emphasizes. This emphasis is, I think, a mistake. Hare's moral theory would, I suggest, be on firmer ground if the logical component were dropped in favor of further development of the empirical component. But I need not pursue these remarks any further here; my objections to the logical component have been stated elsewhere (Haslett 1984), and the approach to justification in terms of self-interest that I try to defend in Part IV of this book will show how I think the empirical component should be further developed.

6
The EC Code

6.1 REQUIREMENTS ANY MORAL CODE MUST MEET

Having seen what sort of moral code the utilitarian standard does not justify, let us now try to determine what sort of moral code it does justify. Let us, in other words, now try to determine what that which I have been calling the "EC" code of personal morality is like.

We may assume, first of all, that the EC code will not be subject to the main objection I made against a code in which the utilitarian norm is fundamental, this objection being that the code is not capable of generating sufficient uniformity of behavior. And, in order for the EC code not to be subject to this objection, it must, for the most part, contain moral norms that are easy enough to comply with so that, with an honest effort, almost everyone could *succeed* most of the time in complying with them. Only if the EC code contained, for the most part, norms of this sort would it be capable of generating the necessary uniformity.

For moral norms to be this easy to comply with, they must, unlike the utilitarian norm, be such that it is normally not necessary to accumulate vast amounts of factual information to know whether or not one is succeeding in complying with them. Furthermore, they must not be so demanding in what they require of us that, short of a prohibitively extreme degree of social pressure, people could not be adequately *motivated* to comply with them. An example of an overly demanding norm might be one that required everyone to work strenuously, say, twenty hours a day every day for the common good; it is hard to see how people could ever be adequately motivated to comply with a norm such as this. So we know the moral code that the utilitarian standard justifies does not contain norms—or at least not many norms—that require substantial factual information to comply with, or that would be unusually difficult to motivate the average person to comply with.

In saying that the norms of the EC code are, for the most part, ones that are easy to comply with, I do not mean they are ones that are *always* easy to comply with; no norms of morality could be easy to comply with all the time. There will be times when determining what some norm of the EC code prescribes is very difficult indeed; all norms, no matter how easy to comply with most of the time, contain a borderline area within which what the norm prescribes is very *unclear* (see sec. 6.8). And there will also be times when summoning the necessary will power to comply with some norm of the code is far from easy, as when, for example, a promise has been made which, according to a norm of the code, must be kept, but can be kept only at great inconvenience. But all that is required in order for a code to generate adequate uniformity of behavior is for *most* of its norms to be easy to comply with *most* of the time, and we may assume that the norms of the EC code are sufficiently easy to comply with to meet this requirement.

We may also assume that the EC code does not, for any given society, contain an extraordinarily large number of norms. Or, at least, it does not contain an extraordinarily large number of norms without having, in addition, a core of a relatively few number of norms that cover *most* circumstances likely ever to arise. The reason for a restriction on the number of norms is simply that the code must be capable of being learned fairly easily by ordinary people. Adequate uniformity of behavior cannot be generated by a moral code people cannot comply with, people cannot comply with a moral code they cannot learn, and people cannot learn a moral code containing too many different moral norms. Similarly, we may assume that the norms of the EC code are not ones that contain so many exceptions, qualifications, and so on, that merely to *learn* what these norms require, as distinct from complying with their requirements, would be very difficult. We may, in other words, assume that the norms of the EC code are ones that are relatively *simple*. And perhaps a norm's simplicity can best be judged in terms of how long and complex its maximally explicit formulation in ordinary, everyday language would have to be. If so, the requirement that the norms of the EC code be relatively simple becomes the requirement that the typical norm of this code be one that, in principle, could be (even if, at present, it has not been) given a maximally explicit, yet simple formulation in ordinary language. Or, if all of its possible applications could not be captured in a simple formulation, it must at least admit of a simple formulation covering *most* cases likely ever to arise. There are, I suppose, those who would claim that at least some simple moral norms are of a sort that, although they can be learned (from the example of others) and followed perfectly well, they cannot, in principle, be formulated in words—and not just because of the inevitable occurrence of "borderline" cases (which are discussed in sec. 6.8). Even aside from borderline cases, a linguistic formulation, they would claim, simply cannot be given. If this claim were true (which I doubt) then we would have to analyze what it means for a moral norm to be "simple" in some terms other than just how complex the norm's linguistic formulation would be. But no matter what the correct analysis is, the need for moral norms to be relatively simple must still be met. Norms that are too complex cannot be learned, and a code consisting of norms that have not been learned obviously cannot be complied with. Moreover, the simpler the moral code, the less (generally speaking) the "social pressure" costs—that is, the less the costs of bringing about and maintaining the social-pressure system of which it is a part. So not only must the EC code meet the requirement of being made up for the most part of norms that, typically, are easy to comply with, but it must also meet the above requirements of simplicity. (The need for a moral code to meet these requirements, or ones similar to them, was, I think, first emphasized in Richard B. Brandt's important works on ethics; see, for example, Brandt 1967. See also Haslett 1974; Hare 1981; Kupperman 1983.)

6.2 STANDARD OBJECTIONS THE EC CODE AVOIDS

I suggest that the only kind of moral code *meeting these requirements* that would have a chance of being chosen from a standpoint of equal consideration for everyone is a code consisting mostly of moral norms not radically dissimilar to those most of us have been brought up to observe—simple, easy-to-comply-with norms specifically forbidding such things as deceptive falsehoods, cheating, stealing, and unprovoked physical violence, and specifically requiring such things as paying our debts, taking conscientious care of our children, and keeping our promises. Also included in this code are, I suggest, certain easy-to-comply-with norms of justice—namely, ones specifically forbidding certain kinds of unequal treatment, such as unequal treatment solely on grounds of race. These norms of personal morality—the ones dealing with unequal treatment—have, I shall argue, counterparts in political morality, where the prohibition against the unequal treatment is directed at governments instead of individuals. And the argument for saying that such anti-discrimination norms are part of the EC code of personal morality is somewhat analogous to the argument to be examined later (chap. 7) for saying their counterparts are part of the EC code of political morality. Another norm that I suggest is probably part of the EC code of personal morality, and has a counterpart in the EC code of political morality, is a norm requiring obedience to the law (with, in the case of personal morality, certain important exceptions). I do not now, however, want to pursue any farther these brief remarks about what *particular* norms are probably found in the EC code; to pursue these remarks any farther is somewhat premature until we have examined still more fully what the norms of the code are probably like *in general*.

But before I proceed, one thing should be noted: if I am right about what sort of norms the EC code consists of, then this moral code is not subject to certain standard objections against the utilitarian norm or, in other words, against a moral code in which this norm is fundamental. Earlier (sec. 3.2) we saw that, among these objections are ones on moral grounds and ones on practical grounds. Objections on moral grounds take the form of showing that the utilitarian norm often prescribes acts that we know, "intuitively," to be morally wrong—acts of promise-breaking, discrimination, "punishing" innocent men, and so forth. But this type of objection cannot be made against the EC code of morality if, as I have suggested, it consists largely of moral norms that correspond with most people's moral intuitions rather well. And I think, as we proceed, it will become more and more apparent that the EC code, both of personal and political morality, *does* consist largely of moral norms that correspond well with most people's moral intuitions. It *must* consist largely of such norms if it is to meet those requirements for a moral code that we can be sure the utilitarian standard endorses—prominent among these being, as we have seen, the requirements of simplicity and easy compliance. And if the EC code does, in accordance with these requirements, consist of a limited number of norms that are, for the most part, simple and easy to comply with, then, of course, the practical objections (elaborated in sec. 5.1) against a code in which the utilitarian norm is fundamental cannot be made against the EC code either.

Incidentally, those familiar with David Lyons's book *Forms and Limits of Utilitarianism* (1965) should note one more thing: if the EC code consists of a limited number of norms that are, for the most part, simple and easy to comply with, then it does not "collapse" into the utilitarian norm as Lyons, in this book, argues that rule-utilitarian codes typically do. Or, to put the matter another way, the indirect utilitarianism advocated here—a utilitarianism in terms of which we are to evaluate moral norms along each of the three dimensions referred to earlier (sec. 4.3), not along just the single dimension of successful compliance—is in no danger whatever of being "extensionally equivalent" to act utilitarianism.

6.3 WHY GENERAL BENEFICENCE IS NOT MANDATORY

The requirement that the EC code not be so demanding that people could not be motivated to comply with it short of prohibitively extreme social pressure has an interesting consequence: it probably rules out any moral codes where doing acts of general beneficence or great self-sacrifice are mandatory—acts such as giving up one's possessions, or even one's life, for people whom one might not even know. In other words, the EC code probably does not impose upon us a *duty* of general beneficence. Opposed to a duty of *general* beneficence are duties of beneficence toward certain individuals—for example, our children, spouses, and parents. The EC code does, no doubt, impose upon us duties of beneficence toward certain individuals, but that is another matter. What I am arguing is that the EC code does not impose upon us a duty to aid others in general—those with no "special" relationship to us. It is true that the more acts of general beneficence there are, the better—that is, the greater the expected utility. The problem is that the costs of achieving general compliance with moral norms demanding such acts—costs in the form of the human energy necessary for maintaining social pressure great enough to achieve this compliance, and in the form of the anxiety such extreme social pressure would engender—would very likely outweigh any benefits that the compliance would bring. And, as I suggested above (sec. 5.1), successfully motivating people through extreme social pressure to make, routinely, great sacrifices might well interfere with *other* motivations, ones that are even more important socially, such as the motivation to work hard and use one's talents in socially beneficial ways. The final result of people being required, say, to give any extra wealth they earn to the more needy may well be that little, if any extra wealth will be earned. In short: although acts of general beneficence are, of course, socially beneficial, motivating people to comply with norms requiring them would be costly indeed, costly enough, probably, to outweigh the benefits.

And there might well be still another problem: it is normally not difficult to determine if a person has violated such duties as those of paying his debts, keeping his promises, refraining from theft, murder, and so on, but how could we normally determine if a person has violated a duty of general beneficence? How could we determine, for example, whether the person who shows little talent for helping others in general actually *has* little talent, or just has not *tried* hard enough? In other words, a duty to perform acts of general beneficence might be both hard to comply with and hard to "enforce" not just because of motivational problems, but because of informational problems as well.

What then is the most appropriate position for a moral code to take with regard to such acts? Probably it is a compromise between ignoring them altogether and making them mandatory, a compromise in the form of placing a very high moral value upon these kinds of acts, but leaving them optional. This high moral value would be achieved through *positive* social pressure in the form of, say, praise and high esteem for those doing them. Such positive social pressure is to be contrasted with negative social pressure, which typically takes the form of condemnation and low esteem for those not doing what is expected. It is true that this compromise would not bring about as many beneficial self-sacrifices as would making acts of general beneficence mandatory, but those it did bring about would be achieved at relatively little cost since *positive* social pressure to perform an *optional* act is "cheap" compared with *negative* social pressure to perform a *mandatory* act: it does not restrict personal freedom, it does not create anxiety over the prospects of social condemnation, and so forth. What is called for by this compromise is more beneficial to society than simply ignoring the acts in question, but at the same time avoids the prohibitively high costs of making them mandatory. It should be no surprise then that what is called for by this compromise is exactly what is called for by the moral codes of most societies; acts of general beneficence are generally thought of as supererogatory—that is, as praiseworthy (to varying degrees), yet *beyond* the call of duty. And, for the above reasons, what is called for by this compromise is, I should think, what is called for by the EC code of morality as well.

But what about more specific duties of beneficence—ones such as a duty to take good care of our children, and a duty of concern for the well-being of our spouse? While these duties certainly do not require that we heap luxuries upon our own families while others are starving, they do require that we attend first to our families' most important needs before turning to similar needs of others. As already suggested, most codes of morality, and no doubt the EC code as well, do impose upon us specific duties of beneficence such as these. These specific duties, as opposed to a general duty, *are* easily justified by comparing costs with benefits. Those toward whom we have these specific duties—our children, our spouse, and so on—we normally know far more intimately than we know most others. And, because we know them more intimately, the efforts we make on their behalf can be expected to be more effective normally than similar efforts on behalf of those whose wants, needs, and problems we do not know so well. So these specific duties make those whose interests we would normally be most effective in advancing the very people whose interests we are normally *obligated* to advance, thereby creating throughout society what amounts to a favorable division of labor or, to be more exact, of beneficence. And since people normally have intense concern anyway for the well-being of those toward whom they have these special duties, the costs of motivating people through social pressure to comply with them are relatively low.

Fortunately, there are people whose efforts on behalf of others go beyond these special duties, even people whose efforts include great heroism or self-sacrifice, people such as Albert Schweitzer and Mother Teresa. Perhaps some of these people have succeeded in developing for all of humanity the same intense concern that most of us have succeeded in developing for a few with whom we are most closely associated—a concern so intense that they would rather suffer themselves than see others, even perfect strangers, suffer. I suggested earlier that those with such a concern, or love, for a few with whom they are closely associated are fortunate indeed; although it carries risks, by means of this concern they will, I suggested, find their lives greatly enriched, and thereby probably end up gaining far more than they will ever lose. Yet would a person not be foolish to develop as intense a concern as this for others in general? Would this not require more self-sacrifice than could possibly be in one's *own* best interests? Perhaps. On the other hand, if the person with this sort of concern for just a few is fortunate, even more fortunate may be the person with this sort of concern for all of humanity. But these speculations are best pursued elsewhere.

6.4 WHY NOT AN ELITIST CODE?

It is tempting to argue that the EC code of personal morality is what might be called an "elitist" code. Let me explain. As we have seen, the most justified code of morality, according to the utilitarian standard, is one consisting of moral norms the prescriptions of which only *roughly approximate* what maximizes expected utility—our toleration of norms that prescribe only rough approximations being necessary for the sake of having them be simple and easy to comply with. But this raises the question: What should be the moral norms of the person who is far more intelligent than ordinary, and thus capable of learning and complying with much more complex and difficult-to-comply-with moral norms? Does not the EC moral code contain a subset of more sophisticated moral norms for such extraordinary people—norms the prescriptions of which are not quite such *rough* approximations of what maximizes expected utility as are the prescriptions of those norms most suitable for ordinary people? These more sophisticated moral norms would, I suppose, be ones allowing exceptions where the simpler norms for ordinary people did not, and ones allowing more discretion in determining what to do. Accordingly, there would be circumstances where the ordinary person would be required by the simpler norms to, say, keep his promise, while the more intelligent person would be allowed by the more sophisticated norms to break his promise—obviously a source of potential trouble. But one is tempted to argue that an "elitist" code—that is, a code containing moral norms of different degrees of complexity for people of different degrees of intelligence—is nevertheless optimal since (we may assume) what such a code prescribes does more closely approximate what maximizes expected utility than what is prescribed by a "lowest-common-denominator" code—that is, a code binding everyone, no matter how intelligent, to those moral norms most suitable for the ordinary person.

To argue that an elitist code is, according to the utilitarian standard, preferable to a lowest-common-denominator code is, however, a mistake, and for the following reasons. In the first place, imagine how we would feel if, having kept our promise to Jones, he breaks a similar promise to us, and not only that but self-righteously proclaims that he is *entitled* to since, being more intelligent than we are, he is not bound by our clumsy moral norms. The resentment engendered by this sort of thing would be a disadvantage which, by itself, would probably outweigh the code's one (I think, relatively minor) advantage of allowing the unusually intelligent in society to more closely approximate maximizing expected utility than otherwise. But an even more serious disadvantage would be the failure of such a code to provide the degree of uniformity of behavior which, as we have seen, is one of the main jobs of a moral code to provide. How, with an elitist code, could we ever be very confident that a person would, say, keep his part of an agreement with us? For all we would know the person might be (or fancy himself to be) one of the super-intelligent who is bound by a different moral norm regarding the keeping of agreements than the norm familiar to us, in which case there would be no telling when this unknown norm of his would allow him to break his agreements. Such unpredictability would generate insecurity and weaken the basis for mutually beneficial cooperation among people—disadvantages of an elitist code that surely outweigh any advantages. Finally, human nature being what it is, I should think it likely that almost everyone would, sooner or later (usually sooner), come to fancy himself or herself among the most morally sophisticated, and thus entitled to use the more complex, difficult-to-comply-with norms. If so, then most ordinary people would end up trying to learn and follow moral norms set at a level of difficulty inappropriate for them, thus placing them farther away from maximizing expected utility than ever. And the number of ordinary people who, for this reason, would end up farther away from maximizing expected utility would no doubt be far greater than the number of extraordinary people who, owing to the "special" norms of the elitist code, would come closer to doing so. So with an elitist code, although those actions prescribed would, to be sure, more closely approximate what maximizes expected utility, those actions actually performed would, due to human fallibility, *less* closely approximate what maximizes expected utility.

I do not mean to suggest that the EC code does not contain *any* special moral norms for certain groups within a society, no matter what kinds of groups these are. I have only tried to show that it does not contain special moral norms for groups that are defined in terms of their members' intelligence, ability to handle complex norms, or something like that. The EC code no doubt does contain special moral norms for, say, different professional groups—doctors, lawyers, businessmen, and so forth (see, e.g., Bayles 1981; Bowie 1982) But I should think that none of these special moral norms are inconsistent with any of its "ordinary" moral norms; otherwise, the code would be objectionable in ways just discussed.

6.5 EXCEPTIONS

We can be sure the EC code does not allow exceptions to its relatively simple moral norms for the sake of what maximizes utility, expected utility, the general welfare, or anything else along such difficult-to-determine lines.

To the extent it did, it would be subject to just the kinds of objections we have already examined (chap. 5)—objections having to do with the lack of uniformity and predictability resulting from moral norms that are too difficult to comply with.

And if the EC code must, for these reasons, disallow exceptions for what maximizes expected utility, it must also disallow exceptions for what is *certain* to maximize expected utility. That is, the moral norms cannot have built into them an exception formulated somewhat as follows: ". . . except when acting contrary to what this norm usually prescribes is certain to maximize expected utility." Why the code must disallow an exception for when we are "certain" may be difficult to appreciate if (along with assuming that moral norms should be designed to maximize utility) we are accustomed to evaluating moral norms from the usual one-dimensional perspective of what the consequences of compliance with them are likely to be. As explained earlier (sec. 4.3), any evaluation that takes into account just this one dimension is liable to be dangerously incomplete; in this case, incomplete in such a way as to prevent us from seeing why this exception cannot be tolerated. In order to see why it cannot be tolerated we must take into account not just successful compliance; we must take into account unsuccessful compliance as well, and we must also take into account the feasibility and costs of social pressure.

Consider, for a moment, unsuccessful compliance: just as allowing an exception for cases that maximize expected utility would surely result in too many mistakes to make such an exception worthwhile (see again the argument in chap. 5), so too would allowing an exception for cases that are "certain" to maximize expected utility. All too many tax evasions, assassinations, governmental cover-ups, and the like, would end up being rationalized on the grounds that they were "certain" to maximize expected utility. The point is simply this: in matters as complex and subject to rationalizations as utility calculations, people are mistaken all too often *even when they feel certain*. (Take, for example, those responsible for Watergate who claimed to have been certain their transgressions would prove justified on utilitarian grounds.) It is considerations such as these—considerations that can only be appreciated fully from the perspective of a three-dimensional evaluation—that show why building an exception of this sort into our moral norms would be a mistake. Any flexibility created by an exception of this sort is the kind of flexibility a moral code can well do without.

On the other hand, a moral code with no exceptions at all to its norms prohibiting such things as taking what does not belong to us would be *too* inflexible. Surely no moral code should demand that we refrain from taking what does not belong to us when, for example, taking a boat that does not belong to us, in order to get to the center of a lake, is the only way we can save a drowning boy. And surely in some circumstances promises *should* be broken, deceptive falsehoods *should* be told, and so on. The problem is: How does a moral code provide for such circumstances without destroying the uniformity of behavior made possible by means of moral norms that are relatively simple and easy to comply with?

The solution is to allow exceptions to be built into these relatively simple and easy-to-comply-with moral norms, but only a limited number of exceptions, each of which is itself relatively simple and easy to comply with. And one of the most important exceptions, which, it seems to me, is very likely built into all the moral norms of the EC code of personal morality, is an exception for emergencies—one that would be applicable to just such a case as that of taking the boat that does not belong to us to save the drowning boy. The scope of this exception for emergencies must be carefully limited, as well as fairly clear-cut; otherwise the moral norms into which it is built would be exposed to a myriad of differing interpretations, making any reasonable degree of uniformity in behavior unlikely. Its scope might, for instance, be limited to cases where it is clear that (1) a genuine emergency, in the ordinary sense of the word, really does exist, (2) the only reasonable way of preventing the imminent disaster (or misfortune) that makes the situation an emergency is by doing something the moral norm in question ordinarily prohibits, and (3) any person harmed by doing what the moral norm ordinarily prohibits will be harmed substantially less than at least one person would have been harmed by the disaster that will thereby be prevented. And perhaps the best way to spell out what is meant by its being "clear" that these three provisos are met is as follows: *most* ordinary persons, on the basis of the evidence available to the agent, would believe that they were met. (I would expect there to be, normally, much more uniformity about whether these provisos were met than about something as abstract as whether expected utility was maximized.) This "ordinary person" test is analogous to the "reasonable person" test prevalent in law, according to which defendants are held to the standard of what a "reasonable person" would have believed in the circumstances.

The third proviso above (or one very much like it) is crucial. Let me try to show why with the help of an example borrowed from John Harris (1975). Suppose that two people will die within hours unless they receive an organ transplant, and that therefore the situation does qualify as an emergency, and suppose further that, since no ordinary donors are available, the only way to prevent this misfortune would be by killing some perfectly innocent, healthy person, say Jones, and transplanting Jones's heart into the first person, and his lungs into the second. This is not the place to go into this matter in detail, but I suggest that the disadvantages of having a morality that permits the killing of innocent people in cases like this far outweigh any advantages. For one thing, if our morality placed all of us in constant jeopardy of being killed for the sake of others, what damage might this do to our peace of mind? And whom could we trust to "play God" and choose those to be killed? (It has been argued that these choices could be made by lottery, but that this would be enough to make the practice in question advantageous is very doubtful. On this matter of a lottery, see Harris 1975, and Singer 1977.) Thus, if I am right, we must formulate the exception so that acts such as killing an innocent person for purposes of transplanting his organs are not permitted, no matter how great the emergency. This is why the third proviso is crucial; this proviso is what precludes the exception for emergencies, as formulated here, from being used to justify these kinds of acts. In killing one person to save two, as in the transplant case, we would be causing not *substantially less* harm for this one person than we prevent at least one of the other two from experiencing; we would instead be causing him *just as much* harm—namely, death—as we prevent each of the other two from experiencing, which is just what this proviso precludes us from doing.

Note that I am assuming here that the death of any one person should count for exactly as much harm to him as the death of any other person counts as harm to that other person, regardless of the persons' age, health, and so on. It would be a mistake for a code of morality to encourage attempts to calculate (for purposes of choosing whom to kill to save whom) just how harmful death would be for different people. Calculations like these are among the sorts that cannot be made successfully often enough for it to be worthwhile for people to try to make them; the results of people trying to do so—and using these calculations for choosing whom to kill— would surely include enough general insecurity, distrust, and resentment to outweigh any benefits. We should instead simply assume that the harm from death is the same for everyone. This assumption then makes it clear that the above exception for emergencies, as formulated so far, cannot be used as an excuse for killing anyone in order to save others.

It is however, tempting to conclude, as B. A. Brody apparently does (1973), that any exception for emergencies should be formulated so as to allow the killing of someone in order to save others in at least one sort of case: the sort of case where the person killed would have died in a "relatively short time" anyway. Cases of this sort include that of the proverbial fat man who is stuck in the only exit from a cave that will soon be flooded, a flood that will drown all those who are trapped in the cave behind him. We are to assume that the fat man happens to be facing inwards, and thus he will drown along with the others. Apparently Brody considers it permissible for the others to save themselves at the last moment by blowing up the fat man with dynamite, since he would have died in a relatively short time anyway. Another case of this sort is where so many people are in a lifeboat that, unless one of them is tossed overboard, the boat will soon sink, drowning them all. Here, assuming that the unwilling victim has been chosen fairly,

Brody no doubt considers tossing him overboard to be permissible, even though this amounts to killing him.

I am inclined to agree that these two emergencies do in fact justify killing an unwilling person; I am, however, unhappy with the *rationale* Brody would use for justifying the killings, this being that the victims would have died in a relatively short time anyway. One trouble with this rationale is that it, once again, encourages the sort of calculations that are so unreliable they are best left unattempted. As Brody points out, to determine whether some given time would count as "a relatively short time" for purposes of this rationale, we would need to calculate to what extent the person in question would, if deprived of this time, suffer "unrealized potentialities"; so we would have to attend to the person's "expectations for this period as well as to its length" (1973, 139n.)—hardly an easy calculation to make. And, if we granted the legitimacy of this rationale, we would have to tolerate some practices of rather questionable value. For example, we would, it seems, have to tolerate the relatives of people who need an immediate organ transplant roaming the corridors of hospitals to find suitable, terminally ill "donors," whom they would then kill on the grounds that these people would have died in a relatively short time anyway. In short, the rationale for killing some to save others needs to be tightened up; and it is Brody himself who suggests (although he does not adopt) what might be the best way to do this. The suggestion he rejects, as I see it, is that in an emergency we may kill one person to save another if and only if doing so is the only way to prevent the occurrence of some disaster that would have killed them both. This rationale allows us to justify killing the fat man and killing someone to keep the lifeboat afloat since, if these people were not killed, they would have died anyway, along with others, in the very disaster that killing them prevents. And, incidentally, this rationale also allows Jim to justify killing one of the twenty innocent Indians in Bernard Williams's famous example of the evil captain who is, then and there, going to have all twenty of them killed unless Jim agrees to shoot one of them himself (Smart & Williams 1973, 98–99). But this rationale does not allow us to justify killing (without their permission) the terminally ill, and giving their organs to others, since the disasters for others that we would thereby be preventing (deaths through their organ failures) would not be the very *same* disasters that would have killed the terminally ill anyway. And determining whether this rationale is applicable to some given case normally does not require any overly difficult calculations, since whether a person we kill would have himself died in the very disaster which our killing him prevents is, in most cases at least, relatively obvious. So, although I agree with the conclusion I think Brody would reach in the fat man and lifeboat cases, I prefer to use the rationale he rejects, not the one he accepts, for justifying this conclusion. And, finally, I suggest we build this rationale into the formulation of that exception for emergencies set out above. This is easily done. As will be recalled, this exception was formulated so as to limit exceptions for emergencies to cases where the harm prevented by doing what the norm ordinarily prohibits is more serious for at least one person than the harm caused is for any person. To this formula I suggest that we add the following: "or any person, harmed by doing what the moral norm ordinarily prohibits, would have been harmed just as much by the disaster that will thereby be prevented."

Other exceptions that the EC moral code might well have built into some or all of its norms include an exception for cases where a person has *consented* to what would otherwise be an act in violation of the norm in question, and an exception for cases, such as self-defense, where what would otherwise be an act in violation of the norm in question is necessary for preventing the person against whom the act is committed from completing or continuing a wrongful act or activity he has already begun—wrongful, that is, according to the EC moral code itself. And, for the latter exception to be applicable, the wrong that is to be prevented must be at least approximately as harmful for some person as any harm to be done to the potential wrongdoer in preventing it; otherwise, it would be permissible to kill a person merely to prevent his wrongfully lying.

Few, if any, exceptions are, I should think, built into the norms of the EC code beyond those, or ones similar to those, already mentioned. A few relatively simple exceptions such as these—ones telling us when deviations from what is ordinarily prescribed are permissible, not mandatory—would be quite enough to provide the flexibility that any moral code needs, without at the same time opening the door too widely.

6.6 CONFLICT CASES

A moral code such as the one I have been describing so far—one that contains a number of independent moral norms—is bound to give rise to cases of conflicting moral duties. These cases are ones where the only way of adhering to one moral duty is by contravening still another moral duty. If, for example, the only way to fulfill our duty to pay back a debt to Jones were to take the amount from Smith in violation of our duty not to steal, then we would be faced with a conflict case; no matter what we did, we would have to contravene at least one of our duties. Or, again, if the only way we could get the funds to fulfill our duty to care for our children were to murder our uncle for his inheritance, then we would be faced with a conflict case. And, incidentally, I am throughout using *duties,* and *acts that are duties,* to refer not only to positive acts that are duties, such as paying our debts, but also to negative acts, or omissions, that are duties, such as not stealing.

One might object to the EC code, as I have described it, by arguing that the conflicting moral duties to which it would give rise would leave people confused about which moral duty to give priority to; some people would give priority to the one duty while others would give priority to the other, it often being impossible to predict who would give priority to which duty. Such uncertainty, so the objection might go, seriously compromises the very uniformity of behavior that the EC code is designed to achieve.

The answer to this objection is that the EC code not only contains the kind of norms that generate such conflicts, namely, norms that are simple and easy to comply with, but it also contains other relatively easy-to-comply-with norms specifically designed for resolving them. These other norms, which become applicable when and only when a conflict occurs, can be called *secondary* norms to distinguish them from the norms among which the conflicts originally arise, which can be called *primary* norms. For example, the EC code, for obvious reasons, probably contains a secondary norm giving the duty not to steal priority over the duty to pay our debts, and a secondary norm giving the duty not to murder priority over all other duties. By people generally adhering to secondary norms such as these, uniformity of behavior would not be seriously compromised after all.

But, if I am right, the most important conflict-resolving norm in the EC code is not one for resolving conflicts between acts all of which are *duties*. It is, instead, a norm for resolving conflicts between, on the one hand, acts that are duties and, on the other hand, acts of beneficence that go *beyond* the call of duty. Such conflicts arise when the only way to perform some act of general beneficence, such as buying food to feed the poor, is by contravening some duty, such as the duty to pay one's debts. Although we are talking here only about acts of beneficence that are not duties, these acts have a special status that distinguishes them from other acts that are not duties; they have the status of being morally commendable (see the discussion of supererogatory acts in sec. 6.2). In other words, these acts of beneficence and acts that are duties are alike in one important respect: they are not morally neutral. So, although the conflicts in question here are not conflicts between acts all of which are duties, they are conflicts between acts none of which are morally neutral. And any moral norms designed for resolving these conflicts, I thus include within the category of "secondary" moral norms.

If I am right, the EC code of morality resolves all these conflicts, that is, all conflicts between duty and beneficence, by one, simple, secondary norm: a secondary norm that prescribes that we always give priority to the duty, no matter how great the benefit to be derived from the conflicting act of beneficence. Take, for purposes of illustration, the case where both your seven-year-old son and some famous person (a well-known politician, perhaps) are trapped in a burning building, and you have time to save only one of them. Which should you save? We may assume the EC code imposes upon you a duty to take care of your children, but does not (largely because of "division of labor" considerations) impose upon you any duty to take care of others in general, which include this famous person. Therefore, since the secondary norm in question requires you always to give duty priority over beneficence, it requires you to save your son instead of this famous person, no matter how beneficial to humanity saving the famous person might appear to be. Notice that the exception for emergencies, as I have formulated it (sec. 6.5), is not applicable here. This is because acting contrary to what normally would be your obligation to your son would result not in *substantially less* harm for him than the famous person would be prevented from experiencing, but in *just as much* harm for him.

The reasons for a secondary norm that gives duty priority over beneficence are practical ones. If people were, in violation of their duties, allowed to steal, cheat, kill, and so on, in order to benefit others, adequate uniformity and predictability in people's behavior would become impossible. In other words, a code that allowed beneficence to be given priority over duty would be subject to essentially the same kind of objection made in section 5.2 against a moral code in which the utilitarian norm is fundamental. Adequate uniformity and predictability can be achieved only by giving *all* duties, no matter how insignificant, priority over *all* acts of beneficence that are not duties, no matter how beneficial. Allowing people to get into the business of weighing the significance of a duty against the extent of a benefit would be fatal. People simply cannot make such calculations with enough reliability and uniformity for this to work. A secondary norm that gives all duties priority, no matter how beneficial the act of beneficence, may seem somewhat harsh. But I suspect that, in many cases where there appears to be a conflict between duty and beneficence, a little ingenuity will reveal that the beneficence can be accomplished without violating the duty after all; that there was no real conflict in the first place. And we must remember also that, although the exception for emergencies is not applicable in the burning-building case set out above, it no doubt *would* be applicable in many other cases, thereby tempering somewhat the harshness of this secondary norm. (For another defense of the priority of duties over beneficence, but for reasons different from those given here, see Murphy 1973.)

6.7 THE CATCH-ALL SECONDARY NORM

I think it fair to say that the vast majority of conflict cases arising from use of the EC code would be resolvable by means of just a handful of frequently applicable, easy-to-comply-with secondary norms like the ones suggested above. But not all conflict cases; there would always be certain relatively unusual conflict cases falling outside the scope of these frequently applicable secondary norms, some of these conflict cases perhaps being so rare as to occur only once throughout history. In fact, given the innumerable number of different conflicts that are possible, in order for the EC code to contain enough simple, easy-to-comply-with secondary norms to cover *all* conflicts that will ever arise, the number of such secondary norms within the code would, I assume, have to be innumerable. So I assume the EC code does not contain enough simple, easy-to-comply-with secondary norms to cover all conflicts; surely social pressure for compliance with *innumerable* such norms would not maximize expected utility. The costs in terms of the human effort necessary for learning and reinforcing an innumerable number of specific secondary norms would be enormous—if learning them were even possible—and since, by hypothesis, the conflicts to which most of these secondary norms would be applicable are ones that rarely ever occur anyway, the benefits derivable from having all these norms within the code would be minimal. The number of times in which such norms would be put to use would be so insignificant compared with the effort necessary for maintaining social pressure for compliance with them that the benefits simply would not cover the costs.

But then if the EC code does not contain a simple, easy-to-comply-with secondary norm for resolving every possible conflict no matter how rare, how should those rare conflicts for which no specific, ready-made secondary norms exist be resolved? I suspect that the EC code contains no fairly specific, simple, easy-to-comply-with secondary norms for resolving such conflicts, but a general, "catch-all" secondary norm for doing so, a norm to which appeal is permitted only after appeal to all other moral norms within the code, both primary and secondary, has been exhausted. (This appeal having been carried out, perhaps, by means of something like the reflective equilibrium methodology described below in chap. 9.) But then what sort of moral norm might be general enough to be applicable to any such conflict whatever? The most likely possibility, I think, is the utilitarian norm, the norm that tells us to choose the alternative we would choose if we were to give equal consideration to the interests of everyone. Say, for instance, that Jones's elderly parents are, for some reason, both in desperate need of some personal care or attention from him, and so it is his duty to provide each with this attention. But say that he can give this attention only to the one or the other but not to both, perhaps because his parents have separated and live too far apart. Anyway, we are to assume that he cannot give the necessary personal attention to both, and hence is faced with a conflict of duties. This is an example of a conflict it may be appropriate to resolve simply by attempting to choose the alternative which maximizes expected utility. This, in other words, is an example of a conflict it may be appropriate to resolve by appeal to the utilitarian norm in the role of a "catch-all" secondary norm of last resort.

As we saw earlier, the utilitarian norm is not the fundamental primary norm of the EC code because its difficulty to comply with would prevent there being a sufficient degree of uniformity in people's moral behavior. If, however, its use is restricted only to resolving rare conflicts not covered by other secondary norms, then it would be used with such relative infrequency that its use would pose no real threat to the uniformity made possible by the more frequently used, easier-to-comply-with norms of the code. It is true that, owing to the difficulty of complying with the utilitarian norm, how to resolve those conflicts to which it is applicable would often be a matter about which there would be differing opinions and thus a certain amount of uncertainty. But this uncertainty would be far better than the even greater uncertainty of there being no moral norm whatever to appeal to for resolving these conflicts. With the utilitarian norm, what the correct resolution is would at least be clear in principle, thus providing a common ground from which differing opinions could be profitably discussed, a common ground that would be lacking were there no moral norm to which to appeal at all. And the human effort necessary for learning just this one general secondary norm for resolving these conflicts would be minuscule compared with the effort that would be necessary for learning instead an innumerable number of *specific* secondary norms for doing so. In other words, the costs of using the utilitarian norm in this role would be minimal and thus not likely to exceed the benefits, as would the much higher costs of using an innumerable number of specific secondary norms instead. So I suggest that the utilitarian norm is found in the EC code of morality after all, not as a fundamental primary norm, but in the very limited role of a secondary norm of last resort.

6.8 BORDERLINE CASES

The uniformity of behavior that the EC code is supposed to provide is subject to another threat: borderline cases. Say, for example, a woman gave birth to a creature that had precisely all the physical, as well as mental, features of a chimpanzee. Would it nevertheless be a human being for purposes, let us say, of our society's moral norm forbidding murder, that is, the premeditated killing of a human being? Fortunately, nature is uniform enough so that most creatures we are likely to encounter are either similar enough or dissimilar enough to the creatures that we have counted as human beings in the past so that we have no trouble classifying them one way or the other. But nature or human technology occasionally presents us with cases that are neither similar enough nor dissimilar enough to past cases so as to allow us to make a confident decision on a norm's applicability one way or the other. Cases to which some norm is neither clearly applicable nor clearly inapplicable we may speak of as falling within the "borderline" area of that norm, while cases to which the norm clearly is or is not applicable we may speak of as ones falling within the "core" area of that norm. Killing the "chimpanzee" described above would perhaps fall within the borderline area of our society's present moral norm forbidding the killing of human beings; while killing one's uncle in order to inherit his money would fall within the core, or clear-cut, area of this norm.

All norms have a borderline area, this area being more conspicuous with some norms than with others. Cases falling within the borderline area of a moral norm introduce an element of uncertainty in the form of differences of opinion about how the norm should be interpreted, and these differences of opinion pose a certain threat to uniformity of behavior. On the other hand, all norms also have a core area that, typically, will be the area into which the vast majority of cases fall. Since borderline cases are thus relatively infrequent, the threat to uniformity that they pose is actually not very great. But we are still left with the question of how such cases, when they do occur, should, according to the EC code, be resolved.

Borderline cases are of two kinds: the kind likely to occur frequently again and the kind not likely to occur frequently, if ever, again. With borderline cases of the first kind—those likely to occur frequently again—it seems clear that the core area of the moral norm in whose borderline area the case falls must be somehow extended so that thereafter cases of this kind fall within the norm's core area. Take, for example, the question of whether or not a fetus should count as a human being for purposes of the norm prohibiting murder. Before safe and easy abortions became possible I assume that, in the interests of simplicity, the norm within the EC code prohibiting murder did not address itself to this case any more than it did to numerous other purely hypothetical cases, such as the "chimpanzee" case above; all such cases simply fell within this norm's borderline area. But with the discovery of a means for having safe and easy abortions, what was previously a purely hypothetical borderline case, one with virtually no chance of occurring, suddenly became a borderline case very likely to occur indeed, and to occur frequently. It stands to reason that, if circumstances change sufficiently, the moral norms justifiable in terms of the utilitarian standard change accordingly. The discovery of a means for having safe and easy abortions surely represented a "sufficient" change in circumstances. Thus I assume that the utilitarian standard, with this change in circumstances, requires that the core area of the norm in the EC code prohibiting murder be expanded somehow so that thereafter cases involving abortions would fall within this norm's core rather than its borderline area. Exactly *how* the core area would expand—that is, exactly how the abortion question should, in terms of the utilitarian standard, be resolved—I do not know. From the standpoint of a theory similar to the one defended here, provocative answers have been suggested by R. M. Hare (1975), and by L. W.

Sumner (1981). But I shall not pursue this matter. The point I wish to make is simply that, when abortions became readily available, the core area of the norm in the EC code prohibiting murder presumably did expand in *some* way so as to address itself specifically to abortions.

Do then the cores of those norms in the EC code of morality thus expand, that is, become more complex, in some way whenever what was previously a purely hypothetical borderline case becomes actual? I doubt it. If these cores were allowed to expand, thus becoming more complex, with every borderline case that became actual then, after a certain period of time, the cores of these norms would become so large and complex that the human effort necessary for learning any one of these expanded norms would be tremendous—so great, in fact, that the benefits of having expanded and thus clarified the norm would no longer be worth the costs of this extra effort. Earlier I suggested that, for the sake of remaining manageably simple, the EC code does not contain a specific secondary norm to cover every kind of conflict of duties that might arise, no matter how rare. I want now to suggest that, similarly, the core areas of its norms do not expand to cover every borderline case that comes along, no matter how unlikely it is ever to occur again. I suggest that only for borderline cases that are likely to occur frequently, or that are otherwise important, is an expansion of a norm's core area warranted, just as only for those kinds of conflicts likely to occur frequently is a specific secondary norm warranted.

How then are borderline cases likely not to occur frequently enough to warrant a change in a norm to be handled? One possibility is that the EC code prescribes that they be handled by appeal to the utilitarian norm, just as are those infrequently occurring conflict cases discussed above. Use of the utilitarian norm for this purpose would not, however, be without its drawbacks. Too often a person might be able to talk himself (and others) into thinking a case fell within some borderline area when in fact it did not, thus too easily gaining access for himself to the utilitarian norm. (There is a similar drawback with using the utilitarian norm for resolving *conflict* cases, although I suspect that, with conflict cases, it generally would be more difficult to talk oneself, and others, into thinking one was faced with a case requiring appeal to the utilitarian norm when in fact one was not.)

It might be thought that another way of resolving these borderline cases, a way that did not involve the utilitarian norm, would be by appealing to the very standard we are to use for "deriving" the norms in the first place—namely, the utilitarian standard. It is, of course, only by appealing to the utilitarian standard that we can determine, definitively, that the case really is a borderline one. But for these sorts of borderline cases, relatively insignificant ones unlikely to occur often, appealing to the utilitarian standard would not, by hypothesis, yield any resolutions. By hypothesis, these sorts of borderline cases are ones that, according to the utilitarian standard, are too insignificant to warrant any increase in the complexity of our norms. The costs of greater complexity (costs in the form of the energy required for people to learn the more complex norms, etc.) outweigh the benefits of greater precision. But without any increase in the complexity of these norms we would, of course, be left with the very same borderline problems with which we began. Thus we cannot, by hypothesis, resolve these sorts of borderline problems by means of the utilitarian standard—that is, by means of the three-dimensional evaluation from which we "derived" our norms in the first place.

It would appear that, for resolving these sorts of borderline cases, we would need to appeal to some norm or norms that had, for this purpose, been built into the EC code itself, or to some method of reasoning applicable to this code. One enticing possibility is that of having us resolve these borderline cases, and perhaps even hard-to-resolve conflict cases, by something like the reflective equilibrium method of moral reasoning proposed by John Rawls, and described here in chapter 9. I argue in chapter 9 that this methodology, or something like it, is appropriate for legal thinking and has a legitimate, although limited, use for moral thinking as well. With moral thinking, this methodology is, I claim, appropriate for reasoning *within* a given social pressure system—for working out the ramifications of its various norms and values, and so on. But, as I conclude there, for comparatively evaluating *alternative* systems, or parts of a system, this methodology is of little value; we must, for this, turn to that three-dimensional evaluation in terms of the utilitarian standard being proposed here. Yet since the resolutions of these borderline cases, or at least some of them, might already be implicit *within* the system, reflective equilibrium methodology might indeed be useful for bringing these resolutions to light.

But if something like reflective equilibrium methodology proves insufficient, as perhaps it would in at least some cases, then I see no alternative norm, or method, than that of appeal, finally, to the utilitarian norm. (Or, alternatively, the reflective equilibrium method itself might lead to the positing of such a norm—cf. sec. 9.4 above.) So I conclude, although somewhat reluctantly, that the utilitarian norm is found in the EC code as a norm of last resort not only for resolving certain conflict cases, but perhaps also for resolving these sorts of borderline cases, or at least some of them, as well. What the utilitarian norm prescribed for such cases might often be difficult to determine. But if used only as a norm of last resort, any uncertainty, rationalizations, and so on, to which it gave rise would, I think, be well within reasonable bounds. Most cases, after all, would be clear-cut ones—ones easily resolvable in terms of the simpler, easier-to-comply-with norms of the EC code.

It should be noted, incidentally, that the reason for moral norms having to remain relatively simple is not applicable to legal norms. The maintenance of social pressure for compliance with moral norms is everyone's job. Successfully maintaining moral norms—involving, as it does, the need for the norms being carefully learned by people in general, taught to the next generation, and so forth—does not come cheaply. If one of the details of a moral norm fails to be learned by people in general, that part of the norm is lost, this detail having been nowhere "officially" recorded, as have the details of legal norms. So to maintain moral norms fully intact, a great deal of effort by a great many people is involved, and, naturally, the more complex the moral norms are, the greater this effort must be and thus the higher their maintenance costs become. Legal norms, on the other hand, are maintained largely through governmental rather than social pressure, the maintenance of this governmental pressure being not everyone's job, but the job of a relatively small number of professionals—judges, lawyers, police. The general public must, to be sure, learn enough about society's legal norms to have at least a *rough* understanding of what they require; but legal norms, as opposed to moral norms, can be maintained fully intact without each of their *details* having to be learned by the general public. Not even the professionals whose job it is to maintain these legal norms need learn their every detail in order for them to be maintained fully intact. All that is necessary is that these details be properly recorded by and easily accessible to these professionals. For this reason, legal norms of great complexity can be maintained fully intact at far less cost than can moral norms of similar complexity. Since with legal norms the costs of complexity are indeed far less, it is reasonable to suppose that these costs do not necessarily, as with moral norms, exceed the benefits after a certain degree of complexity has been attained; and if, with legal norms, the costs of virtually any degree of complexity do not exceed the benefits, there is no conclusive reason for keeping legal norms simple like moral norms.

Finally, if there is no conclusive reason for keeping legal norms simple like moral norms, then how decisions in borderline cases should affect legal norms and how they should affect moral norms may well differ. If legal norms, or their core areas, need not be kept simple, then their core areas need not be left unchanged by decisions in unimportant borderline cases, as with moral norms. Instead, each decision in a borderline case in law, no matter *how* unimportant the case, can be allowed to contribute to the expansion of the legal norm's core area, thus allowing the legal norm to become more and more complex indefinitely.

6.9 THE BRIDGE NORM

Let me conclude the discussion of personal morality by considering briefly the connection between it and political morality. As we have seen, the entities that norms of political morality govern are not people (i.e., natural persons) but governments. On the other hand, it is, of course, people who cause governments to do whatever they do; so without some sort of connection between personal and political morality, norms of political morality would be, if not altogether pointless, certainly weakened with perhaps little capacity for motivating people. Without some sort of connection between personal and political morality a governmental leader who, say, led his nation into an immoral war could always avoid any personal moral responsibility by pointing out that, although it was he who caused the government to act immorally, since norms of political morality are applicable to governments only, he, being a human being and not a government, did absolutely nothing morally wrong himself. Therefore, to preclude public officials from thus avoiding any moral responsibility for their official behavior, some sort of connection between personal and political morality must exist. The most straightforward and, I think, best means of connecting personal and political morality is simply through a norm of *personal* morality requiring us, to the extent that we participate in making governmental decisions, always to do so in a way such as to achieve governmental compliance with political morality. I assume that the EC code of personal morality does contain a connecting or "bridge" norm of personal morality like this. So the governmental leader who knowingly led his nation into an immoral war would personally have acted immorally, but not because he, as opposed to the government, violated the norm of political morality forbidding this war; rather the norm *he* would have violated would be the bridge norm of personal morality requiring us, to the extent we make official governmental decisions, to do so consistently with political morality. And the more serious the foreseeable consequences of a particular violation of this bridge norm are, the more reprehensible the violation is. In sum, norms of political morality do not, on the view I am taking here, *directly* delineate what is morally right and wrong for people to do but, by means of this bridge norm, they *indirectly* delineate what is morally right and wrong for people to do.

This bridge norm of morality is obviously applicable to the decisions of public officials, they being the ones with the biggest role to play in governmental decision-making. But this norm should, in my view, also be applicable to all of us at least to the extent that we participate in public elections since, in doing so, we ourselves are participating in the official governmental decision-making process. Thus if we vote for the candidate representing our own self-interest knowing perfectly well he is the one most likely to steer the government away from the requirements of political morality, we are, in my view, violating this bridge norm of personal morality just as is the candidate himself who, once elected, does steer the government away from these requirements. We ourselves have violated this bridge norm, although I assume our culpability should be mitigated to the degree that it was unclear whether this candidate would steer the government in the wrong direction, and to the degree that (due to the likelihood that the candidate's opponent would have done something equally bad) we had no choice.

A number of important questions might be pursued concerning this bridge norm of personal morality, but I shall not pursue these questions here. One such question is: Which duty, according to the EC code of personal morality, should have priority when there is a conflict between what this bridge norm prescribes and what some other moral norm of the code prescribes? Take, for example, a public official—say, a secret agent of the CIA—who believes that political morality requires that the United States government, through the CIA, murder Fidel Castro for the sake of the general welfare. Assume, furthermore, that this public official, being a CIA agent, is himself the very person who is responsible for carrying out these kinds of governmental acts if they are to be done, and that he is thus faced with what appears to him to be a conflict of duties: because of his sincere, even though perverse, interpretation of political morality, he believes that the bridge norm of personal morality, the norm requiring that he not cause the government to be in violation of political morality, requires him to murder Castro; whereas another norm of personal morality, the norm prohibiting murder, forbids him from murdering Castro. To which norm, according to the EC code of personal morality, should he give priority? Does the EC code contain a secondary norm which *always* gives other norms of personal morality priority over the bridge norm, or just *sometimes*, or perhaps even *never*? Or does it contain a secondary norm that requires that public officials, when faced with such conflicts, always do the only thing that seems to enable them to avoid violating any of the conflicting duties—namely, resign from office? But let us not pursue these and other such questions about *personal* morality any further now. Let us instead turn to political morality.

Part III

POLITICAL MORALITY

7
Human Rights

7.1 PERSONAL AND POLITICAL MORALITY COMPARED

In this part, by focusing upon political morality, we shall complete our investigation into what sort of moral code the utilitarian standard justifies. Since I am referring to any moral code justified by the utilitarian standard as an "EC" code of morality, the question to be investigated in this part becomes: What, in general, is the EC code of political morality like?

The first thing that must be done is to explain more fully than I already have what is meant here by *political* morality. It is, in short, the morality that delineates what is morally right and wrong for governments, or political units, to do. (Note: throughout I shall, for convenience, use the word "government" as synonymous with "political unit," where such things as nations, counties, cities, and states count as political units.) It is by appeal to political morality that one might say, for instance, that the United States' military involvement in Vietnam, or Russia's take-over of Afghanistan was morally wrong.

There are those who hold that, in talking about the morality of governmental actions, the only thing we are really talking about is the morality of the actions of certain people, so that in saying that the United States or Russia acted wrongly, as in the above examples, the only thing we are really saying is that certain people—people such as Lyndon Johnson and Leonid Brezhnev—acted wrongly. Thus, on this view, all talk of the moral duties of governments must, if it is to make any literal sense, be translated into talk of the moral duties of particular people.

But whether this view, which we might call the *translation* thesis, represents the way we do, or should, use language is doubtful. In saying some government (or nation) has a moral duty to do such and such a thing, we do not normally mean that it is the moral duty of one or more particular people within that nation. For example, suppose that, according to the terms of an agreement between the two governments, the United States has received from China some high-quality building stone for government buildings, but that, according to an unexpected loophole in certain legal documents, the United States is relieved of any *legal* duty to pay for the stone. If we were then to say that the United States still had a *moral* duty to pay in spite of this legal loophole, what would we mean? Surely we would not mean that, say, President Reagan himself personally owes this amount to China, and therefore, morally speaking, should sell his ranch in California in order to raise enough cash to settle the debt. Nor would we mean even that each person in the United States is personally obligated to pay off such and such a proportion of the debt so that one might, therefore, fulfill one's personal moral obligation by sending this amount to China. What would be meant is that, morally speaking, the United States or United States government owes the money and is therefore obligated to pay, not that a certain person or persons within the United States owes this money. (For further elaboration of this point, see French 1975.)

I propose that, instead of getting bogged down in some version of the translation thesis, we instead view governments, for purposes of political morality talk, more or less as Anglo-American law views corporations. For a number of reasons—such as convenience and the assurance of continuity in spite of changes in ownership and management—the law, in many contexts, treats a corporation as if it were itself a person and, as such, the subject of legal duties rather than the people who own or manage it being the subject of these legal duties. So if, for example, a corporation reneges on a contract, it is the corporation itself, not its owners or managers, that is liable for any damages resulting from the breach of contract. Therefore, in a legal context, corporations are sometimes referred to as "artificial" persons. Artificial persons in law are nothing mysterious; they are simply convenient fictions. Similarly, for purposes of convenience and continuity in the face of changing personnel, it is desirable in a moral context to speak of governments as if they were persons and, as such, themselves the subject of moral duties, spelled out by moral norms applicable specifically to them; it is, in other words, desirable to view them as artificial persons. On this view, which we might call the *artificial person* thesis, talk about the morality of the actions of governments (or of nations, cities, states, etc.) makes perfectly good sense just as it is; it does not have to be somehow translated into talk about natural persons in order to make sense. This view thus avoids the problem of how, exactly, such translations are to be carried out, and preserves the simplicity of everyday political morality talk. The artificial person thesis need not carry with it excess metaphysical baggage having to do with governments (or nations, cities, states, etc.) being some sort of mysterious beings "over and above" human beings; they are, like corporations, simply convenient fictions. So by *political morality* what will be meant here is the morality that delineates what is morally right and wrong not for natural persons (except indirectly), but for governments (i.e., political units).

Actually, to be perfectly accurate, I must qualify somewhat this conclusion about political morality governing the decisions of *governments* only. There is a type of group the decisions of which should also fall within the reach of political morality, but which is not exactly a government, although it is governmentlike. I am referring to the group that makes a certain kind of *constitutional* decision—namely, a decision as to what a government's jurisdiction is to be. This kind of constitutional decision is one delineating what government, or branch of government, is to have *final say* for what people about what things. In modern-day societies the group that typically makes such constitutional decisions consists of those at a constitutional convention or, by means of a constitutional referendum, the people of the proposed jurisdiction as a whole. These are not ordinary governmental decisions for the simple reason that, until some such decision has been made, there is nothing yet that counts as a government to make governmental decisions. It is constitutional decisions of this sort, written or unwritten, that create governments in the first place. Thus let us call these decisions *metagovernmental* decisions, and groups that make them *metagovernments*.

Sometimes it appears as if a government itself is making a jurisdictional or metagovernmental decision. For example, say that a proposal has been made to amend the United States Constitution so as to make what is now the state of Texas a sovereign nation completely independent of the United States. As specified in the United States Constitution, this proposal will become law if approved by the state legislatures of three-fourths of the states. Since the jurisdictional decision in question is to be decided by the elected governmental officials of the various states— that is, the state legislators—it might appear as if this is one jurisdictional decision at least that would qualify as being a governmental decision also. We shall, however, view the matter differently; we shall consider the state legislators to be "changing hats" and becoming members of a fictitious metagovernmental group for making just this one decision. The importance of thus distinguishing between governmental and metagovernmental decisions will become apparent later. But for the time being I shall, for convenience, refer to both types of decisions covered by political morality—that is, governmental and metagovernmental decisions—simply as *governmental* decisions, and refer to both governments and metagovernments simply as *governments*.

Investigating the EC code of political morality might be easier if we begin by focusing upon the EC code for a small, homogeneous group having no relationship with other societies, and then work our way up to the EC code for more complex societies. Let us begin, therefore, by focusing upon the EC code for an imaginary society brought about, we may suppose, by a nuclear disaster that caused the several thousand men, women, and children who make up this society to flee Earth for a distant, uninhabited planet remarkably similar to Earth. The society these people form is thus made up of a small, homogeneous group of modern-day people like ourselves, but with no relationships with any human beings outside of their own society. The main reason for beginning with a world consisting solely of such a small, compact group of people is that we may safely assume that there is, and should be, only one government in such a world, not a number of independent governments as in our world today. Since we are hypothesizing that the society is made up of modern-day people accustomed to proceeding in a democratic way, we shall suppose that these people select a committee to draw up a constitution that is then submitted to the community as a whole for approval. We shall suppose, furthermore, that the form of government receiving final approval, and the form actually best for them, is a simple representative democracy that, at present, does not recognize any "local" governments under its authority. With the stage thus set, we may now turn to what sort of code is justified in terms of the utilitarian standard.

Since the utilitarian standard is, after all, clearly related to the utilitarian norm, it might be suggested that the utilitarian standard justifies a code of political morality for this community in which the utilitarian *norm* is fundamental—that is, has priority over everything else in the code. It will be recalled that earlier I rejected a similar suggestion made in connection with a code of *personal* morality (sec. 5.1). Let us see if the reasons for this rejection are applicable also to political morality.

The main reason for rejecting a code of *personal* morality in which the utilitarian norm is fundamental—that is, a direct utilitarian code—is that such a code could not generate adequate uniformity in people's moral behavior. It could not simply because the utilitarian norm would always be subject to many differing interpretations. A morality is supposed to create the sort of social climate in which there can be mutually beneficial interaction among numerous people in numerous different ways. But many differing interpretations of the utilitarian norm being simultaneously put into practice, as there would be if it were fundamental in personal morality, would only undermine successful interaction, creating instead insecurity, distrust and, in general, relative chaos (sec. 5.1).

Is then this reason for not having the utilitarian norm be fundamental in personal morality applicable to political morality as well? Not exactly. Since we are hypothesizing now that only one government exists, the code of political morality in question regulates the behavior not of numerous entities, as a code of personal morality does, but of just a single entity: the government. So instead of numerous differing interpretations of the utilitarian norm being simultaneously put into practice, as we have seen there would be if it were fundamental in personal morality, only one interpretation would be put into practice—this one interpretation being, of course, that of the government, owing to its status as the only entity whose practices the code of political morality would be regulating. With only this one interpretation being put into practice, the chaos resulting from numerous differing interpretations being simultaneously put into practice would never occur. And if the chaos resulting from numerous differing interpretations being simultaneously put into practice would never occur, then the above reason for not having the utilitarian norm be fundamental in personal morality is not altogether applicable to having it be fundamental in our hypothetical society's political morality.

Another reason for rejecting a code of *personal* morality in which the utilitarian norm is fundamental is, as we saw (sec. 5.1), that such a code would be too demanding; it would, for example, require that everything we do be for the sake of maximizing expected utility leaving us, in principle, no opportunities to attend solely to our own personal wants and desires. But this reason for rejection is, once again, inapplicable to *political* morality because a government, being an artificial rather than a natural person, has no personal wants and desires to compete against the demands of the utilitarian norm.

The final reason previously given for rejecting the utilitarian norm in the case of personal morality is that a code in which the utilitarian norm is fundamental might well have unexpected negative results, such as depriving society of the means for adequately motivating people to exercise their talents and abilities for the general good (sec. 5.1). But since these unexpected negative results are all of a sort that arise from the incompatibility of utilitarian demands with real people's motivations, wants, and desires, they also would have no direct applicability to artificial persons, such as governments. Thus I conclude that none of the reasons given previously for rejecting a code of personal morality in which the utilitarian norm is fundamental are altogether applicable to political morality.

7.2 THE STRUCTURE OF THE ARGUMENT FOR RIGHTS

In the preceding section we saw that the reasons why the utilitarian norm should not be fundamental in a code of *personal* morality are not altogether applicable to *political* morality. From this we might be tempted to conclude that the utilitarian standard therefore justifies a code of political morality in which the utilitarian norm *is* fundamental—that is, in which it does have priority over everything else. Such a conclusion would, I think, be very much mistaken; in this section I shall try to show that the utilitarian standard justifies instead a code of political morality in which priority over the utilitarian norm is given at least to certain human rights. By a "human" right, I mean simply a basic moral right of human beings. (Since here, as elsewhere, my concern is with justification, not conceptual analysis, I do not attempt any analysis of the concept of a "right;" for such an analysis, see White 1984.) Those human rights which, in the EC code of political morality, are, I claim, given priority over the utilitarian norm are certain relatively specific and easy-to-comply-with rights against the government—ones such as the right to freedom of speech, and the right to freedom of religion. And the reason for their priority is *not,* I shall argue, to make up for some deficiency inherent in what the utilitarian norm prescribes; on the contrary, the reason is that giving them priority actually contributes to, rather than detracts from, the realization of utilitarian requirements.

The argument begins with a few propositions we know to be true. We know, first of all, that the sorts of governmental restrictions upon personal freedom that are forbidden by rights against the government do not *normally* maximize utility, as I have defined it (sec. 3.1). Of course there are always some circumstances in which some such restrictions *do* maximize utility. There may be circumstances in which such restrictions maximize *expected* utility, as I have defined it (sec. 3.1). The existence of circumstances in which they maximize expected utility is not nearly as certain as the existence of circumstances in which they maximize utility, but these circumstances may well exist. Yet surely these circumstances are not especially common. We know quite enough about the potential dangers of such restrictions upon freedom, and the likelihood of these dangers actually occurring, to know the following, which we may take as the first premise of the argument: In most circumstances, the governmental restrictions in question do not maximize expected utility. In other words, we know that most circumstances are not ones "favorable" for such restrictions.

We also know it is incredibly difficult ever to determine what exactly such favorable circumstance are, and when exactly they exist. Why this is so difficult—why, in other words, it is so difficult ever to determine if one of these restrictions upon freedom really does, in the circumstances at hand, maximize expected utility—should require little explanation. For making this determination, not only would the amount of factual information needed be, in principle, virtually infinite, but, with such an emotionally charged matter as this, what relatively few facts we did have would be subject to being distorted by our rationalizations. By a *rationalization* I mean the trick that a person's mind plays on him of twisting the facts so as to make a very bad justification for some position appear to be a very good justification, the cause of this despicable self-deception being that, for personal reasons, the person very much *wants* the position to be justified. In short: whether those relatively rare circumstances currently exist in which a certain one of these governmental restrictions does maximize utility can never be determined very reliably—which we may take as the second premise of the argument.

From all of this we may, I think, conclude the following, which is the third premise of the argument: A belief that those relatively rare circumstances currently exist in which a certain one of these governmental restrictions does maximize expected utility is always more likely to be mistaken than not. Trying to pick out those relatively rare circumstances favorable for one of these restrictions is like the judge, discussed earlier (sec. 1.3), trying to pick out the one defendant in a hundred who, in spite of the blood-test evidence, really is the father. As we saw, a judge's powers of discrimination simply are not great enough to justify this attempt. Likewise, I am now arguing, no one's powers of discrimination are great enough to justify the attempt to distinguish the relatively rare circumstances favorable for one of these restrictions from the ones that are not. It is true that, in the case of the judge, the antecedent probability of a defendant being the father is known exactly—the probability, provided by the blood test, is .01—while it is not known exactly what the antecedent probability is of these favorable circumstances existing. We do know that the antecedent probability of favorable circumstances is relatively low. But, for the sake of argument, say this probability was not as low as the .01 probability of a defendant being the father, but was .10 instead, or even somewhat higher. This alone would not, I submit, be enough to undermine the analogy with the judge, especially since here any greater antecedent probability would be at least partially offset by lesser powers of discrimination; for, in the matter of whether favorable circumstances exist, as complex as this matter is, our powers of discrimination (case by case) are surely even less than those of the judge. This brings us to the fourth and final premise in the argument: For any one of these governmental restrictions, the "harm" from failing to implement it when implementing it is that which maximizes expected utility is, on the average, no greater than the "harm" from implementing it when failing to implement it is that which maximizes expected utility. Given the seriousness of the various kinds of harm that the restrictions upon freedom in question tend to generate, I would not expect this premise to be particularly controversial.

From these premises, we may conclude the following: The governmental restrictions in question are always bad utilitarian gambles. Because of human fallibility, any attempt to maximize expected utility by implementing one of these restrictions does not itself maximize expected utility. That is to say, the attempt does not itself maximize expected utility, assuming, as we should here (see sec. 2.3), that not even a hypothetical "ideal" chooser ever has more insight than we human beings do into whether any of these restrictions maximize expected utility in the circumstances at hand. What does maximize expected utility—or does so *given* our lack of insight into whether any of the restrictions maximize expected utility (without qualification) in the circumstances at hand—is for us human beings always to give norms *prohibiting* these restrictions priority over trying to decide in accordance with the utilitarian norm. Since all governmental decisions are, of course, made by human beings, it likewise maximizes expected utility for *governments* to give norms prohibiting these restrictions priority over the utilitarian norm. From this we may conclude that it maximizes expected utility for there to be *social pressure* for governments to give these norms priority over the utilitarian norm—that is, we may conclude that their priority is justified by the utilitarian standard, and that such norms thus have priority over the utilitarian norm in the EC code of political morality. And finally, since norms prohibiting these governmental restrictions upon freedom are equivalent to rights against the government, we may conclude that, in the EC code of political morality, rights against the government have priority over the utilitarian norm.

7.3 FREEDOM OF SPEECH: AN APPLICATION OF THE ARGUMENT

This then is the general structure of the argument; let us now look more closely at some details, such as what exactly these restrictions, which I claim to be always bad utilitarian gambles, are. As an example of governmental restrictions that are always bad utilitarian gambles, take restrictions upon people's freedom of speech. The restrictions I have in mind include the following: the eighteenth-century ban in England upon Thomas Paine's book *Rights of Man;* the former laws in certain parts of the United States against teaching Darwin's theory of evolution; the legal prohibition upon speeches criticizing Hitler in Nazi Germany; and the present governmental censorship of news coverage in Russia. One way of describing what all these examples have in common is that they are all governmental restrictions upon freedom to express beliefs through ordinary written or verbal means. I shall here be limiting my consideration to restrictions clearly falling within this description—that is, within its core area rather than within the inevitable borderline area around it. What I am claiming is not that *any* restriction that might for some reason be characterized as a restriction upon freedom of speech is always a bad utilitarian gamble, but only that restrictions falling within this particular core area are.

The outline of this core area will perhaps become clearer if I specify some restrictions upon speech that do *not* fall within it. Since this core includes only restrictions upon the freedom to express *beliefs,* it therefore excludes any restrictions upon the sort of pornography and obscenity that is not an essential ingredient in the expression of a belief. For the same reason, also excluded from this core area are governmental restrictions upon deliberately deceptive speech, restrictions that commonly take the form of laws prohibiting perjury, false advertising, and the like. Finally, since this core area includes only restrictions upon freedom to express beliefs through ordinary *written* or *verbal* means, it excludes restrictions upon the expression of beliefs through such (primarily) nonlinguistic means as civil disobedience, protest marches, and other such publicity stunts. So what finally am I offering as one type of governmental restriction that is always a bad utilitarian gamble? The answer is: restrictions upon freedom of speech falling within the above core area. Whenever I refer to restrictions upon freedom of speech (or to censorship), this should be taken to mean restrictions falling within this core area only.

That this type of restriction is indeed always a bad utilitarian gamble can, I think be substantiated well enough in two different ways. The first, most straightforward way is through an appeal to history. There are numerous examples throughout human history of well-intentioned censorship of beliefs doing great harm, and few, if any, examples of its doing any real good. Through such well-intentioned censorship scientific advances have sometimes been held back for centuries; invaluable social, political, and philosophical ideas have been suppressed and, in some cases surely, lost forever. The second way of substantiating that censorship is indeed a genuine example of a bad utilitarian gamble is through rational argument. One might begin with John Stuart Mill's famous arguments for freedom of speech (1859). Mill emphasizes such things as the value of truth, and the greater likelihood of truth coming to light through a free market of competing beliefs than through a belief monopoly imposed by censorship.

Of course circumstances will occur that are in fact "favorable" for censorship, circumstances in which censorship does indeed maximize expected utility. But notice that trying to determine whether such circumstances currently exist is always an *especially* perilous utilitarian calculation to try to make, one more likely than most to be in error. Beliefs that typically are the subject of proposed censorship are ones concerning politics, morality, religion, and other such topics—topics in which the pursuit of truth is unusually prone to miscalculations; and any such miscalculations would likely result in seriously miscalculating the expected utility of the censorship. The difficulty in calculating what is true and false concerning these topics is in part due simply to the inherent difficulty of the topics themselves. But it is also due in part to the fact that these topics are unusually fertile grounds for rationalizations. That human beings are especially prone to rationalizing beliefs concerning politics, morality, religion, and other such topics is well known. And it is to be expected that these rationalizations will not only contaminate a person's thinking about the beliefs themselves, but also contaminate his thinking about the expected utility of their censorship. Furthermore, censorship, more than many other kinds of policies, has built into it certain more or less permanent disadvantages, ones that are present under virtually all circumstances. Mill points out some of these. For example, even if the belief to be censored is in fact false, its censorship still has the disadvantage of eliminating just the sort of healthy criticism of standard beliefs needed for provoking people into rethinking these beliefs, and for thus preventing the beliefs from becoming stagnant and empty. This and other such disadvantages might indeed in certain circumstances be outweighed. But the point is that, in carrying out the balancing calculations, each such disadvantage must be assigned its due weight in order not to invalidate the final result; yet it is impossible to do this with any reasonable degree of accuracy, thus making each of these permanently built-in disadvantages itself a potential source of serious miscalculation. In short, special susceptibility to rationalization along with other sources of potential error all add up to the fact that trying to determine whether circumstances favorable to censorship exist is indeed always an especially perilous utilitarian calculation to try to make, one with an unusually high probability of being mistaken. If then we take this unusually high probability of being mistaken in conjunction with the potential seriousness of such a mistake, we have grounds for concluding that censorship is a bad utilitarian gamble not just most of the time, but all of the time.

I am claiming that freedom-of-speech restrictions falling within a certain core area are always bad utilitarian gambles. But a case-by-case examination of restrictions falling within the borderline area "around" this core would no doubt result in the core's gradual expansion. Furthermore, additional investigation would reveal that my rough delineation of this core area could be improved upon. Additional investigation might reveal, for example, that restrictions not just upon statements of belief, but also upon certain kinds of insincere statements, are always bad utilitarian gambles. If so, this would require expanding the core area so as to include these kinds of restrictions also. Or further investigation might reveal that certain parts of the core area as I have characterized it must be sliced away (i.e., sliced away by building exceptions into it). For example, some have contended that the restrictions upon freedom of speech included in this core are not always bad utilitarian gambles for underdeveloped countries, since only a totalitarian regime that severely limited personal freedom, including freedom of speech, could exercise enough control over the economy to bring about a satisfactory rate of development. I myself seriously doubt the soundness of this contention; yet if it *is* sound, then this would require that we slice off that part of the core area applicable to underdeveloped countries. But let me emphasize that as long as a substantial core area still remained after cutting off this or other slices, and adding others, my main point would remain intact. This point is that within a very substantial core area, at least *roughly* similar to the one I have delineated, restrictions upon freedom of speech are indeed always bad utilitarian gambles.

And, according to the view being proposed here, it is precisely those restrictions which are always bad utilitarian gambles that it is the function of rights to prohibit. So, on this view, a right against the government is justified insofar as it does in fact prohibit what is always a bad utilitarian gamble. How, on this view, justified rights contribute to, rather than detract from, the realization of utilitarian requirements should now be clear: the gambler who makes it a policy never to bet when the odds are against him is likely to have more winnings, on the whole, than without this policy; similarly, the government that, by respecting justified rights, foregoes what are always bad utilitarian gambles is likely to come closer to maximizing expected utility, on the whole, than by not respecting these rights.

Exactly what rights can be justified in these terms—that is, in terms of their prohibiting bad utilitarian gambles? I have already suggested that a right to freedom of speech can. Others that I suggest can, without undue difficulty, be shown to be justified in these terms are a right to freedom of religion, a right to quit one's job whenever one wants (i.e., a right not to be a slave), and a right not to be discriminated against on the basis of one's race, color, sex, national origin, or religion. And were I to attempt a complete inventory here I would surely include certain judicial and political rights as well. Each of these rights prohibits just the kinds of restrictions upon freedom that, I would think, both history and rational argument show to be bad utilitarian gambles. I will not run through the arguments that might be given in each case to show this, but they would be similar to those already sketched in connection with censorship. In other words, the kinds of restrictions that these rights prohibit are all ones that can be shown to be especially susceptible to being justified through rationalizations and related phenomena, such as prejudices and superstitions. (For other, briefer, attempts to provide what amounts to an indirect utilitarian defense of rights, see Braybrooke 1968, 34-43; Lyons 1977 [on behalf of John Stuart Mill]; Dworkin 1979, 272-78 [according to one possible interpretation of these pages]; Gray 1982 [also on behalf of John Stuart Mill]. And for an attack on especially Gray's version [but one inapplicable to the version of indirect utilitarianism proposed here] see Alexander 1985.)

7.4 POSITIVE RIGHTS

The type of rights against the government that I have been talking about so far, however, may not provide the entire remedy against bad utilitarian gambles. All of the rights that I have been talking about so far are ones normally referred to as "negative" rights. Roughly speaking, a negative right is one that *forbids* doing a certain thing *to* whoever has the right, such as, for example, preventing him from expressing his beliefs. Contrasted with negative rights are ones normally referred to as "positive." Roughly speaking, a positive right is one that *requires* doing a certain thing *for* whoever has the right, such as, for example, providing him with the means for necessary medical care. The clarity of any distinction between negative and positive rights has been challenged (see, for example, Davis 1980; Shue 1980, chap. 2); but, for present purposes at least, I think this distinction is clear enough.

Why might negative rights provide only part of the remedy against bad utilitarian gambles? Say, for example, that any number of governmental programs would provide everyone, no matter how poor, with the benefit of adequate medical care, that for everyone to enjoy this benefit is clearly called for from a utilitarian perspective, but that the government, spurred on by the medical profession, persistently rationalizes a refusal to implement any of these programs. An appeal to negative rights would be of little help in remedying this situation; negative rights can only forbid harm; they cannot require a benefit. It is for situations like this that positive rights might have to enter the picture.

When people have a *positive* right against the government, what this amounts to is the government's having a duty to make sure they enjoy a certain benefit—adequate medical care, higher education, or some such thing. Now, on the view being proposed here, a right is justified if and only if it precludes what are always bad utilitarian gambles. Thus a positive right against the government is justified if and only if it requires that the government ensure the enjoyment of a benefit which is such that, for the government *not* to ensure its enjoyment would always be a bad utilitarian gamble. Of course this discussion presupposes that the government is *capable* of ensuring enjoyment of this benefit, and that it would do so by means that were reasonable and that did not create any conflicts with other rights. Not ensuring the enjoyment of some benefit B is always a bad utilitarian gamble if, roughly speaking, (1) our susceptibility to mistakes in trying to pick out the relatively rare circumstances in which not ensuring the enjoyment of B does maximize expected utility, and (2) the seriousness of such mistakes are, in combination, so great that (from a utilitarian perspective) we ought always to act on the assumption that it is *ensuring* the enjoyment of B that maximizes expected utility, no matter what our beliefs to the contrary might be. And if not ensuring the enjoyment of B were in fact always a bad utilitarian gamble, then, of course, the utilitarian standard would justify a moral norm—that is, a positive right against the government—that did require the government to ensure the enjoyment of B, and this norm would have priority over the utilitarian norm in the EC code of political morality.

We have thus seen how, *in principle,* a positive right might be justified by the utilitarian standard, and given priority over the utilitarian norm in the EC code of political morality. But does the EC code of political morality *in fact* contain any positive rights? It is true that positive rights are much more prone than negative rights to fall into conflict with one another, and their implementation and "enforcement" present special difficulties. Nonetheless, I suggest that the EC code of political morality for modern, industrial societies does in fact contain at least the following positive rights, although I shall not attempt to demonstrate this here:

(1) The right to food, clothing, and shelter sufficient for avoiding malnutrition or overexposure to the elements.
(2) The right to adequate medical care.
(3) The right to that degree of education for which one is intellectually qualified.
(4) The right to adequate legal counsel.

7.5 CONSISTENCY WITH COMMON BELIEFS

Utilitarian moral theories are often attacked by pointing out their alleged inconsistency with common beliefs (or "intuitions") about moral rights. Whether this strategy of attack is sound is debatable; about every such inconsistency the utilitarian can always say "so much the worse for common beliefs." In any case, this strategy of attack will not succeed very well against the utilitarian view of moral rights set out here since, as I shall now try to show, this view and common beliefs about moral right happen to be remarkably consistent; in other words, this view, which takes the function of moral rights to be that of precluding bad utilitarian gambles, succeeds remarkably well in providing a rationale for common beliefs.

To begin with, the rights about whose justification there seems to be the greatest worldwide consensus are, for the most part, the very ones that we would find to be justified from the "utilitarian gambler" approach set out here. I am thinking of rights such as the right to express freely one's beliefs, to practice one's religion, to be free from racial and sexual discrimination, to receive adequate medical care, and so on. These are just the sort of rights that could most plausibly be claimed to preclude what are always bad utilitarian gambles. Furthermore, this view of rights provides a rationale for why those rights about which there is the greatest consensus include not just negative, but positive ones as well. Of course not all alleged rights would be capable of being justified in these terms as easily as those mentioned above, and others like them; in some instances it would be very difficult indeed to determine whether an alleged right really is thus justified, or to determine exactly what its scope should be. But of course this is what we should expect; questions about rights are not always easily answered. In fact, some of the alleged rights about which there is the most controversy worldwide might well turn out to be ones that are also most problematic in terms of this approach to their justification. I am thinking, in particular, of the alleged right to private property—if, that is, this right is broadly interpreted so as to include within its scope the private ownership of not just consumer goods, but capital goods as well.

Whether we do have a right to private property (broadly interpreted so as to include within its scope even capital goods) is indeed problematic in terms of the approach taken here, and it may be useful to see why. On the approach taken here, rights serve to delineate what are always bad utilitarian gambles. So to decide whether we have this broad right (that is, whether we have it according to the "utilitarian gambler" approach taken here), we must ask whether governmental restrictions upon the private ownership of property are always bad utilitarian gambles. As we have seen, showing that restrictions of this sort are always bad utilitarian gambles would involve showing that beliefs about such restrictions maximizing expected utility in the circumstances at hand are *especially* subject to being mistaken; that they are, in fact, more likely to be mistaken than not. That this can be shown is doubtful. One of the major causes of mistaken beliefs is rationalization. But the rationalizations of public officials would no doubt tend more to support not restrictions upon private property, but the lack of restrictions, since it is a lack of restrictions that the wealthy normally view as being in their better interests, and public officials are normally wealthy. Furthermore, the issues that divide advocates of socialism, a system favoring restrictions upon private property, and advocates of capitalism, a system favoring the absence of such restrictions, are extremely complex; and at present economics is by no means an exact science. This suggests we cannot even be reasonably sure that in the *great majority* of circumstances today these restrictions have less expected utility than the absence of these restrictions. And if we cannot even be reasonably sure that this is true in the great majority of circumstances, we have little basis for showing that contrary beliefs about *particular* circumstances are likely to be mistaken. From all of this we may, I think, derive an important conclusion: beliefs about restrictions upon private property maximizing expected utility are not the sort of beliefs that can at present be shown to be *especially* subject to being mistaken as can, say, the corresponding beliefs about restrictions upon freedom of speech. And if these beliefs cannot, at present, be shown to be especially subject to being mistaken then, according to the "utilitarian gambler" approach taken here, we should not, as yet, elevate private property to the status of a right; doing so would amount to locking us into a system of *extreme* capitalism, a capitalism that tolerates no restrictions upon private property whatever. I am not denying that extreme capitalism may, in the long run, prove to be the best possible system (although I myself happen to believe that certain more moderate versions of capitalism, even certain versions of market socialism, are more likely candidates). I am only denying that we are, at present, entitled to be so sure that extreme capitalism will prove to be the best that we can assume that the EC code includes a right to property broad enough to preclude any experimentation with alternative systems.

But our not being able, on the approach taken here, to justify, at present, a broad right to property does not, it seems to me, reveal a major conflict between what can be justified in terms of this approach and common beliefs. On the contrary, since even in capitalist countries there is at present great controversy about whether we have any such broad right to property, our not being able to justify it is exactly what we might expect.

Viewing the function of rights to be that of precluding bad utilitarian gambles squares better, incidentally, with what rights we are commonly believed to have than does the traditional view of what their function is. According to the traditional view, endlessly endorsed in political rhetoric, their function is to protect the interests of the minority against the will of the majority. Although the traditional view might seem to square fairly well with one or two of the rights we are commonly believed to have—especially with the right not to be discriminated against on the basis of race, color, creed, and the like—it does not square at all well with most of them. The right to freedom of speech, for example, is for the protection of not just the minority, but everyone, because it is not at all unheard of for governments to censor even *majority* beliefs. Nor surely are positive rights, such as the right to medical care or to an education, just for the protection of the minority; without them it would not necessarily be just a minority of people that would be worse off. In fact, not even discrimination on the basis of race, color, creed, and so on is always directed against a *minority;* take for example, South Africa. Furthermore, it is not necessarily from the will of the *majority,* but from the will of the *government* that these and other rights offer protection. Of course, on the traditional view the will of the government *is* the will of the majority, in a representative democracy at least. But this is simply a mistake. The will of the government is, to be sure, the will of the majority whenever a public issue is decided directly by popular vote; but in a representative democracy most issues are not decided directly. Instead, popular voting is usually for the purpose of deciding upon representatives; it is then these representatives who make most of the actual decisions, and they are far from mere polltakers. Nor indeed *should* they be mere poll-takers; they should exercise a certain degree of independent judgment. In sum: rights against the government are properly characterized as devices for protecting the interests of not just the minority, but everyone, against the will of not necessarily the majority, but the government. This characterization, although inconsistent with the traditional view, is entirely consistent with the approach taken here.

Finally, one especially common belief about rights for which the view set out here provides a rationale is the belief that whenever a utilitarian (or, utilitarianlike) norm conflicts with one of our rights, the right should be given priority. That the right should be given priority becomes perfectly intelligible in light of that function which, on the view set out here, rights against the government serve. They serve the function of prohibiting what are always bad utilitarian gambles; so whenever that which is believed to be required by the utilitarian norm contravenes one of these rights, then obviously the right should be given priority. The right should be given priority since that which contravenes it is, *ex hypothesi,* a bad utilitarian gamble, and thus not the "best" alternative after all. And, therefore, among the secondary (i.e., conflict-resolving) norms of the EC code of political morality is a secondary norm that gives these rights priority over the utilitarian norm, without exception (or over the "general welfare" norm—see chap. 8).

It might be objected that, in arguing that rights *always* should be given priority over utilitarian requirements, I have overshot my mark since, according to common belief, utilitarian requirements, in at least certain circumstances, do have priority over what certain rights normally prescribe—especially in circumstances characterizable as states of emergency. For example, were an innocent country on the verge of being overwhelmed by the invading forces of an overly ambitious dictator, then most people would believe the fulfillment of, say, the right of everyone to that degree of education for which he or she is intellectually qualified should be temporarily sacrificed if it conflicted with the utilitarian goal of producing enough armaments to turn back the invasion. So it might be argued that, at least in cases such as these, common belief does give priority to utilitarian requirements. My reply would be as follows. As already mentioned, some of the rights recognized by the EC code surely have certain exceptions to what they normally prescribe that are best (though not necessarily) thought of as being built into the rights themselves. Among these exceptions might be an exception for emergencies built into this right to an education, and perhaps into certain other positive rights (but probably not into any negative rights recognized by the EC code of political morality). This exception would be applicable to just such cases as the invasion case mentioned above. In such cases, therefore, this right to an education *itself* would allow utilitarian requirements to be given temporary priority over what it normally calls for; so, strictly speaking, there would be no genuine conflict between it and utilitarian requirements after all.

But, in attributing exceptions to the rights of the EC code of political morality, we must be careful. The same rationale behind the establishment of these rights in the first place limits the number of exceptions that may be built into them, and limits the extent to which any one of these exceptions may be vague or hard to comply with. One exception which, from this rationale, we know that none of these rights could ever have built into it is a general exception for whatever is required by the utilitarian norm; such an exception would, of course, gobble up the right entirely. So, in my view, rights most definitely are *not* mere utilitarian rules of thumb. Utilitarian rules of thumb delineate not what are always, but just *most* of the time, bad utilitarian gambles. They are merely rough-and-ready guidelines for whenever there is not sufficient time or data to work out whether or not something really is a bad utilitarian gamble; as such, whenever there do happen to be sufficient time and data, they may be overridden. To turn rights into rules of thumb would be to turn them into the same farce as they are in the Russian Constitution. The Russian Constitution grants the Russian people what would be a magnificent array of rights except for the fact that these rights allow exceptions to them for any cases in which the Russian government thinks they should be overridden. Thus, for the Russians, rights against the government work just like rules of thumb; they are no more than rough-and-ready guidelines. Most people would not consider these to be genuine rights at all, which, again, is consistent with the view of rights taken here. If rights against the government allow exceptions to them for any cases in which the government thinks they should be overridden, then they are allowing the government to take those very gambles which, according to the view being proposed here, it is their function always to disallow. If this view is correct, it is therefore no wonder that such easily overridden rights do not appear to be genuine.

7.6 HOW NOT TO JUSTIFY REVERSE DISCRIMINATION

At the beginning of this book I mentioned that some philosophers hold that giving everyone's interests equal consideration has priority over any moral norm specifically forbidding racial discrimination; therefore, these philosophers argue, certain "benign" forms of racial discrimination, such as reverse discrimination for wiping out the effects of prior racial discrimination, can be justified by appealing directly to equal consideration (Dworkin 1977, chap. 9; Singer 1978). But a norm prescribing that we decide what to do by giving everyone's interests equal consideration is equivalent to the utilitarian norm, as it has been interpreted here. And a moral norm specifically forbidding racial discrimination is, in effect, equivalent to a *right* not to be discriminated against on the basis of race. Furthermore, such a right is, if I am not mistaken, among those which can be justified in the way proposed here—that is, contravening it can be shown to be always a bad utilitarian gamble. So, if I am not mistaken, these philosophers are making a serious mistake: no governmental racial discrimination can ever be justified by appealing directly to equal consideration. For a government to justify reverse discrimination in this way would be for it to do the very thing I claim a government should never do—namely, give the utilitarian norm priority over one of our rights. If for justifying "benign" forms of racial discrimination, such as reverse discrimination, public officials and others are allowed to appeal directly to what is, in effect, the utilitarian norm, it will be only a matter of time, it seems to me, before they start appealing to the utilitarian norm for justifying forms of racial discrimination that are not so benign.

But I might now encounter an objection of the following sort. According to the theory proposed here, moral norms, including of course any in the form of rights, can have exceptions built into them. Furthermore, we are to decide whether some proposed exception is justified by appeal to the utilitarian standard, which obviously is closely related to the utilitarian norm. If we appeal to the utilitarian standard for deciding whether to build an exception for reverse discrimination into the right, we are (so the objection might go) appealing to utilitarian considerations to decide whether to give reverse discrimination priority over the right. But then is this not doing essentially the same thing I say we should never do?

The answer is no. Appealing to the utilitarian standard for deciding whether to build the exception for reverse discrimination into the right, and appealing to the utilitarian norm for deciding whether to give reverse discrimination priority over this right are far from being essentially the same. And to understand why is to understand a crucial aspect of the theory proposed here. To appeal to the utilitarian norm for deciding whether to give reverse discrimination priority over this right is to evaluate reverse discrimination along one dimension only; it is to ask only whether the likely consequences of successfully adhering to reverse discrimination are better than those of not doing so. But (according to this theory) to appeal to the utilitarian standard for deciding whether to build an exception for reverse discrimination into this right, we must broaden the scope of our evaluation considerably. As explained earlier (sec. 4.3), we must ask not only about the likely consequences of successfully complying with reverse discrimination policy, but also about the extent to which people *would* be likely to comply successfully—not just now, but in other circumstances that are likely to arise as well. Along with this, we must ask about the likely consequences of attempts that failed. (Might, for instance, an attempt at reverse discrimination that failed be perceived as ordinary discrimination instead?) And, finally, we must ask about the likely costs of any social pressure designed to bring about this compliance. In other words, according to the theory proposed here, deciding whether to build an exception for reverse discrimination into the right requires not merely the one-dimensional evaluation called for by the utilitarian norm, but the three-dimensional evaluation called for by the method of justification that appealing to the utilitarian standard represents (sec. 4.7).

And what would the result of such an evaluation be? I do not know; I suggest, however, that it would show that building an exception for reverse discrimination into the right not to be discriminated against would be a mistake. Currently, this right is so fragile, apparently so difficult for people to comply with, that to complicate it by building this exception into it might well, I suspect, do more harm than good—by generating misinterpretations, miscalculations, and so on. Yet, even if my suspicions are correct, perhaps reverse discrimination, or something very much like it, might be justified nevertheless, not as an exception built into our right not to be discriminated against, and certainly not as a policy that, for utilitarian reasons, has priority over this right, but as a form of *compensation*—compensation for the wrongs of past discrimination. Viewed as compensation, reverse discrimination would not be discrimination at all and, accordingly, would not violate the right not to be discriminated against. Any advantages that, say, blacks received through the policy in question they would receive not because they possessed the characteristic of being black, but rather because they possessed the characteristic of being victims of a prior wrong—namely, the wrong of discrimination against a person for being black—and as such deserved to be compensated for this wrong (e.g., see Boxill 1972; Nickel 1975). If this approach to justification is taken, then so-called reverse discrimination becomes no more a form of racial discrimination than is, say, requiring a white to compensate a black for a bicycle he has stolen from him. This, of course, would be just the first step in the argument, and certain objections to this approach to justification (e.g., see Fullinwider 1975) would have to be overcome for it to be successful. I shall not, however, pursue these matters here. The main point is simply that any justification of reverse discrimination should proceed along some line other than that of allowing the requirements of the utilitarian norm to override the right not to be discriminated against on the basis of race. These utilitarian requirements should never override this, or any other right justified according to the theory proposed here because, once again, overriding the right for the sake of expected utility is always a bad utilitarian gamble. For this reason, the EC code of political morality does indeed contain a secondary norm prescribing that utilitarian requirements never, as such, be given priority.

And, if I am right, this secondary norm does not give utilitarian requirements priority even in cases where we feel *certain* about our utilitarian calculations. As explained earlier (sec. 6.5), in matters as complex and subject to rationalizations as this, we are likely to be mistaken all too often even when we feel certain. If so, even when we feel certain about our calculations, even when we have what appears to be a clear "counterexample," overriding a right solely for the sake of expected utility remains a bad utilitarian gamble; mere feelings of certainty are not enough to bring about a sufficient change in the odds.

7.7 HUMAN FALLIBILITY: ONE MORE NATURAL FACT

I have been arguing that adherence to rights is always our best utilitarian gamble, even when we feel "certain" about an alleged counterexample. Of course any alleged counterexample, if merely a hypothetical one, must, in order to be taken seriously, at least be a realistic one. If we are willing to abandon the constraints of reality altogether, then circumstances in which adherence to rights would not be our best utilitarian gamble can be easily hypothesized. Since the argument for adhering to rights is based upon human beings being fallible, the most obvious way to hypothesize circumstances in which adherence to them would not be our best utilitarian gamble is to hypothesize a world in which human beings were *not* fallible. If, in this world, adhering to rights were not our best utilitarian gamble, then the rationale presented here for a secondary norm giving rights priority over the utilitarian norm would, for this world, be inapplicable. This is exactly what some opponents of utilitarianism with intuitionist sympathies will no doubt find objectionable. They apparently expect any sound rationale for a moral norm to be applicable to any hypothetical world or circumstances, no matter how fantastic and unlikely. Since the rationale set out here for this secondary norm is, admittedly, inapplicable under circumstances in which human beings are not fallible, these opponents of utilitarianism will no doubt find the rationale deeply disturbing.

But with circumstances so fantastic that they have no *reasonable* possibility of ever occurring, it is hard to see why the mere *logical* possibility of their occurring should be so disturbing. The rationale for no moral norm holds up under any circumstances conceivable. The most we can reasonably expect is a rationale that holds up under any circumstances likely ever to occur; and since the utilitarian rationale set out here for a secondary moral norm giving rights priority over utilitarian requirements does meet this condition, opponents of utilitarianism should be satisfied. Let me elaborate these points somewhat. H. L. A. Hart argues that there is what he calls a "minimum content of natural law" (1961, 189–95). What he means by there being a minimum content of natural law is that we can easily deduce what part of the content of any adequate legal or moral code would have to be merely from certain facts about all human beings all of the time—facts that are so basic and unlikely ever to change that, to distinguish them from more transitory facts about the world, Hart suggests we call them "natural" facts. The natural facts Hart lists are (1) vulnerability, (2) limited altruism, (3) approximate equality, and (4) limited resources. (Hart also mentions limited understanding of long-term interests and limited goodness of will, but for purposes of this discussion I am assuming that we can assimilate these facts to the fact of limited altruism.) Hart argues that, were it not for these natural facts, codes of law and codes of morality would have no point at all, or would at least be radically different from any such codes that have ever existed. As Hart points out, some species of animals have a physical structure that renders them virtually immune from attack by other members of their species, and some species of animals have no organs enabling them to attack; people, however, *are* vulnerable to physical attack from one another.

Were it not for this vulnerability, moral and legal norms prohibiting such attacks obviously would have no point. Likewise, Hart says, these norms would have no point if people were perfectly altruistic, and never *wanted* to attack or otherwise harm one another. Or, if people were not approximately equal, but some were so much more powerful than all others that they needed never fear any harm from these others then, at least as far as these superpowerful individuals were concerned, this also would deprive these norms of any point. And, finally, if people had as much of everything as they wanted—if, in other words, resources were unlimited—then such moral norms as those protecting property would have no point.

I want to add another natural fact to the list Hart has drawn up: the fact of human fallibility. It is true that human fallibility is just a contingent fact, not a logical necessity; we can easily imagine a world without it. But the susceptibility to being mistaken that is in question here has been a fact about all human beings at all times, and is likely always to be so; people, in matters as complex and emotionally charged as those concerning rights, will no doubt always be susceptible to rationalizations, faulty reasoning, incomplete or mistaken factual information, and so on. And, just as with the natural facts Hart lists, were it not for this fallibility, moral and legal codes would have no point at all, or would at least be radically different from any such codes that have ever existed.

It would be unreasonable to demand that the rationale for norms forbidding attacks work under any factual circumstances no matter how fantastic, even circumstances in which people have become forever invulnerable to such attacks. Likewise, I am claiming, just because there *are* circumstances—namely, those of human infallibility—in which the rationale given here for the secondary moral norm that gives priority to rights would not work, this certainly does not mean that this rationale is inadequate. To find it disturbing that this rationale depends upon the contingent fact of human fallibility is no more reasonable than finding it disturbing that the rationale for norms prohibiting violent attacks depends upon the contingent fact of human vulnerability. In moral theory it is, I suggest, time we abandon the ancient philosophic quest for *a priori* certainty, and learn to live with probability instead. Until we do, I doubt if we make any more progress in understanding morality than ancient philosopher-scientists, likewise committed to *a priori* certainty, did in understanding the natural world.

7.8 A POSSIBLE MISINTERPRETATION

The argument for there being a secondary norm in the EC code that gives rights priority over utilitarian requirements is, of course, analogous to the argument (set out in sec. 1.3) for there being a rule in paternity cases that gives blood-test evidence priority over contrary evidence. This analogy, however, suggests an interpretation of my position that is seriously mistaken. The rule giving blood-test evidence priority in paternity cases does not, if followed, always yield a correct legal decision; the blood test that this rule has us treat as conclusive is in reality correct only 99 percent of the time. Since following this rule does sometimes (namely, 1 percent of the time) yield an incorrect decision, this rule cannot strictly speaking be said to be itself the criterion for what a correct decision in these paternity cases would be; instead it merely provides us with a procedure that, if followed, will yield a decision that, given our limited knowledge, has the *highest probability* of being correct. It is, in other words, merely a norm of good procedure. Likewise, it might be thought, the norm in the EC code giving rights priority over the utilitarian norm does not itself serve as a criterion for what is morally correct; it might be argued that, on my view, the utilitarian norm does this; the norm giving rights priority merely tells us, so it might be said, what moral decision, given our limited knowledge, is *most likely* correct. Thus, it might be concluded, this priority norm is, like the rule of evidence for paternity cases, merely a procedural norm of some sort, and is not itself a norm of morality. This conclusion would be seriously mistaken. The norm giving rights priority over the utilitarian norm most certainly is meant to be, along with the rights themselves, a norm of morality and, as such, a norm that does provide us with a criterion for what is morally correct. And since this norm is itself a criterion of the morally correct, giving rights priority, as the norm prescribes, it not just *most likely* correct; it *is* correct.

But how, it might be objected, can this norm be a *criterion* of the morally correct when it is clear that if we did have vastly more knowledge—enough knowledge to determine accurately what the utilitarian norm calls for in every case—then it would be the utilitarian norm, not these rights, to which the EC code would give priority? My reply is: yes, with this knowledge the utilitarian norm would then be given priority, but so what? Any code of law and any code of morality would be different if our knowledge were vastly more extensive in certain respects than it is. For example, if we knew vastly more than we know today about what the safe driving speeds are at different places, our speed limit requirements would no doubt be at least somewhat different. But just because, with vastly more knowledge, speed limits would be different, this clearly does not mean our current speed limits are not requirements of law itself. Likewise, just because, with vastly more knowledge, the priorities within the EC code would be different, this does not mean the current priorities are not requirements of morality itself, but are mere procedural requirements of some sort.

Yet why not, it might be asked, view the norm giving priority to rights as a norm of procedure rather than of morality—a norm of procedure for determining what is most likely required by the "real" norm of morality, namely, the utilitarian norm? After all, so it might be argued, whether the norm giving priority to rights is labeled a norm of "procedure" or of "morality," the results would be the same, so why not label it a norm of procedure? The answer is that the results would not be the same; the label does matter. Why? The reason should by now be clear. If labeled a norm of procedure, this norm would inevitably come to be viewed as a mere "rule of thumb," a rule to be ignored whenever one is quite sure one does know what morality really requires. In short: unless this norm is clearly given the status of morality itself—thus making compliance with it subject to that special social pressure reserved only for norms of morality—it would be all too easy to rationalize, in the name of morality, the very gambles that this norm is designed to preclude. So, to summarize, I grant that the justification for a moral norm giving priority to rights does depend upon the fact that human beings do not possess unlimited knowledge, that human beings are, in other words, fallible; but as long as human beings are indeed fallible, a moral (not procedural) norm giving priority to certain rights is thus justified, along with, of course, the rights themselves.

7.9 OTHER NORMS OF POLITICAL MORALITY

Finally, it is not just moral norms of the sort normally thought of as "human rights" that have priority over utilitarian requirements, or the utilitarian norm, in the EC code of political morality. What the distinction is between moral norms defining human rights and ones defining other kinds of governmental obligations; whether, indeed, such a distinction really does, in the final analysis, make sense, we need not decide here. The distinction is, however, commonly made; let us simply accept it, and concentrate, for the remainder of this chapter, on those moral norms within the EC code which have priority over the utilitarian norm, but do not define what we normally think of as a human right.

For each of these moral norms, the rationale for admitting it to the EC code with priority over the utilitarian norm is essentially the same as that for admitting human-right moral norms: violating the norm is always a bad utilitarian gamble no matter how sure a public official might be that its violation in the circumstances at hand does maximize expected utility. One moral norm that does not define what we normally think of as a human right, but that, I suggest, the EC code contains nevertheless, is a norm requiring governmental obedience to the law of the land (the very law created by the government itself). If, for example, the law forbids unauthorized wiretapping, or requires the government to pay damages for breach of contract, then, according to this moral norm, if the government does conduct unauthorized wiretappings, or refuses to pay damages, it is acting immorally. The norm requiring governmental obedience to the law does not, of course, forbid any governmental change or repeal of a law, but as long as a law has not been "officially" changed or repealed, this norm requires the government to obey it.

The reasons it is always a bad utilitarian gamble for the government to violate the norm requiring its obedience to the law are, I think, related to the reasons why the best form of government is one with a separation of powers—that is, a form of government where the legislative, judicial, and executive branches of government are separate from one another. If, say, the legislative and executive branches of government were one and the same, then surely public officials in this combined branch of the government would, for the sake of expediting the fulfillment of their executive duties, at times rationalize the desirability of, and thus pass, very bad laws—ones that never would have been passed by a legislative branch that was separate and hence not so partial. For example, because it would make their job of maintaining national security a lot easier, the officials in such a combined branch might rationalize the desirability of, and thus pass, overly lenient laws about wiretapping and other invasions of privacy. It is largely in order to minimize vulnerability to these kinds of rationalizations that the checks and balances provided by the separation of powers are desirable. But if public officials were, in the name of the government, allowed to violate the law whenever they believed it maximized expected utility to do so, then the very point of having a separation of powers would be largely defeated, and the vulnerability of public officials to all sorts of vicious rationalizations would be greatly increased. In short, there is reason to believe that, owing to these sorts of rationalizations, to other sources of mistaken calculations, to the seriousness of such mistakes, and so forth, governmental violation of the law is always a bad utilitarian gamble, just as is governmental violation of our rights. And, just as the utilitarian standard therefore justifies a code where rights are given priority over the utilitarian norm, so also, I suggest, it justifies a code where compliance with a moral norm requiring governmental obedience to the law is given priority over the utilitarian norm.

Another of the moral norms, other than those defining human rights, which I think is always a bad utilitarian gamble for a government to violate, and which I claim is therefore given priority over the utilitarian norm in the EC code, is a norm prohibiting governmental lying or deceit. By *governmental deceit* I have in mind such things as the United States' "deemphasis" of its involvement in Vietnam and, what was perhaps the most despicable governmental deceit of all time, Hitler's staging of a false confrontation between German and Polish troops in order to rouse the German nation for a war against Poland. Many of the potentially damaging results of governmental deceit are obvious. Take, for example, the damage resulting from governmental deceit in the United States regarding Vietnam and Watergate. This damage included, among other things, a serious loss of confidence by the

American people in their public officials (Harward 1974). Yet considering the intense pressure public officials are usually under to carry out their programs successfully, it is easy to see how, were it not morally prohibited, a public official might well talk himself into believing a little deceit here and there would not hurt, when in reality it would be disastrous. (For more on the potential harms and ease of rationalizing governmental deceit, see Bok 1978, chap. 12.)

Another moral norm that I believe is given priority over the utilitarian norm in the EC code is one requiring the honoring of agreements, and there are no doubt still others, although I shall not attempt to itemize them all here. In general, I would say that many, if not most, of the relatively easy-to-comply-with primary norms of the EC code of personal morality, and no doubt some secondary norms as well, have an analogue in the EC code of political morality.

As I noted earlier (sec. 3.2), one standard objection against the utilitarian norm is based upon the difficulty of complying with it, this difficulty being a result of the enormous amount of factual information one must have to be sure about what the utilitarian norm prescribes. The utilitarian norm is so difficult to comply with, so this objection goes, that it is forever vulnerable to dangerous misapplications caused by misinformation and rationalizations. I do not want to deny that the utilitarian norm is every bit as difficult to comply with as is alleged; as a matter of fact, if I did deny this I would be undermining my own argument for showing that rights and other moral norms have priority over it. But if these rights and other moral norms do indeed have priority over the utilitarian norm, then the objection that is based upon the difficulty of complying with the utilitarian norm loses its sting. This objection loses its sting because the priority of these rights and other moral norms serves the function of keeping damage from misapplication of the utilitarian norm within reasonable bounds. The utilitarian norm's vulnerability to misapplication does provide us with sufficient reason for believing that, in the EC code, certain rights and other moral norms have priority over it; but as soon as we have reason for believing these norms have priority over it, we no longer have reason for believing that its vulnerability to misapplication is a fatal objection.

8
The General Welfare Norm

8.1 THE NEED FOR A GENERAL WELFARE NORM

With rights against the government, as well as other moral norms, all having priority over the utilitarian norm, its role in the EC code of political morality is considerably more modest than it would be otherwise. But its role in the EC code of political morality is not as modest as its role in the EC code of personal morality. In the EC code of personal morality its role, it will be recalled, is limited to that of resolving conflict and borderline cases when appeal to all other norms within the code has been exhausted. The utilitarian norm probably has this role in the EC code of political morality too, but its role in the EC code of political morality goes far beyond just this. In political morality the utilitarian norm fills in what would otherwise be a glaring void in the system of norms applicable to governments—a void not found in the system of norms applicable to persons.

What I mean by the utilitarian norm filling in what would otherwise be a "glaring void" in political morality requires explanation. Norms of morality applicable to people rather than governments regulate only a relatively small area of personal decision-making. Negative (personal) moral duties—duties *not* to murder, *not* to steal, *not* to lie, and so forth—tell us only what we should *not* do, never what we *should* do. Positive (personal) moral duties—duties such as our duty to take good care of our children—do tell us what we should do, but only to a very limited extent. For one thing, positive duties do not specify exactly *how* we are to do what we should do and, in any case, are very limited in scope, thus leaving a very large area of personal decision-making to which no moral norms at all are applicable. In other words, much of what we do is neither required nor forbidden by the EC code of personal morality, but is, according to this code, outside the scope of morality altogether. If then there is no *moral* norm applicable to a large area of personal decision-making, what norm is applicable? The answer is, needless to say, that this area is (at the very least) covered by the norm of personal welfare—that norm which delineates what is in a person's best interests (see chap. 2). Turning now to political morality, we find that the relatively specific rights against the government and other moral norms discussed above—that is, those norms having priority over the utilitarian norm—cover only a relatively small area of potential governmental decision-making, just as the norms of personal morality cover only a relatively small area of personal decision-making. Since these rights and other norms cover only a relatively small area of potential governmental decision-making, were it not for the utilitarian norm there would be a large area of potential governmental decision-making not covered by any moral norms at all. Governments are not real people; so this void could not be filled by the norm of personal welfare, as is the analogous void in personal decision-making. Thus, in the EC code of political morality, the utilitarian norm's role goes far beyond its use in resolving conflict and borderline cases; it takes up the slack where the relatively specific norms of political morality, including our rights, leave off, just as the personal welfare norm takes up the slack in personal decision-making where norms of personal morality leave off.

Because, in this role, the utilitarian norm's function is analogous to that of the personal welfare norm, I shall refer to the utilitarian norm, in this role, as the *general welfare* norm. As far as I am concerned it might, in this role, just as accurately be called the *public interest* norm or the *common good* norm, because I fail to find the distinctions some philosophers draw between the general welfare, public interest, and common good to be very useful. But I shall use the label "general welfare" norm simply to emphasize the analogy between the utilitarian norm, in this role, and the *personal* welfare norm. It should be noted, however, that the analogy between the general and personal welfare norms is not complete since the general welfare norm is itself a part of that code of morality-namely, the EC code of political morality—for which it, in effect, takes up the slack, while the personal welfare norm is not, of course, a part of the EC code of personal morality. (And, incidentally, closely related to the general welfare norm is a *standard*—the *general welfare* standard—in terms of which alternatives can be comparatively evaluated. This discussion, however, will focus on the general welfare *norm*.)

8.2 THE SPATIAL DIVISION OF GOVERNMENTAL LABOR

So far I have, for simplicity, been talking about a code of political morality exclusively for a hypothetical world in which there exists only one government (see sec.7.1). It is now time to complicate this hypothetical world somewhat and see how this complication entails a change in the code of political morality justified in terms of the utilitarian standard. Let us say that, after the government in this hypothetical community becomes established, some men, who are sent out to explore, make an unexpected discovery; hundreds of miles away, the find another close-knit community of several thousand people. This community is made up of refugees from another part of Earth who, having taken longer to reach the new planet, are just now deciding what sort of government for themselves they should establish. One of the first questions they would have to answer is: Should the two communities unite under a joint government, or should each have its own independent government?

The usual advantages of joint governments are, I assume, that joint endeavors and intercommunity relationships of all sorts are facilitated through laws, regulations, policies, and so forth, that are uniform. But these advantages would be minimal in the case of the two communities in question here since the distance between them would probably, for a while at least, prevent there from being much in the way of joint endeavors and intercommunity relationships to facilitate.

It is, on the other hand, easy to see major advantages in separate governments for each community. First and foremost, separate governments for each community would provide each with a government that could specialize in the community's own particular needs and problems. In other words, separate governments can be viewed as a kind of division of labor—a division of *governmental* labor; and a division of governmental labor can be expected to yield gains in effectiveness similar to that normally yielded by any division of labor—gains made possible by the fact that the smaller the area in which there is specialization, the greater the mastery of that area can be. Since it would be easier to master the problems of just one community than of two, each of two separate governments in this hypothetical world could be expected to gain a greater mastery of the problems it is responsible for handling than could one government responsible for handling the problems of both communities together.

But even if (unrealistically) the needs and problems of both communities were always exactly the same so that there was thus no basis for any gains from a governmental division of labor, separate governments would still provide an important advantage. Governing a group of people is at present, and no doubt always will be, a very inexact science. Progress in finding better governmental approaches to the solution of community problems is often possible only through the slow process of trial and error. If there were two separate governments in our hypothetical world instead of one, then, to the extent that their approaches differed, comparisons of the merits and demerits of two different approaches in use at the same time would become possible. This would be an important advantage since, if such comparisons were made, we could expect more progress in finding better approaches than if there were only the one approach of a single government in effect at any given time, with nothing to compare it with. Whereas the first advantage of having separate governments is, I suggested, analogous to that of having an economy with a division of labor, this advantage is analogous to that of having economic competition rather than monopoly.

Which alternative then would be, for our hypothetical communities, most consistent with the requirements of the EC code of political morality: a joint government, separate governments, or perhaps some form of federalism that attempts to combine the advantages of both joint and separate governments by having each community be self-governed with respect to some matters and jointly governed with respect to others? The issue to be decided is the constitutional issue of what jurisdictional arrangement should prevail in these communities. As such, the decision to be made qualifies as being a metagovernmental decision (see sec. 7.1); it is the sort of decision by means of which governments and their jurisdictions are created in the first place. But even though it qualifies as metagovernmental rather than governmental, it is still the sort of decision that should be governed by political morality, and within the EC code of political morality the norm that should be appealed to for making such decisions is, if I am right, the general welfare norm. Thus, if I am right, the question at issue here is: Which jurisdictional arrangement is most in the general welfare?

I doubt if we could make a very intelligent guess as to the answer without knowing still more information about these hypothetical communities—information such as exactly how much interaction, if any, there probably would be between them. But if we grant, as surely we must, that in reality the general welfare norm often does call for separate governments (either within some sort of federation, or not), then we must also grant that the general welfare norm itself is not, as it now stands, appropriate for morally evaluating the decisions of these governments; each of two or more separate governments trying seriously to comply with the general welfare norm would defeat the very point of these governments being separate. Let me explain. Say that a separate government is established in each of the two hypothetical communities. The advantages of having separate governments are, once again, greater efficiency, made possible by a governmental division of labor, and greater progress, made possible by comparing diverse approaches. If each of the hypothetical governments tried, as is required by the general welfare norm, to give equal consideration to the interests of *everyone*—which would necessarily include even those within the jurisdiction of the *other* government—then obviously neither government could specialize in the needs and problems of just those within its own jurisdiction; each government would have to give *equal* consideration to the needs and problems of *everyone,* no matter which jurisdiction the person happened to be in. If neither government specialized in the needs and problems within just its own jurisdiction, then the efficiency of a division of governmental labor—and thus the first advantage of separate governments—would not be realized.

And if both governments tried to give equal consideration to the interests of everyone, then surely the second advantage of separate governments—

that of greater progress through comparing diverse approaches—could be realized only at far too great a cost in chaos for its realization to be worthwhile. Let us say, for example, that the government of community 1 was contemplating building some public tennis courts within its community. If, however, the government of community 1 had to give equal consideration to the interests of everyone in both communities before going ahead with the courts, then it would have to try to determine whether or not those in community 2 needed them more. And if it were determined that those in community 2 did need the courts more, then giving equal consideration to the interests of everyone would probably call for the government of community 1 to donate the funds to community 2 for the purpose of building the courts there instead. Similarly, the government of community 2, in contemplating whether to build some tennis courts, would have to give equal consideration to the needs of those in community 1. In general, both governments would sacrifice much in the way of time, effort, and expense investigating the needs and problems of the other community—hardly the most efficient way of proceeding. And, because of governmental fallibility, without any coordination of their efforts the results of each seriously trying to give equal consideration to the interests of all would no doubt often be absurd. For example, each government, knowing the other government is giving equal consideration to the interests of everyone in both communities, might fail to appropriate any funds for tennis courts in either community, each thinking that the other government will do so; or community 2 might end up with tennis courts from both governments, and community 1 with none. Without any coordination of their independent approaches, having both governments seriously attempt to give equal consideration, not just to the interests of those within its own jurisdiction, but to the interests of everyone, would be bound to result in endless duplication and confusion. There would indeed be diversity, but the costs of this diversity would outweigh any of its benefits.

If, on the other hand, in order to avoid such chaos the two governments did get together and formed, say, a central committee with representatives from both to coordinate their approaches then, to the extent that their approaches were in fact successfully coordinated, they would surely be less diverse. In other words, in order to eliminate the unacceptable costs of maintaining diverse approaches, this diversity itself would have to be somewhat compromised, in which case the second advantage of having separate governments would, I suspect, not be adequately realized either. In short: a separate government for each community—one that is autonomous in all or almost all respects—is incompatible with each of these governments trying to give equal consideration to the interests of everyone.

Fortunately, the general welfare norm as it now stands can be easily modified so as to make it perfectly compatible with there being more than one government in the world. All that needs to be done is narrow the norm's domain so that, for purposes of making governmental decisions, its domain includes, not everyone, but only those within the jurisdiction of whatever government is making the decision. That is to say, the general welfare norm must be changed so that it prescribes that governments give equal consideration only to the interests of those within their own jurisdiction rather than everyone. This would mean that city governments should give equal consideration to the interests of those and only those within the city over which they have jurisdiction, state or principality governments to those and only those within the state or principality over which they have jurisdiction, national governments to those and only those within the nation over which they have jurisdiction; only a world government, such as the United Nations is supposed to be, should give equal consideration to the interests of everyone.

I hasten to point out, however, that the reasons for thus narrowing the general welfare norm's domain when this norm is used for making governmental decisions are not applicable to when this norm is used instead for making metagovernmental decisions—that is, jurisdictional decisions that delineate what is to count as a government and its jurisdiction. Thus, for making jurisdictional decisions I assume that the requirement that equal consideration be given to the interests of everyone remains intact. And I assume this holds even for the case where the jurisdictional decision is made by the representatives of an existing government, thereby taking on the appearance of a governmental decision. The example given earlier of a jurisdictional decision that might appear to be a governmental decision was of a decision made by representatives of the existing state governments of the United States concerning whether or not to allow the state of Texas to become independent of the United States. In discussing this example I suggested that we view the representatives of the state governments as "changing hats" and becoming members of a fictitious metagovernmental group for purposes of making this one decision. The reason for viewing the matter this way can now be appreciated: with jurisdictional decisions equal consideration should be given to the interests of everyone, not, as with governmental decisions, to just those in some already established jurisdiction. So within the EC code there are, I am arguing, two somewhat different standards for what counts as being in the general welfare, one applicable to governmental decisions, and the other applicable to metagovernmental or jurisdictional decisions. We can, if we want, capture both of these standards within a single norm by reformulating the general welfare norm somewhat as follows: "If you are a government, choose that and only that which someone would choose who gave equal consideration to the interests of all those within your jurisdiction; if a metagovernment, choose that and only that which someone would choose who gave equal consideration to the interests of everyone."

8.3 BUT WHAT ABOUT GREAT NEED ELSEWHERE?

This change in the domain of the general welfare norm does not, needless to say, affect the priority that rights against the government and other moral norms have over it. The change does, however, create the need for still another norm of political morality having priority over the general welfare norm. Let me illustrate why with the help of our two hypothetical communities. Say that a disastrous flood, which destroyed most of the crops in community 2, has resulted in widespread starvation within this community, and the community's government lacks the resources for coping with this emergency. But say that the necessary emergency aid could easily be provided by the government of community 1. The only problem is that the general welfare norm as now formulated requires a government to concentrate only on the interests of those within its own jurisdiction, and all the victims of the famine lie outside the jurisdiction of community 1's government. This means that those responsible for making governmental decisions in community 1, if guided only by the general welfare norm as now formulated, might well conclude that community 1's government is morally forbidden to render the aid (or at least is not morally obligated to do so), since the aid would be at the expense of those within the government's own community. Or, again, say that community 1, favored with easily accessible natural resources and a good climate, makes great strides in economic development, becoming rich and powerful, while community 2, with less accessible resources and an unfavorable climate, remains poor and weak but, with proper aid from community 1, it too could make great strides in economic development. Yet, once again, if guided only by the general welfare norm, as now formulated, those responsible for making governmental decisions in community 1 might well conclude that community 1's government is forbidden to render this aid. These examples thus illustrate the need for some moral norm that clearly does require that aid be given in cases such as these, and that has priority over the general welfare norm.

But is there any reason for believing that the EC code of political morality contains any such norm? I think so. It must always be kept in mind that, although some norms within the EC code—in particular, the general welfare norm—might allow the interests of certain people to be given *special* consideration, the EC code itself is derived by giving everyone's interests *equal* consideration. Because of this fact—that is, because the EC code is derived by giving everyone's interests equal consideration—there is indeed reason for believing that this code contains some moral norm with priority over the general welfare norm, clearly requiring that a government render aid to those outside its own jurisdiction in cases of emergency, or any other cases where some misfortune or disadvantage cannot otherwise be satisfactorily overcome. In order to realize the substantial advantages of having a division of governmental labor, the domain of the general welfare norm must, as we have seen, be narrowed so as to include only those within a government's jurisdiction. But in order to allow the general welfare norm's domain to be thus narrowed, the EC code must also contain some other moral norm clearly requiring governments to step outside of this narrowed framework in those sorts of cases in which, from the "universal" standpoint of the utilitarian standard, it would be necessary to do so—cases like those described above. Such a norm, which I think we may conclude that the EC code does contain, might be formulated somewhat as follows: "Render aid to other jurisdictions for overcoming misfortunes or disadvantages that cannot be satisfactorily overcome by those within the jurisdiction itself." And, for purposes of this norm, we should not view some misfortune or disadvantage as one capable of being overcome "satisfactorily" by those within the jurisdiction itself unless it can be overcome by them within a reasonable amount of time.

8.4 THE TEMPORAL DIVISION OF GOVERNMENTAL LABOR

The main reason for narrowing the domain of the general welfare norm is, as we have seen, to allow the advantages of a division of governmental labor to be realized. By thus allowing governments to specialize in the needs and problems of those within just their own territory, everyone's needs and problems are likely to receive better attention than if governments tried instead to attend to the needs and problems of everyone. The territorial or spatial division of governmental labor that the above reformulation of the domain of the general welfare norm allows is, therefore, most likely to be to everyone's advantage. This is precisely why such a reformulation is in accordance with the utilitarian standard. But if it is to people's advantage everywhere that there be this *spatial* division of governmental labor, then might it not, for similar reasons, be to people's advantage in every generation that there be a *temporal* division of governmental labor too? (It must be remembered that we are focusing here, as elsewhere, upon what it is to people's advantage to have governments *try* to do, as opposed to *succeed* in doing, a focus that enables us to take governmental fallibility fully into account.) A government would have a temporal division of labor if it, before all else, concentrated on the needs and problems of only those alive *at present*, rather than trying to give equal consideration to the needs and problems of those in every future generation as well.

I suggest that a temporal division of governmental labor is, in fact, to the advantage of all generations. If, instead, a government tried to give equal consideration to the needs and problems of every generation, then in no generation would people have a government able to achieve a mastery of their own needs and problems, a mastery that only a specialization in just those needs and problems could achieve. With each generation's government trying to give as much attention to the needs and problems of future generations as they do to those of their own generation, there is no reason to believe that there would be any less in the way of inefficiency, confusion, and absurd results than we saw there would be with each government trying to give as much attention to the needs and problems of other jurisdictions as they do to those of their own jurisdiction. In fact, there is one reason why the results of equal attention to all generations might be even somewhat worse than that of equal attention to all jurisdictions. With governments from different jurisdictions, a central committee composed of members from these different governments could, if worse came to worst, always be formed (although at a cost) to help coordinate somewhat their various efforts, but no such central committee is, for obvious reasons, ever possible with governments from different generations. But if the government in each generation did concentrate on the needs and problems of just those *at present* within its jurisdiction, then each generation would enjoy the benefits of governmental specialization in its own needs and problems and, therefore, those in *all* generations would likely be better off.

In light of the above, I suggest that the utilitarian standard justified a temporal narrowing of the general welfare norm's domain just as it justifies a spatial narrowing of the norm's domain. If I am right, then we must reformulate the general welfare norm one more time so that it requires a government to give equal consideration to the interests of not everyone (anytime) within its jurisdiction, but everyone *at present* within its jurisdiction.

This narrowing of the general welfare norm's domain has important ramifications for governmental population policy. According to this norm governments should, other things being equal, encourage population growth up to and not beyond the point of diminishing returns—that is, up to and not beyond the point where the benefits from further increases in population are outweighed by the costs. But determining even roughly when this point had been reached would be all but impossible if the domain of the general welfare norm included all future generations. Doing so would require balancing the "happiness" and "unhappiness" of beings not even in existence yet with that of beings that were—a very difficult balancing act indeed. On the other hand, with the general welfare norm's domain being narrowed so that equal consideration need be given only to those existing, governments would be required to encourage population growth only up to the point of diminishing returns for those *already* alive. This would mean that governments could do their balancing without having to throw any projections of future happiness for those as yet unborn onto the scales. Not having to take the happiness of those as yet unborn into account has at least two advantages. First, since it simplifies the necessary calculations, more accuracy can be expected. Second, if a government need not, in calculating the utility of further population increases, offset the detriments of an increase by the "happiness" that can be expected to be experienced by those as yet unborn, then clearly the point of diminishing returns will be reached much sooner than if the government does have to offset these detriments by the "happiness" of those as yet unborn. Not having to take into account the "happiness" of those as yet unborn would therefore allow nations already dreadfully overpopulated to adopt policies discouraging further population increases that they might not feel justified in adopting if they did have to take this potential "happiness" into account. With millions of people today either starving or undernourished, the fact that a temporally narrower domain makes it easier to justify policies discouraging further population growth is perhaps no small advantage.

It might be objected that since the utilitarian standard does give equal consideration to the interests of everyone, including those as yet unborn, a general welfare norm that did not give equal consideration to the interests of those as yet unborn could not be justified in terms of it. This objection is, I think, mistaken. It is true that by thus narrowing the general welfare norm's domain, it is probable that some utility will be sacrificed through there being fewer people around to be "happy." But there are two things that, when taken together, more than offset this loss in utility. First of all, taking into account the happiness of those as yet unborn is such an extremely difficult thing to do that, by miscalculating and going too far in encouraging population growth, governments might well end up losing as much through too many people as they would lose through too few people with the narrower domain. Second, and even more important, a wider domain requiring that equal consideration be given to the interests of those in all future generations is obviously incompatible with a temporal division of governmental labor, and thus with the gain in utility that this division of labor represents. This virtually certain gain in utility—a gain that has nothing to do with population policy— would, I should think, more than offset any loss in utility resulting from there being fewer people around to be "happy," especially since, as we have seen, any such loss in utility is far from certain anyway. In other words, trying to adhere to the narrower domain has greater *expected* utility.

It might be suggested that governments should use both the wider and narrower domains—the wider domain for determining population policies and the narrower domain for everything else—thus combining use of the wider domain for population policies with the benefits of a temporal division of governmental labor. How this would work is as follows. Using the wider domain a government might, for example, decide to encourage a population increase. Then the government would switch to the narrower domain for determining all other matters, such as what policies *vis-à-vis* food, housing, and so on, to adopt or encourage those in these industries to adopt. The problem is that by proceeding in this way the government's policies on food, housing, and so on, would be appropriate only for the number of people already in existence, and thus dangerously out of kilter with its policy of increasing population. Thus I conclude that the equal consideration norm prescribes the use of just one domain for all governmental decisions, this domain being the narrower one of everyone *at present* within the government's jusisdiction.

8.5 BUT WHAT ABOUT FUTURE GENERATIONS?

Although this temporal restriction upon the general welfare norm's domain helps resolve problems in the area of population policy, it seems to create problems of another sort; it would seem that allowing governments to concentrate upon the interests only of those *at present* within their jurisdiction would lead to short-sighted decisions on such matters as the rate at which natural resources are to be used. Would not a concentration on the interests of only those currently alive lead, it might be asked, to the immediate, selfish consumption of all resources, leaving nothing for future generations? It is not at all obvious that the answer to this question is yes. People currenlty alive do have a genuine interest in the welfare of their as-yet unborn children, grandchildren, great-grandchildren, and so on; so concentrating on just the interests of those currently alive assures at least some regard for the interests of those of future generations. But still, it might be argued, this is not assurance enough; the interests that those currently alive have in the welfare of future generations is all too easily miscalculated, thereby resulting in disaster for future generations after all.

By limiting the general welfare norm's domain to only those currently alive, some additional moral norm probably does, I admit, become necessary for helping protect the interests of future generations. But whatever norm is necessary, we can be sure the EC code contains it. We must remember that, even though the general welfare norm's domain does not include future generations, the domain of that criterion form which the general welfare norm, and all other norms of the EC code, are "derived"- namely, the utilitarian standard—does include future generations. So whatever may be necessary to help protect the interests of future generations, we can be sure that the utilitarian standard justifies, and the EC code thus contains it. And what *is* necessary is, I suggest, a relatively simple, easy-to-comply-with norm that (1) has priority over the general welfare norm, and that (2) does clearly forbid the government from doing, or allowing those within its jurisdiction to do, any thing that is very likely to cause future generations grave harm. Such a norm is the analogue of the moral norm requiring emergency aid to those in other jurisdictions, this latter norm having been made necessary, as we have seen, by the *spatial* narrowing of the general welfare norm's domain . Both of these norms, and perhaps still others like them, can be viewed as necessary insurance against interpretations of the general welfare norm that would be disastrous for those in other jurisdictions or generations—an insurance policy that, by eliminating the main risks of a spatial and temporal division of governmental labor, allows us to enjoy the very substantial benefits that such a division of governmental labor affords.

Besides those norms designed to minimize the risks of a narrower domain, still other moral norms with priority over the general welfare norm become necessary when there is more than one government in the world. The most obvious of these are moral norms clearly specifying what sort of military force is permitted against other governments, and when. In other words, with more than one government in the world, relatively easy-to-comply-with moral norms dealing with war, which have priority over the hard-to-comply-with general welfare norm, become necessary. These norms are necessary as safeguards against miscalculations of what the general welfare norm calls for with respect to military matters. And safeguards against miscalculations are necessary in matters dealing with war not only because of people's unusually high susceptibility to rationalizing about such matters, but also because miscalculations about such matters obviously carry an unusually great potential for harm.

But, aside from the ones we have already considered in this chapter, I doubt if many additional moral norms with priority over the general welfare norm become necessary when there is more than one government in the world; as we have already seen (sec. 7.9), the EC code for a world where there is only one government includes moral norms (other than human rights) regulating the government's interaction with persons—norms that require such things as the keeping of agreements and the payment of debts, norms that thus no doubt already cover most of the ways in which a government's interaction with other governments needs to be regulated. In sum: the relatively few, but crucial changes in the EC code considered in this chapter should come close to being sufficient for transforming it into a code of political morality appropriate for a world as complex as ours is today.

One final note: codes of morality for governing the behavior of persons, and ones for governing the behavior of governments are not necessarily the only kinds of moral codes to be found in the equal consideration system. It might also contain—that is, the utilitarian standard might also justify—still other codes of morality, ones for governing the behavior of various types of organizations other than governments, perhaps many such codes. Included among these specialized codes—let us call them EC codes of "organizational" morality—might be, for example, an EC code of business morality (governing corporations, and other business establishments), EC codes of team morality (perhaps different ones for different sports), EC codes of club morality, and so on. Any EC moral code for governing the behavior of some type of organization other than a government would, I assume, be similar to, yet much simpler than, the EC code of political morality. A code for governing the behavior of certain types of organizations might consist of a norm analogous to the general welfare norm (although with a much smaller domain) and little else. For example, the basic norm for governing the behavior of social clubs might be one requiring any such club (in making whatever decisions are within its agreed-upon scope) always to give equal consideration to the interests of all its members. And perhaps the EC code of personal morality imposes a moral obligation upon the decision-makers of any such club to steer it within the confines of this simple code of organizational morality. It may also impose a certain moral obligation upon the members of the club to obey (with certain exceptions) whatever formal social norms the club might promulgate, this moral obligation being analogous to our moral obligation to obey the law. But to pursue these thoughts any farther here would take us too far afield.

9
Judicial Reasoning

9.1 THE TRADITIONAL VIEW

If we were to observe the legislative debates of legislators all of whom were fully committed to the EC code of political morality, we would find that their debates over proposed legislation appeared to be no different from those of almost any modern-day legislators anywhere. Even though these legislators would be using the general welfare norm and the other moral norms of the EC code as their ultimate criteria for deciding upon proposed legislation, these moral norms, especially the general welfare norm, would not, I submit, be the criteria mentioned most often in the course of their debates; their debates instead would be conducted at a much less abstract level, in terms of goals and values of a sort we would expect modern-day legislators anywhere to conduct their debates in terms of—ordinary, everyday goals and values such as full employment, a clean environment, good schools, highway safety, equal opportunity for all, the elimination of disease, and so forth. The general welfare norm, or general welfare, would probably be mentioned most often in summations such as: "I conclude, therefore, that passage of this legislation is in the general welfare." Otherwise, however, the general welfare norm would, I suspect, remain for the most part in the background—constantly being put to use by these legislators in justifying specific legislation, and determining priorities, but rarely having to be mentioned. Other more specific moral norms of the EC code might have to be mentioned somewhat more often, but even these norms would not be mentioned as often as would very specific, everyday goals, ideals, and values, such as those alluded to above. So the difference between legislators committed to the EC code and ones not would not show up as a difference in the level of abstraction at which debates were conducted; the difference would show up instead in the results reached. (As an example of what I mean, see my investigation into the justification of inheritance, where I attempt to reach a satisfactory conclusion by appealing only to values, ideals, etc., less abstract than the general welfare—Haslett 1986.)

In this chapter, however, it is not on using the EC code for making legislative decisions that I want to focus, but on using it for making judicial decisions. Although the code's use at the executive and legislative levels of government decision-making is, I think, straightforward enough, its use at the judicial level is somewhat more complicated, requiring special discussion. Moreover, the claim that this code is applicable to judicial decision-making appears, without further explanation, to contravene some sound points about judicial reasoning made by Ronald Dworkin and others (Dworkin 1977 and 1985; Sartorius 1967; McCormick 1978). Thus some special attention to judicial reasoning clearly is in order. Let us begin by looking very briefly at what might be said to be the traditional view of judicial reasoning, and then at what some of Dworkin's criticisms of this view are.

It is generally agreed that the main function of the judiciary should be to interpret the law as it is, not to make law. Laws, however, are notoriously "vague at the edges," thus giving rise to borderline cases, as do any norms. And there are cases where the law appears to prescribe alternatives that are inconsistent with one another—that is, there are conflict cases. Now, according to the traditional view, existing law is not sufficient for resolving all conflict and borderline cases and, therefore, if any decision at all is to be reached in such cases, judges must create what amounts to new law; to this extent, judges must play a legislative role whether they want to or not.

But there are very pressing reasons for keeping the judge's legislative role to a bare minimum. First, judges normally do not, and probably should not, have to run for reelection every few years; it would be difficult for judges, facing such political pressure, to remain sufficiently impartial. But if judges thus are not to be accountable to the electorate for their decisions, as are legislators, then (assuming it is not desirable to undermine the ideals of democracy) they ought to avoid creating new law as much as possible. Next, to the extent that judges do create new law, defendants thereby become subject to the requirements of law that did not exist at the time they did whatever they are being tried for. In other words, they become subject to the requirements of retroactive law, which hardly seems fair, and constitutes another reason for keeping judicial legislation to a minimum. Other reasons include the fact that judicial proceedings are, by their very nature, particularly poor forums for the creation of new law since judges are equipped with only very limited fact-finding apparatus, must normally act under severe time constraints, and must, for the most part, focus only on the controversies raised by the parties before them. So, according to the traditional view, judicial legislation, though necessary, should be kept to a bare minimum.

This goal of keeping judicial legislation to bare minimum is realized through the observance by judges of certain norms of judicial procedure. One of the two most important of these norms of judicial procedure is the principle or norm of *stare decisis*, which, roughly speaking, states that once a court has held a certain rule of law to be applicable to a certain set of facts, it (and other relevant courts) shall follow this same rule of law in all future cases where the facts are substantially the same. A court must, in other words, follow its own prior decisions (and those of other relevant courts), these prior decisions being known as *precedents*. This requirement has some exceptions—that is, prior decisions may sometimes be overruled—but these exceptions are limited in scope and need not concern us now. Also, it should be noted that the norm of *stare decisis* requires a court to follow a decision laid down in a prior case only if the relevant facts of the present case and those of the prior case are substantially the same. So to the extent that a rule of law laid down in some case is broader than necessary for covering the facts of that particular case, courts in future cases need not follow it; they are free either to qualify the rule of law or to disregard it altogether if presented with a factual situation that, even though "covered" by the rule of law, is substantially different from the factual situation found in the case in which the rule was formulated or in any of the cases in which it has been followed. What this means is that, in principle, a court can effectively "legislate" only for the particular facts of whatever case is before it. Thus, according to the traditional view, with each court being limited to "legislating" for only those facts presently before it, judicial legislation proceeds very slowly, by numerous tiny steps rather than by occasional big leaps. From these numerous tiny steps general rules of law do gradually take on a definite shape, but only gradually.

The second of the two most important procedural norms that serve to keep judicial legislation to a minimum is the principle or norm of "legislative supremacy." This norm requires courts always to adhere to valid rules of law, in the form of statutes, regulations, and so on, passed by the legislative branch of government (or, to the extent that it has power to do so, by the executive branch of government). The only exception to this requirement, an exception not recognized in all legal systems, is for laws that are unconstitutional.

The norms of *stare decisis* and legislative supremacy obviously place drastic limits upon any judicial legislation. Still, according to the traditional view, judicial legislation must occur; even the most carefully drafted statutes and most fully worked-out rules of law will occasionally give rise to borderline or conflict cases that cannot be resolved by norms already within the legal system; to decide cases such as these—we may call them *hard cases*—a judge must resort to something other than the law itself. This something else might be the judge's personal morality, the morality of the community, the public interest, or whatever; but some criteria beyond the law must be used, and to the extent that the judge does resort to criteria beyond the law, he is thereby legislating.

9.2 CRITICISMS OF THE TRADITIONAL VIEW

Let us now turn to recent criticisms of the traditional view, the best-known being those made by Dworkin. He begins by directing our attention to the fact that the law—that is, a legal system—is made up not just of the legal rules "that appear in statutes and are set out in bold type in textbooks," rules of the sort that we are all familiar with, such as "The maximum legal speed on the turnpike is 55 miles/hour," and "A will is invalid unless signed by three witnesses." Just as much a part of the law, even though less well known by the average person, are what Dworkin calls legal "principles" or "maxims." The formal difference between legal rules and legal principles is, according to Dworkin (1977, 22–28), that legal rules operate in an all-or-nothing fashion, whereas legal principles do not. If a legal rule is applicable to a case then it always determines its outcome, or else the rule is abandoned or changed. In other words, rules may conflict with other rules; when, however, there is such a conflict, one of them must be abandoned altogether or changed by, say, a new exception being added permanently to it so as to eliminate the conflict. Principles, on the other hand, are not applicable in an all-or-nothing fashion; a principle might be applicable to a case yet neither determine its outcome nor be abandoned or changed When in hard cases there is a confrontation among conflicting legal *principles,* some, of course, must be given priority over others; all, however, remain intact, being neither abandoned nor changed, to be used again to help some judge decide some future hard case. Examples Dworkin gives (1977, 23–24) of legal principles are as follows: "No one shall be permitted to profit from his own wrong"; ". . . one who does not choose to read a contract before signing it cannot later relieve himself of its burden"; ". . . the courts will not permit themselves to be used as instruments of inequity and injustice"; and ". . . the courts generally refuse to lend themselves to the enforcement of a bargain in which one party has unjustly taken advantage of the economic necessities of others." Also qualifying as legal principles would be more general and fundamental norms, such as one that, Dworkin says, requires that all people be treated with "equal concern and respect."

What exactly are these legal principles or maxims to which Dworkin directs our attention? I suggest that, for the most part at least, they are not norms addressed to the general public, as is the typical legal rule; rather, they are general directives to judges on how to interpret legal rules. The principle "No one shall be permitted to profit from his own wrong," for example, is not meant to apply directly to the general public; it would be ludicrous to treat profiting from one's own wrong as providing a legal cause of action against an individual on a par with, say, driving over 55 miles an hour on the turnpike. The principle "No one shall be permitted to profit from his own wrong" should instead, I suggest, be seen as saying something like "Courts shall not interpret legal rules—i.e., statutes and common law rules—so as to allow a person to profit from his own wrong in cases where allowing this is likely to reduce people's incentives to comply with the law." In other words, what Dworkin calls legal principles are, for the most part, what might be called *canons of* (legal rule) *interpretation;* they are norms that are called into play only for the purpose of resolving borderline and conflict cases involving other norms; they are thus the legal analogue of those norms of personal morality which, likewise, exist only for resolving conflict and borderline cases, and which I have been referring to here as "secondary" moral norms. (For a similar interpretation of legal principles, see Smith 1976, chap. 9, written jointly with Coval.)

In any case, what the traditional view fails to appreciate, according to Dworkin, is the role legal principles play in hard cases. The advocate of the traditional view talks as if law consisted solely of legal rules; he seems to be saying that, with borderline or conflict cases where the judge must therefore resort to standards beyond the legal rules themselves, the judge is forced to go outside the law altogether. What the advocate of the traditioinal view fails to recognize fully, Dworkin says, is that there is much more to the law than legal rules: there are also legal principles.

But to understand Dworkin's critique of the traditional view we must understand that he is saying much more than merely that legal principles provide still further legal standards that must be taken into account before a judge must resort to nonlegal standards. The main claim Dworkin and others want to make is that the role of legal principles in judicial reasoning is such that they make it unnecessary for judges *ever* to have to resort to standards beyond the law itself. Dworkin argues for this claim by hypothesizing an ideal judge with superhuman powers whom he calls "Hercules," and demonstrating how Hercules would go about arriving at an ideal decision in some hard case. I cannot reproduce Dworkin's exact argument without discussing his thorny distinctions between principles and policies, and rights and goals—distinctions that Dworkin considers essential, but that I have doubts about and prefer not to go into here. I shall in what follows, therefore, sketch an argument that is, at best, only similar to Dworkin's, but that, in my view, captures what is most interesting about his criticism of the traditional view.

The first thing the ideal judge would do in order to arrive at an ideal judicial decision would be to gather together all the prior judicial decisions (i.e., legal "precedents") and statutes of his jurisdiction, and included among the "statutes" (in the broad sense in which the word is being used here) would be constitutional provisions, as well as governmental regulations with the force of law. All of these common-law precedents and statutes together would be an imposing set of legal materials. Then the ideal judge would ask himself: what set of legal principles taken together would be necessary to justify this set of precedents and statutes? In other words, he would start from these precedents and statutes and work out a set of legal principles from which they and future judicial decisions could (with the help of relevant factual information) be deduced. The correct decision in the hard case presently before the judge would then be whatever decision was entailed by this set of legal principles. The principles of which this set was comprised would be the *true* legal principles for the jurisdiction in question. If these legal principles had been properly worked out, then from them, in conjunction with the precedents and statutes of the jurisdiction, the correct decision in any hard case could, in principle, be deduced—and, it will be noticed, deduced without appeal to any standards beyond those within the legal system itself. Thus no judicial legislation at all would be necessary. All that would be necessary is the initial data in the form of statutes and precedents from which the judge can reason "backward" to legal principles, and from these legal principles then reason "forward" to a decision in the case at hand.

According to this argument, judicial reasoning is strikingly analogous to scientific reasoning. The scientist, very roughly, starts with certain empirical observations and then reasons "backward" to construct a scientific theory from which these and still further observations can (if the theory is "correct") be deduced. The judge uses this same sort of reasoning, except that in place of empirical observations he uses precedents and statutes, and instead of constructing a scientific theory from which existing and future empirical observations can be deduced, he constructs a *theory of law* (consisting of legal principles) from which existing precedents and statutes can be deduced, and from which decisions in future hard cases should be deduced. The analogy with scientific reasoning may be carried even further. Just as the ultimate constituents of a scientific theory do not seem to exist in quite the same sense as the original observations from which they were constructed, but are merely "theoretical" constructions, so the ultimate principles of a theory of law do not seem to exist in quite the same sense as the precedents and statutes from which they were constructed, but are also "theoretical" constructions.

Now, since human beings are fallible, some of the "data" from which a theory of law is constructed—namely, existing precedents and statutes—will inevitably be the result of faulty logic, misinformation, rationalization, and other human failures; consequently, existing precedents and statutes will in some instances contradict one another and, in general, display a certain lack of "harmony" with one another. Because of this lack of harmony, we should not expect a judge, even an ideal judge, to be able to construct a theory of law encompassing *all* existing precedents and statutes—not, that is, if we expect the principles that make up this theory to serve as viable standards for arriving at future decisions. In order for such principles to serve as viable standards for arriving at future decisions, the theory of which these principles are a part must meet certain criteria of practicality, criteria that would include the criterion of not being so overwhelmingly complex as to be incapable of being learned or understood by ordinary judges. Any theory of law encompassing *all* the existing statutes and precedents of an advanced legal system would be so complex as not to meet these criteria of practicality. In short, to construct a theory of law meeting these criteria, some compromise with the past is necessary; no adequate theory of law for an advanced legal system will be able to accommodate all existing precedents and statutes; some, the least "important," must be discarded in constructing the theory.

A precedent's "importance" for these purposes is determined by such matters as the following: the extent to which the arguments upon which the precedent was originally based can be shown to contain faulty logic or misinformation, the status of the courts and judges that propounded it, the length and extent of public reliance upon it and, most important, the extent of its harmony with other precedents, statutes, and legal principles. Any precedents discarded in constructing the theory of law are to be viewed as abandoned or officially overruled. The abandonment or overruling of certain precedents is, incidentally, all perfectly consistent with the principle of *stare decisis,* which, as I mentioned earlier, does allow some exceptions to its requirement of adherence to precedents. The exceptions it allows are, in fact, for just those precedents which, according to criteria such as the above, are "unimportant." Because of the principle of legislative supremacy a court is never, of course, free to abandon or overrule a (constitutional) statute as it can a precedent. But if, according to much the same criteria used for determining a precedent's importance, a statute is very unimportant, then, even though it must continue to be enforced, it too will have little or no influence in the construction of the jurisdiction's theory of law.

Other things being equal, the fewer the precedents and statutes that are abandoned or disregarded in constructing the theory, the better; but, as we have seen, the abandonment of some is unavoidable. Thus theory construction in law is a two-way process. In constructing legal theories we must work not just from precedents and statutes up to theory, but also at the same time from tentative theory down to precedents and statutes, abandoning some precedents and changing others for the sake of a more viable, practical theory. By thus working back and forth, sometimes adjusting the theory and sometimes adjusting the data from which it is constructed, we arrive finally at a satisfactory resting point, which John Rawls (in speaking of an analogous process used for constructing a moral theory) calls a "reflective equilibrium." When a reflective equilibrium is reached the theory is, for the time being at least, complete.

Judges, of course, do not and could not actually base their decisions in hard cases upon a *full* theory of law of the sort just described; no ordinary judge is capable of constructing such a theory in its entirety. But, it is argued, judges do reason "backwards" from precedents and statutes to construct *partial* or *rudimentary* theories from which they deduce their decisions in hard cases and, what is even more important, the construction of a full theory of this sort does represent the *ideal* that judges should strive to approximate as closely as possible. By appeal to a full theory of this sort a judge could, so it is claimed, decide any hard case that might arise without appeal to any principles outside the theory. And since the legal principles that make up the theory are properly viewed as being just as much a part of the legal system (i.e., of existing law) as are the precedents and statutes upon which these legal principles are based, a judge need never, in principle, go beyond existing law in reaching his decisions. So, it is concluded, a judge need never legislate. And, with this conclusion, my sketch of a Dworkin-like argument against the traditional view of judicial reasoning is complete.

9.3 THE ROLE OF PREEMPTIVE MORAL NORMS

The method of decision-making I have been describing—let us call it the *reflective equilibrium* method—is, I think, indeed one to which judges should conform as closely as possible. We have seen that the key norms of *stare decisis* and legislative supremacy require a judge to decide cases in conformity with precedents and statutes. The reflective equilibrium method of judicial decision-making simply draws our attention to what is already implicit in the ideal of conformity to precedents and statutes as required by *stare decisis* and legislative supremacy. Conformity to precedents and statutes is surely not just a matter of following them only in cases where they are *clearly* applicable, thus leaving the judge on his own in all other cases—that is, in the hard cases. Surely conformity to them is also a matter of following, in hard cases, whatever general principles these precedents and statutes best exemplify, even if these general principles have not yet been formulated by anyone.

But is deciding judicial cases by appeal to precedents and statutes compatible with deciding them by appeal to the EC code of political morality? It might seem that, in using the norms of the EC code to make a judicial decision, a judge would be required to start with the moral norms of this code—including the general welfare norm—and deduce the decision from *them,* thus ignoring any precedents and statutes, at least to the extent that the precedents and statutes were inconsistent with these moral norms. This appears to be just the opposite of the judicial procedure Dworkin and others recommend—namely, that of starting with precedents and statutes, not moral norms. If, as I grant, something very much like the procedure Dworkin and others recommend is the appropriate one, how then can this be reconciled with the use of the EC code for making judicial decisions?

If I am not mistaken, this reconciliation is a very simple matter: something very much like the norms of *stare decisis* and of legislative supremacy—those very norms which give rise to the requirements of conformity to precedents and statutes and hence to the reflective equilibrium method itself—are, I suggest, themselves part of the EC code of political morality and are, for purposes of judicial decision-making, to be given priority over all other norms in the code. If I am right, these two norms—*stare decisis* and legislative supremacy—can thus be thought of as "preemptive" norms of political morality in that, by means of them, all other norms of political morality are, for purposes of judicial reasoning, *preempted* in favor of precedents and statutes. Thus, if I am right, there is no conflict between using the EC code for making judicial decisions and using precedents and statutes; there is no conflict simply because conformity to precedents and statutes in judicial decision-making is required by the EC code itself, by means of these preemptive norms. And, incidentally, just because these preemptive norms are norms of political morality does not mean that they cannot be norms of law also, as indeed they typically are.

Why am I so confident that, for purposes of judicial decision-making, the EC code would contain moral norms preempting all other moral norms in favor of precedents and statutes? As we saw earlier, there is obvious utility in minimizing or eliminating judicial legislation, which compliance with these preemptive norms achieves. There is, in particular, utility in having a legal code that "stays still" for the most part—that is, in other words, predictable—so that people can use it as a basis for making plans for the future without undue fear of their plans' being upset. If judges, in making judicial decisions, turned first to the general welfare norm and other norms of political morality before turning to precedents and statutes then, owing to the extreme difficulty there normally is in discovering exactly what the general welfare norm calls for, it would normally be impossible to predict with any confidence what their decisions would be. Thus the predictability that a reasonable legal code must provide would not exist. This preditability would exist, however, with conformity to preemptive norms that require judges instead in turn to precedents and statutes first. For these reasons, I am confident that the utilitarian standard does indeed justify, as part of political morality, preemptive norms very much like those of *stare decisis* and legislative supremacy. And this code might contain other, less important, preemptive moral norms as well, such as one preempting (in certain kinds of cases) the rest of political morality in favor not of precedents and statutes but of certain established commercial practices—that is, "customs"; but we need not pursue these fine points here. (On the status of customs in legal systems see, for example, Hart 1961, 44–46.)

It might be objected that preemptive norms are not really necessary; a moral code that contained the general welfare norm would, it might be argued, generate predictability quite well enough without any preemptive norms. After all, so the argument might go, judges in deciding cases primarily by appeal to the general welfare norm would, in calculating what decision maximized the general welfare, be required to give due weight to the need for predictability anyway; so would not the use of preemptive norms for the sake of this predictability be unnecessary?

The answer to this question takes the form of an argument similar to the one used earlier for showing that rights against the government always have priority over the general welfare norm. There are, no doubt, some circumstances in which it maximizes expected utility within a jurisdiction to depart from the norm of *stare decisis,* and other circumstances in which it maximizes expected utility to depart from the norm of legislative supremacy. But clearly it is always very easy to be mistaken about whether such favorable circumstances currently exist, and the damage (in the form of undermining people's confidence in the legal code, undermining predictability, etc.) from mistaken departures from *stare decisis* and legislative supremacy is always potentially very great. In short, the chance of being mistaken and the potential damage from such mistakes are always great enough so that, for a judge to contravene one of these preemptive norms on the chance that he has successfully determined that such favorable circumstances exist is always a bad utilitarian gamble. This being so, the utilitarian standard justifies always giving these preemptive norms priority over the general welfare norm, thus disallowing all such bad gambles altogether.

9.4 WHY JUDGES MAY HAVE TO LEGISLATE AFTER ALL

If Dworkin and others are correct in claiming that the reflective equilibrium method of reaching judicial decisions is self-sufficient in that, by means of it, a judge can (in principle) arrive at a single right answer for every case without appeal to anything beyond precedents, statutes, common law rules, and legal principles, then political morality would have no role to play in judicial decision-making other than that of setting the reflective equilibrium method in motion in the first place (by means of preemptive moral norms). Is then the reflective equilibrium method self-sufficient or not? In other words, must judges, at least to some extent, legislate after all? Some philosophers, such as Joseph Raz (1972), argue that this method is not self-sufficient. They ask us to consider cases such as those involving conflicting legal principles; how exactly, they then ask, are we to determine, by means of this method, which of the conflicting legal principles is to be given the greatest weight? By reference, it will be replied, to still other legal principles. But, as has been pointed out (e.g., see McCormick 1978), legal principles tend to "hunt in pairs," in that, for every legal principle that one can find in support of some decision, there seems to be another legal principle in support of just the opposite decision. So it would seem that, in some cases at least, the point eventually will be reached where appeal to further legal principles must end and one legal principle (or set of legal principles) must be given greater weight than its competitors on the basis of some criterion other than still further legal principles, thus forcing the judge to go beyond the reflective equilibrium method.

In reply it might be pointed out that a legal theory could easily have built into it a "catch-all" conflict-resolving legal principle; this would assure that all conflicts, as well as borderline cases, could be resolved without appeal to standards outside the legal system itself since, if worse came to worst, a case could always be resolved by appeal to this "catch-all" legal principle. Such a legal principle might, for example, be a judicial analogue of the general welfare norm. In fact, in a society committed to the EC code of political morality, it is to be expected that the theory of law that best "fits" the precedents and statutes of that society would include, along with other legal principles, ones very similar to the moral norms of the EC code. It is to be expected since the statutes turned out by public officials committed to the moral norms of the EC code would naturally tend to reflect this commitment, and if the statutes reflected a commitment to the moral norms of the EC code, it follows that the theory of law that best "fits" these statutes would likely contain legal principles similar to these same moral norms. And if the society's legal theory contained, along with other legal principles, ones similar to the moral norms of the EC code—including a judicial analogue of the general welfare norm—then obviously it would be unnecessary for a judge, in resolving a conflict or borderline case, ever to go beyond this legal theory to these moral norms themselves; he would need only to appeal to their judicial analogues. Furthermore, the preemptive norm of *stare decisis* in the EC code is, I assume, formulated (as it is in current Anglo-American law—see sec. 9.1 above) so as to require adherence to those and only those legal rules and principles which are not broader than necessary for covering the facts of previous cases. This, in effect, requires judges to give narrow, specific legal rules and principles priority over broader, more general ones. This priority of the specific over the general would serve the purpose of preventing excessive appeal to the judicial analogue of the general welfare norm which, I take it, would be the most general of all legal principles available. It would relegate the judicial analogue of the general welfare norm to the role of being a principle of last resort, a principle to be appealed to only after appeal to all the other numerous legal rules and principles within the legal system had been exhausted, which is a role similar to that played by the utilitarian norm in the EC code of personal morality.

An argument along these lines might indeed be sufficient to show that all ordinary conflict and borderline legal cases could be decided without having to resort to standards outside the law itself and that, therefore, the reflective equilibrium method is self-sufficient to this extent. But now consider questions of the following sort. As we have seen, the set of legal principles constructed from the data of precedents and statutes by using the reflective equilibrium method cannot possibly encompass *all* precedents—not, at least, without making the resulting set of legal principles unacceptably complex and difficult to apply; so, for the sake of simplicity, some precedents must be disregarded or overruled. But how are we to determine exactly how *many* precedents should be disregarded for the sake of simplicity? In other words, in constructing a theory of law, how much importance should be given to the goal of inclusiveness (i.e., having the theory encompass all precedents vis-à-vis the goal of simplicity (i.e., having the theory be easy to understand and apply to new cases)? Even if ordinary conflict and borderline cases could be decided without appeal to standards outside the law, it seems that cases raising questions such as these could not be; for it seems that cases raising questions such as these—questions about which to choose from among alternative legal theories, each *equally* consistent with the data—could not be decided by appeal to the alternative theories themselves, and so could be decided only by appeal to standards outside the law. Finally, it might be somewhat plausible to claim that the reflective equilibrium method is self-sufficient when put to use within a mature legal system, such as that of the United States, a legal system containing numerous precedents and statutes with which to work; but every legal system must have a beginning, and it is much less plausible to claim self-sufficiency for this method when put to use within a relatively young or primitive legal system, one as yet containing few (if any) precedents and statutes with which to work. In light of considerations such as these, it would appear that some "judicial legislation" may be necessary after all.

But my main purpose in discussing judicial reasoning has not been to settle the complex issue of judicial legislation; my main purpose has been to show how using the EC code for making judicial decisions can be reconciled with giving priority to existing precedents and statutes. This reconciliation is, as I have tried to show, achieved by means of what I call the preemptive moral norms of the EC code. The role of the EC code of political morality in judicial decision-making is that of supplying these basic preemptive moral norms. All I need really say about judicial legislation is that, to the extent that the reflective equilibrium method is not self-sufficient, the EC code has an additional role to play in judicial decision-making: it has the role of taking up where the reflective equilibrium method leaves off, so to speak. It has, in other words, the additional role of being a code of last resort. Therefore, according to the EC code of morality, every case, no matter how "hard," should be decided either by means of the reflective equilibrium method or, as a last resort, by appeal to the EC code of morality itself. This view entails that, for every case, no matter how "hard," there is indeed one and only one correct decision, although, to find this decision, once in a while a judge may, in theory, have to go beyond what is ordinarily thought of as law, and into morality. Whether these judicial excursions into morality should count as "judicial legislation," I shall not try to decide.

9.5 REFLECTIVE EQUILIBRIUM AND MORAL JUSTIFICATION

Reflective equilibrium methodology is now widely viewed as appropriate not just for judicial justification, but for moral justification as well, the most widely discussed proponent of its use in moral reasoning being John Rawls (1971, see esp. sec. 9). Other proponents of its use in moral reasoning include C. F. Delaney (1976), Stuart Hampshire (1977), Norman Daniels (1979, 1980a, and 1980b), Jane English (1980), and Kai Nielsen (1982a, 1982b, and 1985). Although I have suggested that this methodology has a certain plausibility for purposes of judicial reasoning, its use for purposes of *moral* reasoning is, I think, less plausible. But I shall argue now that this methodology, or something very much like it, nevertheless does have a legitimate, although limited use in moral reasoning as well.

When using reflective equilibrium methodology for moral justification, instead of beginning with precedents and statutes, we are to begin with what Rawls calls "considered moral judgments"—the moral analogues of legal precedents. Considered moral judgments are not ones made simply on the spur of the moment, without much thought, rather, they are ones made under conditions generally favorable for deliberation and judgment. In other words, they are pre-equilibrium judgments to which we have given careful consideration, and in which we, therefore, have confidence, judgments such as "that religious intolerance and racial discrimination are unjust" (Rawls 1971, 19; see also 48–49). From our considered moral judgments we are then to construct a set of moral principles that, when conjoined with our beliefs about circumstances, would entail these judgments. And, as in constructing a theory of law, we are then to "work back and forth," between judgments and principles, at times discarding or modifying some of our considered moral judgments, and at other times discarding or modifying some of our constructed moral principles. These decisions about what to keep, what to discard, and what to modify that we are to make in thus working back and forth, we may refer to an *adjustment* decisions. By means of these various adjustment decisions, we arrive, finally, at a satisfactory resting point, a "reflective equilibrium," at which point the process of moral justification is complete—complete, that is, until some new "evidence" of some sort upsets the delicate balance, thus necessitating that we work out a new reflective equilibrium.

I have two major reservations about the use of this methodology for moral justification. The first is that it is circular. By working back and forth, one in effect uses one's considered moral judgments to justify one's moral principles, and one's moral principles to justify one's considered moral judgments. Accordingly, it is to be expected that different people, starting out with different moral judgments (a radical Marxist and a fundamentalist Christian, let us say) will arrive at quite different reflective equilibria, between which this methodology provides no rational means of choosing. Yet is it not just such a means of choosing between the moralities of those with different considered moral judgments that we want from a method of moral justification? (There are, incidentally, two ways that proponents of this methodology have tried to meet the circularity objection. One is through a shift from what they call "narrow" reflective equilibrium methodology, which is what has been described here, to what they call "wide" reflective equilibrium methodology, which is much the same except for bringing "background theories" into the reasoning process [see, e.g., Daniels 1979]. The other way is by comparing the circularity of this methodology to that found in scientific reasoning, and arguing that just as the latter is "benign" circularity, so is the former. I argue elsewhere that both these attempts to avoid the circularity objection fail [Haslett 1987].)

Notice that the circularity objection is less applicable to use of reflective equilibrium methodology for legal reasoning. Precedents and statues, the judicial analogues of considered moral judgments, derive an "initial credibility," which considered moral judgments lack, from the powerful rationale that supports the doctrines of *stare decisis* and legislative supremacy. Moreover, the precedents and statutes upon which judges are to operate are identical from one judge to the next within any given jurisdiction, while the considered moral judgments upon which people are to build their reflective equilibria differ markedly from one person to the next.

But the second major reservation I have about this methodology is just as applicable to its use for legal as it is for moral reasoning. As we saw, this methodology requires working back and forth between our starting point (considered moral judgments or precedents and statutes, as the case may be) and our constructed principles, making a number of "adjustment" decisions along the way, thus removing the inconsistencies between them. My objection is that we are given no specific criteria in terms of which it can be determined, definitively, whether these adjustment decisions have been made correctly or not. So we are, in effect, "free" either to discard any given considered moral judgment in favor of preserving intact some principle with which it conflicts, or to retain the judgment and modify the principle instead. Adjustment decisions are, in other words, very much "underdetermined." Thus, because of their differing adjustment decisions, even two people starting out with *identical* considered moral judgments are likely to end up with different reflective equilibria, between which, once again, this methodology provides us with no rational means of choosing. Without any rational means of choosing, this methodology can therefore, with enough ingenuity, be used in support of virtually any "starting point" prejudices whatever (Haslett 1987).

But, in spite of these reservations, I suggest that reflective equilibrium methodology—or something very much like it—can play a legitimate, although limited, role in moral reasoning after all. We can, I suggest, legitimately use it as a method by means of which we may reason *within* any given social-pressure system, a method to which we may turn for uncovering the system's various implications, for working out its ramifications. As such, this methodology might be of genuine use in resolving hard cases within the system; in other words, in resolving conflict and borderline cases (see secs. 6.7 and 6.8).

Yet, for challenging any aspects of the social-pressure system, for changing any aspects, or for justifying the system in the first place it is not, I claim, to reflective equilibrium methodology that we should turn, but to the method being proposed here (as set out in chap. 4). To put it another way, what I am claiming is this: perhaps we may be able to use reflective equilibrium methodology profitably for *infra*-system evaluation, but for any serious *inter*-system evaluation we should turn instead to a "three-dimensional" evaluation carried out by means of the utilitarian standard. However, a crucial question about this claim remains unanswered: Why, exactly, use the *utilitarian standard* for this purpose? It is to this question that we now, in Part IV, turn.

Part IV

THE RATIONALE

10
Equal Consideration and Self-Interest

10.1 THE PROJECT AND THE STRATEGY

The method or moral justification being proposed here calls for an evaluation of moral norms, or codes, in terms of the utilitarian standard; that is, by giving everyone's interests "equal consideration." As pointed out earlier (sec. 4.7), an evaluation in terms of the utilitarian standard is by no means all there is to this method; it also calls for an evaluation of moral norms, or codes, not solely from the perspective of compliance with them, but as part of social-pressure systems; in other words, this method also calls for a three-, rather than merely one- or two-dimensional evaluation. But the justification for the "three-dimensional" aspect of this method has already been explained (chap. 4). What remains to be explained is why the other aspect of this method—use of the utilitarian standard for carrying out these evaluations—is justified. Thus the question to which we must now turn is: Why exactly should moral norms, codes and, in general, entire social-pressure systems be evaluated in terms of the utilitarian standard? With the answer to this question we arrive, finally, at what is most fundamental, thereby completing the rationale for the method of moral justification being proposed here.

The social-pressure system that, according to the utilitarian standard, is most justified I have been calling the "equal consideration" system. In Parts II and III, to set the stage for the argument presented here, I examined what certain aspects of this ideal system might be like. In particular, I examined what codes of personal and political morality are part of this system—that is, I examined the "EC" codes of morality. One noteworthy fact emerging from this examination is that probably most of the norms in these moral codes are not radically different from the moral norms most people in most present-day societies already accept. The EC code of personal morality no doubt contains norms prohibiting such things as killing, taking what does not belong to one, telling falsehoods, breaking promises, and so on, and these norms are no doubt ones with relatively simple, easy-to-comply-with cores. The EC code of political morality probably contains a norm requiring the government to act in the general welfare, but this code no doubt also contains various rights against the government and other relatively specific moral norms that have priority over the general welfare norm. All of this, in general outline, corresponds notably well with the moral intuitions and judgments of most people.

There are philosophers today who would view this correspondence as being itself justification for the utilitarian standard—in fact the only justification for it that is possible. Take, for example, those philosophers who adhere exclusively to the reflective equilibrium method of justification (see sec. 9.5). They might interpret this correspondence as showing that the utilitarian standard is the most satisfactory "theoretical construct" from which our "considered moral judgments" can be "deduced," which, for them, amounts to justification. That the utilitarian standard might well be justified even from the standpoint of many who adhere to the reflective equilibrium method of justification is of interest. But, as we saw (sec. 9.5), the reflective equilibrium method when used for purposes of *inter*-system justification, has serious limitations. Other, more traditional, intuitive methods are even more objectionable. Thus, in my attempt to show that the utilitarian standard is justified, our moral intuitions and considered moral judgments will not play a leading role. Instead, I shall try to show that the utilitarian standard is justified the only way I think it possible to show this: by appealing to our own well-being, or best interests. I shall not be trying to show that it is always in our best interests to comply, personally, with those norms which, according to this standard, deserve to be evaluated the most highly. The extent to which our compliance with those norms may be in our best interests is examined in the next chapter. Here I shall try to show that, regardless of whether our compliance with the norms that deserve to be evaluated the most highly is always in our best interests, it is nevertheless always in our best interests to use the utilitarian standard *as our criterion of evaluation*.

In trying to justify the utilitarian standard by appealing to what is in our best interests it is time, finally, to put to use the fundamental norm of personal welfare (as formulated in sec. 2.2), and the standard of personal welfare implicit in it. As will be recalled, this standard of personal welfare can be used to tell us which alternatives are in our best interests from among alternatives whose *actual* effects are not known; all that need be known are their possible sets of effects along with, for each possible set, its *probability* of occurring. Where only probabilities, not actualities, are known, the alternative that is most justified from the standpoint of our self-interest may be referred to as the alternative that maximizes for us "expected" personal utility. If, however, the actual effects *are* known—that is, if all the probabilities are 100 percent—then this alternative may be referred to as the one that maximizes not "expected" personal utility, but "actual" personal utility.

Equal Consideration and Self-Interest 171

Of course the alternative that maximizes our expected personal utility will not always end up maximizing our actual personal utility, in spite of favorable probabilities. Nevertheless, the alternative that maximizes our expected personal utility is our best personal "bet," and for convenience shall be referred to here simply as the alternative that is in our "best interests."

How then might I go about showing that it is in our best interests to use the utilitarian standard as our criterion for evaluating social-pressure systems? The most obvious strategy would be by trying to show that the social-pressure systems that, according to the utilitarian standard, is most justified—that is, the "equal consideration" system—is also the system that is most in everyone's interests. If this social-pressure system was always in everyone's best interests, then obviously for us to use the utilitarian standard as our criterion for evaluating social-pressure systems would, from a perspective of self-interest, make sense. Unfortunately, this strategy will not work simply because the equal consideration system—that is, its existence—probably is *not* always in everyone's best interests. So rather than trying to show that the equal consideration system is always in everyone's best interests, I shall try to do the next best thing: I shall try to show that, even though the equal consideration system is not always in everyone's best interests, it nevertheless is always in everyone's best interests to *act* as if it were. If the system that is most justified according to the utilitarian standard is also the one that, for purposes of deciding what to do, we should always *assume* is in everyone's best interests, then (even though it may not always *be* in everyone's best interests) it still makes sense for us to use this standard as our criterion for evaluating systems. So what I shall be trying to show in this chapter is that it is indeed always in our best interests to act on the assumption that the equal consideration system is more in our interests than any alternative.

At this point it might be asked: What exactly would be the *practical consequences* of our assuming this—that is, of assuming that the equal consideration system is more in our interests than any alternative? If it is always in our best interests to make this assumption, does this, for example, mean it is always in our best interest to *comply* with the norms of the system? My answer, as we shall see in the next chapter, is: not necessarily. But then exactly what effect upon our actions should this assumption have—if we decide to make it? I shall return to this question later in this chapter, and in the next chapter. But first, in this chapter I must try to show that this assumption is indeed one we should decide to make.

So, once again, my strategy for justifying the utilitarian standard in terms of self-interest is to try to show that, for deciding what to do, we should always assume that the equal consideration system is more in our interests than any alternative. And "any" alternative means, of course, any factually possible, as opposed to merely conceivable, alternative, and includes even the alternative of there being no social-pressure system at all. What I shall be trying to show then is that, whenever we believe it is more in our personal interests for there to be some social-pressure system in the world other than the equal consideration system, we resist this belief and act instead on the assumption that the equal consideration system is the one in our best interests (just as the judge, discussed earlier (sec. 1.3), should resist his belief that the defendant is the father whenever this belief is contrary to the blood-test evidence).

My strategy can be made more precise by means of that rather subtle distinction drawn earlier between what is in our "unqualified" and our "qualified" best interests (sec. 2.3). As will be recalled, an alternative is in our *unqualified* best interests if it is the one that would be chosen by us from a standpoint that included *all* the knowledge that one choosing from an ideal standpoint for determining self-interest is, in principle, supposed to have. An alternative is in our *qualified* best interests, on the other hand, if it is the one that would be chosen by us from a standpoint that included all the knowledge that one choosing from this ideal standpoint is supposed to have, *except* for certain facts—certain facts that in real life we do not know and are to assume that in choosing from an "ideal" standpoint we still would not know. If these facts are not known, a choice from this "qualified" standpoint thus represents not what is in our *un*qualified best interests, but what is in our *qualified* best interests—that is, our best interests *given* that these facts are not known. In the example presented earlier (sec. 2.3), it was in Jane's qualified best interests to ask for a kiss. It was in her *qualified* best interests because it was the alternative she would choose from a standpoint that was ideal in every respect except for her being unaware of what John's current willingness to consent to such a request was. What I shall be trying to show in this chapter is this: even though the equal consideration system is not always in our *unqualified* best interests, acting on the assumption that it is in our unqualified best interests is always in our *qualified* best interests; it is always, in other words, our best personal "bet." Acting on this assumption is always in our qualified best interests in the sense that it is always what we would choose to do, if we were choosing from a standpoint that was ideal in every respect *except* for our not having certain crucial knowledge.

What then is the crucial knowledge that (we are to assume) we would not have in choosing from this qualified ideal standpoint? We are to assume that we would not have any more *or* less knowledge than we do, in real life, about whether, in the particular circumstances at hand, the equal consideration system is in our unqualified best interests. From this qualified ideal standpoint we do, of course, have far greater knowledge than we do in real life about what the probabilities are of our opinions on what is in our unqualified best interests being correct, and about what is true of *most* circumstances, as opposed to the particular circumstances at hand. But about this one matter—whether, *in the particular circumstances at hand,* the equal consideration system is in our best interests—we are to assume that we do not have any more or less knowledge than we do in real life. And we are to make this assumption for a good reason. It is obviously of practical value for us to try to determine what it is in our best interests to do, given that no more is known about the particular circumstances at hand than we actually *do* know.

Trying to show that it is always in our qualified best interests to act on the assumption that the equal consideration system is more in our unqualified interests than any alternative will obviously involve comparing the extent to which the equal consideration system is likely to be in our interests with the extent to which alternatives are likely to be. I cannot, however, compare the equal consideration system with *all* possible alternatives, and for this reason the argument will not be conclusive. But I do compare it with the alternative that, I think, most people would consider to be its *most likely* competitor—competitor, that is, for being that social-pressure system most in our interests. If I can show that it is always in our best interests to act on the assumption that we are better off with the equal consideration system than with this particular alternative, then even though this will not establish conclusively the corresponding claim about *any* alternative, it should make it much more plausible.

The particular alternative with which I shall compare the equal consideration system is one that is blatantly biased or discriminatory. What I mean by a "biased" (or "discriminatory") system is one that has the effect of distributing what is in people's interests *less evenly* among groups than does the equal consideration system—giving a greater percentage than does the equal consideration system to some groups and a lesser percentage to others—with these groups being identified by a characteristic such as the skin color, national origin, or religion of its members (i.e., some characteristic of a sort that ordinarily would be viewed as reflecting a bias). For example, the sort of informal social norm that I would expect to find in a biased system if the bias were directed against, say, blacks would be a norm making aid to a person in dire need mandatory if the person is white, but only optional if the person is black, or a norm requiring that all high-paying professional positions be reserved for only whites. And in such a social-pressure system we might find, for example, that social pressure for discouraging blacks from raping whites took the form of lynchings, while social pressure for discouraging whites from raping blacks took the form of mild verbal reprimands. I am assuming, of course, that our discussion of personal and political morality has provided us with good reasons for believing that any such blatantly biased norms or practices as these would always be bad *utilitarian* gambles, even if not bad *personal* gambles, and that therefore such norms and practices would never be found in the equal consideration system.

It would appear that if any social-pressure system were more in the interests of some people than the equal consideration system, then it would be a *blatantly* biased one; those people for whom such a system would be the better one being, of course, those in the "favored" group—that is, those in the group doing the discriminating. I shall argue, however, that, even for those in the favored group, it is always in their best interests to act on the assumption that the equal consideration system is more in their interests. And what I mean by a "blatantly" biased system is one that (at least with respect to the society of the person whose interests are in question) is biased enough for the bias to be obvious to virtually anyone. Although my argument focuses only upon *blatantly* biased systems, the conclusion may well be applicable to mildly biased systems also. Finally, the argument relies upon factual premises that cannot very well be proven true by scientific experimentation, but that I think we have reason to believe true nevertheless. As background for these premises let me now draw attention to certain ways in which (blatantly) biased systems are generally disadvantageous for everyone.

10.2 SOME OBSERVATIONS ABOUT DISCRIMINATION

First, with a biased system, everyone would, in some respects, be somewhat less secure—and everyone includes, of course, even those doing the discriminating. For one thing, those against whom a biased system is directed would not feel as much of an obligation to act consistently with the moral code within this system as they would were it unbiased. This biased code would not be viewed by them as *their* code—that is, the code would not be "internalized" by them—so naturally they would feel less compunction about breaking the norms of this code than they would otherwise, especially when, in doing so, they would be harming those doing the discriminating. Furthermore, those who openly discriminate are leaving themselves wide open to the possibility of receiving "a dose of their own medicine" through being, in some way or other, discriminated against themselves. And, incidentally, this discrimination would not necessarily be at the hands of the same group against whom they have discriminated.

Next, many mutually beneficial cooperative endeavors between individuals depend upon there being a degree of trust and good will between them that, in all likelihood, would be lacking between discriminators and those against whom they were discriminating, a lack of which would be to the disadvantage of everyone.

Also, to the mutual disadvantage of everyone in both groups, it would be more difficult, if not impossible, to enjoy fully even the ordinary benefits of friendship and companionship with those not in one's own group. Even if two individuals were, for the sake of a friendship, willing to ignore the hostility between their two groups, the general atmosphere of *blatant* bias in their society would hardly be one in which their friendship could be expected to flourish fully. (An exception to this might be sexual discrimination; the natural attraction between men and women is, I suppose, strong enough to form the basis for a satisfying relationship no matter how blatant the bias but, even here, the relationship surely would not be all that, without the discrimination, it could be.)

As a final example of the disadvantages even for those in the favored group, take the overall decrease in society's productivity that would result from discrimination that precluded large numbers of people—namely, those being discriminated against—from ever realizing their full productive potential. For instance, potential discoverers of a cure for cancer might well, as a result of the discrimination, end up digging ditches instead and, of course, discriminators get cancer too. In general, the positions in society that those being discriminated against would have held if positions were handed out on a nondiscriminatory basis would instead be held by less-qualified people who would never have succeeded in getting these positions had they not been favored through the discrimination. To the extent that such a mismatch between qualifications and positions existed, overall productivity within the society would be lost, a loss that probably would be far from insignificant. (It has, for example, been estimated that, in terms of *1969* dollars, the loss in overall productivity in the United States resulting from discrimination against blacks is no less than $19 billion per year [Thurow 1969].)

Next, as against these disadvantages, consider the likely advantages to those in the favored group from there being a biased system. First and foremost, discrimination increases the job prospects of those in the favored group. If the number of good people against whom they have to compete for the better positions in society are, through discrimination, considerably reduced, it stands to reason that many of those in the favored group will end up with higher-level positions than they would otherwise have had. For example, a person in the favored group who otherwise would have qualified only for simple manual labor might end up with something he considered somewhat better if those being discriminated against were forced to do this labor instead.

But would such a person likely end up with a position that was *much* better? If he had otherwise been qualified only for simple manual labor, then even with the help of discrimination he is not likely to end up with very much; he still would lose out to many who were more qualified from his own group. Or if, alternatively, he were a highly qualified individual, then, in order to get a high level position, he probably would not need the discrimination. In general, if, through discrimination, a person did gain a higher level position than he would otherwise have got, the gain is not likely to be dramatic.

And even if the gain were dramatic—that is, even if the person did succeed in getting a position that was at a level *far* higher than he would otherwise have got, he well might not end up happier as a result. Continually struggling with a position that is at a level far higher than one's qualifications would have enabled one to get would not appear to be the way to happiness; it might instead be the way to a nervous breakdown.

How else then might one gain through discrimination? I have heard it argued that discrimination in the form of slavery might result (or has resulted) in great gains to humanity in general. The argument is that the leisure that slavery makes possible for some provides them with the time necessary for making great discoveries, cultural advances, and the like, that dramatically benefit all of humanity. It would seem, however, that any such great advancements would not be a result of the discrimination as much as a result of the leisure, and if such leisure really were necessary for these great advancements, then surely this leisure could be more effectively arranged on a nondiscriminatory basis through competition open to all, or even through random selection. Thus it is difficult to see how any such great advancements could very well be said to be among the benefits of discrimination *per se*.

I have also heard it argued that those in the favored group derive certain subtle, psychological benefits from discrimination, like that of having a group to which they can feel superior. But how secure can any psychological benefits be if derived from an alleged superiority that has no basis in fact? And may there not also exist, for those in the favored group, equally subtle psychological detriments—detriments that may more than offset any such benefits? For example, discrimination may, for all we know, diminish our capacity for having the love for others that great religions of the world tell us is what is most meaningful in life. Anyway, it is far from certain whether any significant psychological benefits actually do exist. And if they did, I should be very surprised if the same benefits were not attainable by some means far less disadvantageous than discrimination.

Of course, if one were a rapist, or a sadist, I suppose one might gain through those forms of discrimination which allowed people to cruelly assault those in the discriminated-against group without being punished. But fortunately, few of us are rapists or sadists, and those of us who are would no doubt benefit more by going to a good psychiatrist than through discrimination.

Aside from a better job (and it might well not be much better), it is hard to think of ways in which one, even though a member of the favored group, would be likely to gain much from discrimination. On the other hand, it is easy to think of ways in which one, even though a member of the favored group, would be likely to lose—less security, fewer and less-satisfying relationships with those in the other group, less overall productivity from one's society, and so on. In sum, it does not take a very extended investigation into the likely gains and losses from discrimination for one thing to become apparent: even for members of the favored group, losses from a biased system would be likely to outweigh gains—not necessarily in all circumstances, but in most.

10.3 THE PREMISES

From these observations comes the first premise of the argument, which is as follows: under not all, but most circumstances, a biased system is not in one's best interests, even if one is in the favored group. The favored group would, to be sure, get a greater *percentage* of the "pie," but in most circumstances the "pie" would be so much smaller than with the equal consideration system that, for most discriminators, their share, in spite of being bigger in relative terms, would be smaller in absolute terms.

It might be objected that this premise is true enough if we are talking about discrimination directed against some large and powerful group, such as American blacks, but not if we are talking about discrimination directed against some relatively small group, such as American Indians, or some relatively helpless group, such as those in need of institutionalization because of severe metal or physical disability. Surely, it might be claimed, with discrimination directed against some small or helpless group, a group that could not very effectively fight back, it would normally be the *biased* system that was in the best interests of those in the favored group. But, I submit, not even this claim is warranted. Admittedly, since small or weak groups would lack the retaliatory capacities of larger, more powerful groups, certain obvious disadvantages of discrimination for the favored group would be minimized. But discrimination against a small or weak group would also lack the same capacity for *benefiting* the favored group; so not only would disadvantages for the favored group be minimized, but advantages would be too. Thus the advantage of having minimal disadvantages would tend to be canceled by the disadvantage of having minimal advantages, making discrimination against a small or weak group generally no more advantageous than discrimination against a larger, more powerful group. Furthermore, although for many of us the probability of ourselves eventually being among a group of disabled individuals who are discriminated against might (with some such groups) be minimal, there is always the chance of someone we care about, say a future son or daughter, a close friend, or the son or daughter of a close friend, being among this group. This is a disadvantage that would not be minimized. Finally, among the benefits of not discriminating against any group, no matter how small or weak, is what might be referred to as a certain "solidarity" with others and, along with this solidarity, a certain peace of mind and comfort that only the knowledge that *all* are given equal consideration can generate. All, without *any* exceptions. In a world in which, for example, a momentary lapse at the wheel of an automobile can, instantly, transform the most well off of us into the most piteous, in a world as uncertain and tragic as this, to underestimate the value of this solidarity would be, I suggest, a grave mistake; few things of as much value to everyone as this could be purchased at what would be such a relatively small cost. For these various reasons, I claim the premise above is applicable even to discrimination directed against a group that is small or weak.

Let us turn now to the second premise of the argument, which is that, although for each of us there are no doubt certain circumstances in which certain biased systems *are* more in our interests that the equal consideration system, our calculations concerning exactly what these circumstances are, and exactly when they exist, are bound to be highly unreliable. Human affairs are simply too complicated and unpredictable, involving too many indeterminable, interrelated variables, for this to be otherwise. One need only ponder for a moment the overwhelming difficulties in the way of carrying out such calculations successfully to see that this is so. There might sometimes be grounds for being reasonably sure about *some* of the results for ourselves of a blatantly biased system; the fact is, however, that the number of possible different results are innumerable, and there could hardly be grounds for being reasonably sure about enough of these possible results so as to be reasonably sure about the *overall* value for us of discrimination in the circumstances at hand. If, in certain circumstances, we did have grounds for being reasonably sure that blatant discrimination against certain people would not result in, say, a rebellion against us, causing us untold grief, there would always be other possible results, just as disadvantageous, about which we could not be so sure. Perhaps, for example, the discrimination would, by excluding these people from certain professions, prevent from ever occurring what otherwise would have been unparalleled contributions to humanity. And, in trying to make these calculations, we must contend with more even than major fact-finding difficulties. Being human beings, we are all subject to rationalizations (some of us more than others); and rationalizations about this matter would often distort whatever relatively meager facts about the particular circumstances we did have, thus making any conclusions reached even more unreliable. In short, our susceptibility to mistakes in making any such complicated and emotionally charged calculations as these is, as was pointed out earlier (sec. 7.7), a fact so basic and unlikely ever to change that it might well be called a "natural" fact to distinguish it from more transitory facts about human beings.

To summarize, I have been arguing so far for the following two premises: (1) Take any blatantly biased system; it is not more in one's unqualified interests than the equal consideration system in most circumstances; (2) Whether the relatively rare circumstances currently exist in which the biased system is more in one's unqualified interests can never be determined very reliably. These two premises, taken in conjunction, are, I submit, strong enough to yield a third premise, which is as follows: A belief that those relatively rare circumstances currently exist in which the biased system is more in one's unqualified interests than the equal consideration system is always more likely to be mistaken than not. Trying, on a case-by-case basis, to distinguish those relatively rare circumstances favorable for a biased system from the majority of circumstances that are not is, again, like the judge, discussed earlier (sec. 1.3), trying to pick out the one defendant in a hundred who, in spite of the blood-test evidence, really is the father. As we saw, a judge's powers of discrimination are simply not great enough to support an attempt to pick out this one defendant. Likewise, I submit, no one's powers of discrimination are great enough to support an attempt to pick out those relatively rare circumstances favorable for a biased system. This analogy with judicial reasoning is not perfect: we know *exactly* what the antecedent probability is of a defendant being the father—the antecedent probability, as shown by the blood test, is .01—while we do not know exactly what the antecedent probability is of circumstances favorable for a biased system. But we do know at least this much: the existence of these circumstances is relatively rare. To be sure, the antecedent probability of favorable circumstances existing may be somewhat greater than that of a defendant being the father (I am not convinced it is; yet it certainly may be). But, given the incredible complexity of the matter, in trying to spot these favorable circumstances our powers of discrimination are surely somewhat less than those of the judge in trying to spot the real fathers; and these lesser powers of discrimination would at least partially offset any greater antecedent probability. Thus, although the reasons we have for holding premise (3) to be true are not, of course, conclusive, they do, I submit, establish at least a prima facie case.

As between the assumption that the equal consideration system is more in our interests and the assumption that a biased system is more in our interests, no matter which assumption we act upon, we are taking a gamble. The only question is: Which is the best gamble? Premise (3) tells us that a belief that a biased system is the one most in our interests is more likely to be mistaken than not. This strongly suggests, of course, that our best gamble is to act upon the assumption that the system most in our interests is the equal consideration system. But before we can conclude this, one more premise is necessary: a premise telling us whether or not our best gamble lies with the biased system anyway, on the grounds that the difference between the likely "winnings" from such a system and those from the equal consideration system is great enough to override the greater probability of the equal consideration system being the "winner." We need, in other words, a premise comparing the likely *extent* of our winnings from each alternative. I think we have already seen enough of the potential benefits and detriments from each type of system to be reasonably confident that, by consistently "gambling" on a biased system being most in our interests, our "winnings" would (when we did win) be no greater, on the average, then they would be were we gambling instead on the equal consideration system. Actually I think we would be warranted even in claiming that, on the average, our "winnings" from the equal consideration system would be not just equal to, but greater than, those from a biased system; however, the weaker claim expressed above is *more* than strong enough for present purposes. Let us, therefore, take the following as the fourth, and final, premise: In those circumstances in which a biased system is more in one's unqualified interests, the difference between the extent that it and the equal consideration system are in one's unqualified interests is, on the average, no greater than is the difference in those circumstances in which it is the equal consideration system that is more in one's unqualified interests.

In might be objected that premise (4) addresses itself only to what is the case *on the average;* but, so this objection would go, *in the particular circumstances at hand* our potential "winnings" from a biased system might *far* exceed those from the equal consideration system. They might indeed. But, once again, we can never know enough about the particular circumstances at hand for a *belief* that they do to be little more than mere speculation. And, as already explained, we are assuming that an ideal chooser would be no more enlightened about the particular circumstances at hand than we ourselves are. Thus, for premise (4) to address itself only to what is the case on the average is, for present purposes, quite sufficient.

10.4 THE CONCLUSION

The role premise (4) plays in this argument is exactly the same as the role a certain assumption played in the argument set out earlier (sec. 1.3) for showing that, in paternity cases, judges should never act upon the belief that someone who has "passed" the blood test really is the father anyway. Its role is exactly the same as the role played by the assumption made there that incorrect decisions against mothers are no better or worse than incorrect decisions against alleged fathers. Both premise (4) and this assumption show that the potential gains from acting upon an improbable belief are not sufficient to override its improbability. The improbable belief in question here, of course, is a belief that, in the circumstances at hand, a biased system is more in one's interests than the equal consideration system. The improbability of this belief, as expressed by premise (3), combined with premise (4), yields, finally, the conclusion of the argument: Acting upon the belief that a biased system in more in one's unqualified interests than the equal consideration system is never in one's qualified best interests. It is always a bad personal gamble. What really is in one's qualified best interests—that is, what really does maximize one's qualified expected personal utility—is, once again, acting on the assumption that the equal consideration system is more in one's interests.

One of the two underlying themes of this book is that we should never act upon certain kinds of beliefs. The belief that, in the circumstances at hand, a biased system is more in our interests than the equal consideration system is one of those kinds of beliefs. A norm prohibiting our acting upon such a belief is a sound norm of personal welfare, one that it is always in our best interests to try to comply with. And, I might point out, it is always in our best interests to try to comply with this norm even when we feel *certain* a biased system would turn out best for us. For, as pointed out earlier (sec. 6.5), in matters as complex and subject to rationalizations as this, we are mistaken all too often even when we feel certain.

The rationale for this norm of personal welfare is similar to that which would be used to support other norms of personal welfare that most of us take for granted. Let me provide one example. We know that experimenting with heroin often leads to addiction, and that those who become addicted are worse off than had they never taken any heroin in the first place. On the other hand, we also know that those who do stop short of any addiction probably will have experienced a certain amount of pleasure without any negative consequences, and thus might end up *better* than had they not taken any heroin. The catch is that whether or not we shall be among those who stop before any addiction is a matter about which we can never be very sure. So, in view of our limited knowledge as well as our tendency to rationalize, rather than gambling on the possibility of our being one of the lucky ones who are able to stop, it is a sound norm of personal welfare always to act on the assumption that experimenting with heroin is not in our best interests. Similarly, I am arguing, it is a sound norm of personal welfare always to act on the assumption that a biased system is less in our interests than the equal consideration system, never gambling on the possibility that just those circumstances exist in which bias really is in our best interests. Although a biased system will, for some people in the favored group under some circumstances, maximize expected personal utility (without qualification), our susceptibility to error in calculating exactly when these exceptional circumstances exist, their relative infrequency, and the potential dangers of biased systems, all make it in our best interests always to "bet" on the equal consideration system instead. Betting on a biased system would be analogous to taking one of the bad utilitarian gambles discussed earlier (see esp.

chap. 7), the only difference being that the gamble in question here would not be a *utilitarian* gamble, but a *personal* one.

10.5 THE PRACTICAL EFFECT

So far I have argued that it is always in our best interests to act on the assumption that the equal consideration system is more in our interests than a biased one. But there are alternatives to the equal consideration system other than biased ones (e.g., an alternative derivable from a Rawlsian "original position," which is discussed in chapter 12). Therefore, even if sound, this argument does not establish that it is always in our best interests to act on the assumption that the equal consideration system is more in our interests than *any* alternative. However, a biased system is—assuming that we are in the favored group—perhaps the alternative *most likely* to be more in our interests than the equal consideration system; therefore, if (as I have argued) we should nevertheless act on the assumption that it is not, then it becomes considerably more plausible to claim that the same is true about *any* alternative to the equal consideration system.

In any case, let us, for the sake of argument, assume that this claim *is* true, that it *is* always in our best interests to act on the assumption that the equal consideration system is more in our interests than any (factually possible) alternative. The next question is: Exactly what practical effect—that is, exactly what effect upon our actions—should this assumption have? If we are always to assume that the equal consideration system is more in our interests than any alternative, does this mean we should always *comply* with the norms of this system? We are, of course, considering everything in this chapter from a perspective of self-interest, so the preceding question is: Does this assumption mean that, *from the perspective of self-interest,* we should always comply with the norms of this system? We shall consider the answer to this question in more detail in the next chapter, but for now the following will suffice. Just because it may be in our best interests for the equal consideration system to *exist* (or so we are to assume), it does not follow that it is in our best interests to *comply* with the norms of this system. It especially might not be in our best interests if an altogether different social-pressure system currently existed in the world—one with moral norms inconsistent with those of the equal consideration system—for then compliance with the moral norms of the equal consideration system would mean contravening those currently supported by social pressure, which it might be very much against our interests to do (society "punishes" those who contravene its current moral norms).

Earlier, however, I pointed out that the main practical application of our norm evaluations (or, more generally, *system* evaluations) is not that of guiding our *compliance* decisions, but that of guiding our *support* decisions—

that is, of guiding our decisions as to which norms and values to support with social pressure, in what way, and to what extent (sec. 4.4). Similarly, the main practical effect of assuming that the equal consideration system is more in our interests than any other should be upon not our compliance decisions, but our support decisions—our decisions concerning praise, blame, persuasion, and so on. If the norms and values of the equal consideration system are the ones most in our interests to have backed by social pressure (and this would follow from our assumption that the equal consideration system is the one most in our interests) then it follows that, normally, it is *these* norms and values that it is most in our interests personally to support—that is, support through praise, blame, persuasion, and, in general, social pressure. Or, stated more generally, it is the equal consideration system, rather than some alternative, the existence of which it is most in our interests to help bring about and maintain.

Does this mean it is *always* most in our interests to help bring about and maintain the existence of this system? Probably not quite. It would appear we can, reliably enough, recognize certain circumstances in which helping to bring about or maintain the equal consideration system would *not* be in our best interests; take, for example, those circumstances in which the most effective means of doing this would be by standing up against the biases of an enraged mob poised to lynch anyone who stands up against it.

But, if I am right, even though it may not always be in our overall best interests to help bring about and maintain the equal consideration system, there is, from the standpoint of self-interest, always at least *one* crucial reason for doing so: the equal consideration system is more in our interests than any other, or so we are to assume. What this amounts to is that there is always, from the standpoint of self-interest, a *presumption* in favor of helping to bring about or maintain this system. Whether, from a standpoint of self-interest, this standing presumption in favor of the equal consideration system should be overridden in some given set of circumstances can, in the final analysis, be determined only by appeal to the fundamental norm of personal welfare (sec. 2.2). I should think this presumption strong enough so that to override it would require the prospect of being harmed more substantially than, say, having to endure the mild disapproval of friends.

Yet, the fact that, from a standpoint of self-interest, there is only a *presumption* in favor of helping bring about the equal consideration system, or a part of it such as the EC code, might be said to constitute a serious weakness in the connection between self-interest and equal consideration. It might be argued that, in a society with a deeply entrenched biased morality, for example, this presumption would be rendered altogether impotent; the hostility directed against anyone who helped bring about the EC code would, so it might be argued, always be harm enough to override the presumption. I do not find this very convincing. No matter how morally biased and intolerant of other moralities the society to which one belongs might be, there will always be *some* occasions where one could, in *some* way, help bring about the EC code without suffering substantial harm. As a first step in helping bring about the change, perhaps one could at least refrain from praising acts of bias, even if one could not, without suffering substantial harm, actively criticize such acts. And there no doubt would be intimate friends whom one could, without fear, attempt to influence through more positive means. Those whom one succeeded in influencing might then influence others, and these others might in turn influence still others until, eventually, most people were no longer helping to maintain the old, biased morality, but were helping to maintain a reasonable approximation of the EC code instead.

10.6 FUTURE GENERATIONS AND ANIMALS

Before moving on we should, I think, give at least some attention to future generations and animals. First, let us consider future generations. Earlier I concluded that future generations are excluded from the domain of the *general welfare norm* (sec. 8.5). But, I noted, the utilitarian standard, in terms of which the general welfare norm is justified, does not exclude future generations from *its* domain. By means of this standard, I argued, we can justify moral norms that, contrary to the general welfare norm, do explicitly offer some protection to future generations. We need not consider any further here how future generations are to be treated according to moral norms justifiable in terms of the utilitarian standard. But we need now to consider a more fundamental matter: Is there any justification for my assumption earlier that future generations *are* within the domain of the utilitarian standard? As will be recalled, to be within the domain of this standard is to be among those whose interests are given equal consideration in any evaluations carried out in terms of it. My argument so far in justification of this standard, being in terms of what is in our best interests, might appear to justify our giving equal consideration to the interests of only those existing now, not those in future generations. After all, we need have little fear of those in far-off future generations getting back at us for denying them equal consideration. And there is another matter to consider: If future generations were indeed excluded from the domain of the utilitarian standard, would this standard not then justify a moral code (or, more generally, a social-pressure system) with "disastrous" implications for the use of natural resources, a code that allowed, or perhaps even required, using up all the world's natural resources for the enjoyment of those of us existing now, leaving little or nothing for those in future generations?

I very much doubt if excluding future generations from the utilitarian standard's domain would have these "disastrous" implications; the interests of those in future generations are linked to the interests of those of us currently existing in such a way that it would be impossible for us to follow our interests without taking their interests very much into account. For one thing, those of us currently existing do not want to spend the latter part of our lives being despised by younger generations for having selfishly used up natural resources to the point where extreme scarcity and hardship will set in after we have gone. We especially do not want to observe the unhappiness of our own children, grandchildren, and great-grandchildren over this bleak prospect. (That is, being despised and observing their unhappiness makes *us* unhappy, and our being unhappy is not in *our* interests.) Furthermore, the harmful effects of unrestrained resource depletion are so unpredictable that those responsible for it might well, much to their surprise, find many of these harmful effects occurring even during their own lifetime. Thus protecting future generations has the additional benefit of guarding us against the totally unexpected and potentially disastrous effects upon the environment, upon productivity, and so on, likely to occur *even during our lifetime* if we have no regard for what happens after us. In other words, protecting future generations has the additional benefit of helping protect us against ourselves. Considering how susceptible we are to miscalculating even the *immediate* effects of unrestrained resource depletion, this additional benefit is by no means insignificant. This, combined with the fact that, as already noted, present generations do have a direct interest in the happiness of at least the more immediate future generations, shows that there are powerful reasons for considering the interests of future generations in "choosing" a moral code, even if they are not included within the utilitarian standard's domain.

Nevertheless it is important, I think, that the utilitarian standard be formulated so that future generations *are* included within its domain. As we have seen, no matter which way it is formulated, we would have to give some consideration to the interests of future generations anyway. The crucial question is: Which makes it more likely that we will give future interests the consideration that it is in our interests to give them: (1) building equal consideration for future interests into the utilitarian standard itself, or (2) not doing so, and relying instead upon our being able to recognize the extent to which these interests should be given consideration nevertheless? The danger for us in building equal consideration for the interests of future generations into the utilitarian standard itself is, of course, that this might cause us to err against our own interests by giving the interests of future generations too *much* consideration. The danger for us is not building it into the standard is that this might cause us to err against our own interests by giving the interests of future generations too *little* consideration. In view of the human being's natural self-centeredness and notorious propensity toward rationalization, I am much inclined to think that the greater danger is the latter.

Put somewhat more exactly, the argument (which parallels the one set out in sections 10.3 and 10.4 above) is, in outline, as follows. Our susceptibility to error in trying to calculate exactly when social-pressure systems "biased" against the interests of future generations do maximize our expected personal utility, the frequency with which such systems do not, and the potential harm to us from such systems are, in combination, great enough to make it in our (qualified) best interests always to act on the assumption that social-pressure systems "biased" against the interests of future generations are not in our (unqualified) best interests. Accordingly, in evaluating social-pressure systems, it makes sense (from a perspective of self-interest) to give equal consideration to the interests of future generations; that is, to include future generations within the domain of the utilitarian standard.

But now what about animals, another group that, like future generations, can hardly fight back if we deny them equal consideration? Should animals be included within the domain of the utilitarian standard, among those whose interests should be given equal consideration in determining what social-pressure system is most justified?

I do not know the answer to this question; the inclusion of animals within this standard's domain would appear to be even more difficult to justify according to the approach taken here—that is, an appeal to self-interest—than the inclusion of future generations. My suspicious are, however, that a successful argument can be made for including animals within the domain also—an argument similar to the one just sketched for including future generations within the domain. This argument would be designed to show that, owing to the dangers for us inherent in neglecting animal interests, and to our susceptibility to misinformation, rationalization, and the like, we are always in greater jeopardy of choosing a system contrary to our best interests if we exclude animals from the utilitarian standard's domain than if we include them.

Such an argument might appeal to considerations like the following. First, most of us find displeasure in being confronted with any suffering, even if it be that of an animal. Second, the more we disregard animal suffering, the more we may become insensitive to the suffering of human beings—an insensitivity that might have grave ramifications for us all someday. Third, animals provide us with many benefits; they provide us, among other things, with companionship, transportation, and unending amusement. And there is no telling in what additional ways animals in general, or certain species of animals, might be of service to humanity in the future, or in what ways they are important for maintaining the fragile ecological balance necessary for our well-being. The mere existence of animal species other than *homo sapiens* makes the world incalculably more fascinating for us. But given the excessively crowded conditions in most parts of the world today, and the virtual certainty of even greater crowding in the future, the continued existence of many animal species is threatened, and once a species is gone it is, of course, gone forever.

So it clearly is in our best interests to give some consideration to animal interests, at least enough to assure that most species of animals continue to thrive in this world along with us. The crucial question, once again, is whether we would, in evaluating social-pressure systems, be more likely to give animal interests the amount of consideration that it is in our own interests to give them by including animals within the domain of the utilitarian standard, or by excluding them. Considering especially our susceptibility rationalizations, the safest alternative for us may well be that of including them. I myself, in any case, am inclined to think so, and to think, therefore, that the argument for their inclusion within the domain, along with future generations, can be made successfully. But I shall not pursue these matters further here; they are not essential to the main argument of this chapter.

11
Why We Should Act Morally

11.1 TWO VERSIONS OF THE QUESTION

The social pressure system that, according to the utilitarian standard, is most justified I have been referring to as the "equal consideration" system. In the last chapter I argued that our use of the utilitarian standard for evaluating social-pressure systems is itself justified not because the equal consideration system is always more in our interests than any alternative, but because it is always in our best interests to *assume* that this system is more in our interests than any alternative, rather than trying, on a case-by-case basis, to pick out those relatively rare circumstances in which it is not. But then this raised the question of exactly what influence this assumption should have upon our actions. I argued that, from a perspective of self-interest, the main influence it should have is upon our "support" decisions—that is, upon our decisions as to which norms and values to support with social pressure through blame, praise, persuasion, criticism, and so on. Its influence upon our "compliance" decisions—that is, our decisions as to which norms to comply with—should not, I argued, be so direct.

In this chapter I shall, in effect, continue the discussion of compliance. The question upon which I shall focus is: Why should we, individually, comply with the requirements of morality? Why, in other words, should we act morally? Take, for example, the person who feels confident he can embezzle large sums of money from the bank where he works, and never be caught. Why, in these circumstances, should he comply with the moral prohibition against theft? The question of why we should act morally might be said to be an especially pressing question for an ethical theory such as the one advocated here, one that is based on self-interest; it might be said that such an ethical theory can only provide a reason for doing what is in our self-interest and, since morality and self-interest are not definitionally equivalent, such a theory cannot provide us with a reason for acting morally. I happen to disagree; I believe the question of why we should act morally *can* be satisfactorily answered within the theoretical framework set out here. Thus, in this chapter, I shall sketch what I believe the answer to this question to be. (For well-known valuable previous discussions of this question, see Baier 1958, esp. chap. 12; and Nielsen 1963.)

The first thing we must consider in trying to answer the question, Why should I act morally?, is what morality this question refers to. Does it refer to society's current morality, so that the question then becomes: Why should I comply with the moral norms of the social-pressure system (or moral code) that happens to prevail at the present time? Perhaps this is how the question would be interpreted by some people, an interpretation I shall refer to as the *first* version of the question. Others, however, would point out that the social pressure-system that happens to prevail at any given time does not necessarily prescribe what is *really* moral; they, therefore, would interpret the question as: Why should I comply with the moral norms of the social-pressure system that prescribes what is really moral? I shall refer to this as the *second* version of the question.

But in order to understand the second version of the question, we need to know what is meant by moral norms that prescribe "what is really moral." I suggest that the only way to make much sense of this phrase is to interpret it as referring to the moral norms of that social-pressure system which is *most justified*. With this interpretation, the second version of the question thus becomes: Why should I comply with the moral norms of the social-pressure system that is most justified? But then what system is it that is in fact most justified? The answer to this question depends, of course, upon what theory of moral justification happens to be correct; let us, however, for purposes of argument, assume that the theory proposed here is correct, and that therefore it is the equal consideration system that is most justified. Given this assumption, the second version of the question becomes finally: Why should I comply with the moral norms of the equal consideration system? (Or, to be slightly more accurate: Why should I comply with the moral norms of that part of the equal consideration system applicable to my society?) I have thus distinguished two different versions of the question: Why should I act morally? In what follows I shall try to sketch the answer to each version, beginning with the first.

11.2 NONCOMPLIANCE FOR REASONS OF GREED

The first version of the question, once again, is: Why should we comply with those moral norms, applicable to our society, of the social-pressure system that prevails at the present time? More simply put, this asks why we should comply with our society's current morality (especially when it appears that our noncompliance would not be detected). Throughout the discussion I shall be talking only about that part of society's morality which is fairly well established, and only about noncompliance with this morality that is serious, which a typical person within the society would be likely to view as no trivial matter. Finally, throughout the discussion I shall assume that "our society" is a society, such as are all twentieth-century Western societies, whose morality (1) does not require—that is, make morally mandatory—acts of unusually great self-sacrifice, heroic or saintly acts like giving up one's life to save another or donating all one's wealth to the poor; and (2) does recognize an exception for emergencies not too dissimilar from the one discussed earlier (sec. 6.5). With these important qualifications in mind, let us proceed.

I shall try to show why we should comply with our society's current morality by first pointing out two different reasons one might have for *not* complying. The first type of reason for noncompliance is a serious disagreement with one's society about what moral norms are justified. The person who fails to comply with his society's moral norms for this type of reason is doing so for what we may call reasons of *conscience*. In order for noncompliance to qualify as noncompliance for reasons of conscience, as I am using this term, the noncompliance not only must stem from a serious disagreement with society's morality, but must also be directed toward helping change this morality or the laws that reflect it, or toward otherwise helping people (other than just oneself) avoid wrongful treatment stemming from this morality. Reasons of conscience may include personal gain, but *only* personal gain that would result from that change in morality or law which one thinks should occur, or from helping bring this change about or otherwise helping people avoid any allegedly wrongful treatment stemming from the morality or law that is current. To the extent that Martin Luther King, for example, failed to comply not only with the law, but also with the morality of his society, his noncompliance would qualify as noncompliance for reasons of conscience. King's noncompliance was directed at bringing about a change both in current morality, which relegated blacks to the status of "second class" citizens, and in the law that reflected this morality.

The second type of reason for noncompliance with society's morality is for any personal gain of a sort other than that just specified in connection with noncompliance for reasons of conscience. In other words, the second type of reason for noncompliance is, typically, more wealth for oneself (or one's family, friends, etc.), or the advancement of one's career, or one's experiencing of certain pleasures. Reasons of this type I shall call reasons of *greed*. Obviously noncompliance for reasons of greed is far more common than noncompliance for reasons of conscience.

What I shall argue is that, although noncompliance with society's morality for reasons of conscience either may or may not be in our best interests, noncompliance for reasons of greed never is. I shall, in other words, argue that, no matter what the circumstances, it is in our best interests to try to comply with the norm: "Do not fail to comply with society's morality for reasons of greed," and that this norm therefore qualifies as a subsidiary norm of personal welfare (just as does the norm discussed above in sec. 10.4).

And in presenting the argument for complying with this norm I must emphasize the role played, again, by that rather subtle, and hence potentially confusing, distinction: the distinction between what is in our *unqualified* best interests, and what is in our *qualified* best interests. As will be recalled, an alternative is in our unqualified best interests if it is the one that would be chosen by someone from a (prudential) ideal standpoint that includes *all* the knowledge that one choosing from such a standpoint is, in principle, supposed to have. An alternative is in our qualified best interests, on the other hand, if it is the one that would be chosen by someone who is choosing from an ideal standpoint that includes all the knowledge that one choosing from such a standpoint is supposed to have, *except* for certain facts—certain facts that we in real life do not know and are to assume that not even an ideal chooser knows, thereby placing the ideal chooser in a position where his choice represents not what is in our *unqualified* best interests, but what is in our best interests, *given* that the facts in question are unknown. Why, it might be asked, are we interested in what is in our qualified, as opposed to unqualified, best interests? As explained earlier (sec. 2.3), in reality we often do not possess certain crucial facts relevant to making a personal choice; therefore knowing what is in our qualified best interests—that is, our best interests given that these facts *are* unknown—is often what is of practical value for us to know.

What I shall try to show is that, although contravening the norm requiring compliance with society's morality is no doubt sometimes in our unqualified best interests, it is never in our qualified best interests; that is, it is never in our best interests given that we have no more (or less) knowledge about a certain crucial matter than in real life we actually have. This crucial matter is whether circumstances currently do exist in which our noncompliance with society's morality for reasons of greed is in our (unqualified) best interests. So, for trying to determine whether such noncompliance is in our best interests, the assumption that an ideal chooser is "omniscient" is to be qualified as follows: we are to assume that an ideal chooser never has any more, or less, insight than we do ourselves into whether acting contrary to society's morality for reasons of greed is in our best interests in the circumstances at hand. Of course, an ideal chooser does have far greater insight than we do into the probability of human insights of this sort being correct in general, and an ideal chooser does have far greater insight than we do into what is true of *most* circumstances, as opposed to merely those currently existing.

This then, in general outline, is how the argument will proceed; let me now fill the outline in. (Since this argument is so similar to the one set out in chapter 10, I can be briefer here than I was there.) First of all, it must be admitted that the very noncompliance with society's morality that is forbidden by the norm I am trying to justify (i.e., noncompliance for reasons of greed) does, in some circumstances, maximize our (unqualified) expected personal utility. That is to say, in some circumstances the possible sets of effects upon our lives of this noncompliance combined with their probabilities of occurring are such that noncompliance would indeed be chosen over compliance if the choice were made from the ideal standpoint, specified earlier (sec. 2.2), for choosing what is in our personal welfare. So in some circumstances this noncompliance is indeed in our unqualified best interests.

But these circumstances are, I submit, relatively uncommon. Surely society has arranged its total system of punishments and rewards so that, in most circumstances at least, noncompliance is *not* in our unqualified best interests. And by society's "total" system of punishments and rewards, I am referring to both *formal* punishments and rewards—those specified by law, such as fines and jail sentences—and *informal* punishments and rewards—ones such as criticism, ostracism, and high and low social status. (A society's total system of punishments and rewards could, incidentally, be referred to as its "total social-pressure system," a system that consists of its "formal social-pressure system"—i.e., its laws, governmental regulations, etc.—and its "informal social-pressure system,"—i.e., what I have been referring to here simply as its "social-pressure system.") A society can arrange its total system of punishments and rewards so as to make noncompliance with its morality as contrary to our unqualified best interests as it pleases; by making its punishments for noncompliance and rewards for compliance great enough (with extensive enough "enforcement"), I suppose a society could even make noncompliance contrary to our unqualified best interests in virtually all circumstances. But the costs of a total system extreme enough to do this—costs in terms of both the money and human energy necessary for maintaining the system, not to mention the anxiety and suffering such a system might engender—would probably be enormous, more than any society would be willing to pay. On the other hand, a society can, without incurring unacceptable costs, arrange its total system of punishments and rewards so that noncompliance is contrary to our (unqualified) best interests in at least *most* circumstances. And if a society can do this, surely it has done so; for a society not to have arranged its total system so as to make noncompliance contrary to our best interests in most circumstances would be to invite a degree of noncompliance with its morality so extensive as to be to virtually no one's advantage. Thus we arrive at the first premise of the argument: In most circumstances, noncompliance with society's morality for reasons of greed is not in one's best interests.

The second premise of the argument is as follows: Whether those relatively rare circumstances currently exist in which noncompliance for reasons of greed really is in one's best interests can never be determined very reliably. This is where our unavoidable human fallibility once again enters the picture. A human being can never know enough about the circumstances at hand to be able to calculate very reliably if they are circumstances where noncompliance is in his unqualified best interests or not. This is another of those kinds of calculation involving too many indeterminable, interrelated variables ever to be made with much reliability. In the first place, it is questionable whether one is ever warranted in being very confident that noncompliance, be it anything from embezzlement to adultery, will go undetected. Of course circumstances do occur in which detection would be virtually impossible but, in view of the numerous, altogether unforeseeable things that normally can go wrong, it is questionable if one is ever warranted in placing much trust in one's ability to *recognize* these circumstances. (For illustrations of how, even in those circumstances which appear most favorable for avoiding detection, something may still go wrong, we might read a few good detective novels.) And even in those relatively rare circumstances where detection really is virtually impossible, there will still be many other bad, maybe disastrous, potential consequences for oneself of one's wrongdoing that are *not* virtually impossible. For example, as a result of one's wrongdoing one may suffer agonizing guilt, loss of peace of mind, or loss of self-respect; one may even be edged farther along toward what, for lack of a better phrase, might be called a *criminal life-style,* a life-style that precludes one from experiencing certain satisfactions that only those with a deep concern for others can experience, and that give a certain meaning to our existence that cannot be got any other way (e.g., see Singer 1979, 202–20). The point is that there are simply too many unforeseeable ways in which noncompliance can very well turn out badly ever to justify one in being confident that one has spotted just those circumstances in which it would not. And it must not be forgotten that, in trying to spot these circumstances, one must contend with more than just a vast lack of information; one must contend also with one's rationalizations, which might distort whatever meager information one does have.

Considering then how relatively rare those circumstances are in which noncompliance really is in one's best interests (as stated by premise (1)), and considering especially how unreliable one's attempts are to pick out these circumstances (as stated by premise (2)), we are, I submit, justified in putting forth the following as premise (3): A belief that those relatively rare circumstances currently exist in which noncompliance for reasons of greed really is in one's best interests is always more likely to be mistaken than not. Trying, on a case-by-case basis, to pick out those relatively rare circumstances favorable for noncompliance is, once more, analogous to the judge trying to pick out the one defendant in a hundred who, in spite of the blood-test evidence, really is the father (sec. 1.3). One's powers of discrimination are simply not great enough to make the attempt worthwhile.

I think it fair to say also that, in gambling on noncompliance being in one's best interests, what one gives up if one "loses" is likely to be at least as great as what one gains if one "wins"; things one might give up if one "loses" include one's freedom, one's reputation, the love and respect of others and, *even if the noncompliance goes entirely undetected,* one's peace of mind (as a result of, say, guilt or remorse, or continual fear of detection) along with one's *self*-respect. In short: the potential sacrifices are indeed likely to be as great as the potential gains, which gives us the fourth and final premise: In those circumstances in which noncompliance for reasons of greed is in one's best interests, the difference between the extent that it and compliance are in one's interests is, on the average, no greater than is the difference in those circumstances in which it is compliance that is in one's best interests.

Premise (4), along with premise (3), allows us to conclude, finally, the following: Noncompliance for reasons of greed is always a bad personal gamble. It is always a bad personal gamble *given* our fallibility in calculating which, as between compliance and noncompliance, is in our best interests in the circumstances at hand. So what this argument boils down to is that, although admittedly noncompliance for reasons of greed is, in some circumstances, in our *unqualified* best interests, it is never in our *qualified* best interests; it is never in our best interests given that we do not know any more than, in real life, we ever do about whether the noncompliance is in our (unqualified) best interests in the circumstances at hand. It is thus, *for all practical purposes,* in our best interests always to adhere to the following norm of personal welfare: "Do not fail to comply with society's morality for reasons of greed." A belief that, in the circumstances at hand, noncompliance for reasons of greed is in our best interests is, therefore, still another of those types of factual beliefs which, in view of our fallibility, we should resist acting upon.

And, I might add, it should make absolutely no difference even if we were very sure about such a belief, or felt certain. For, as suggested earlier (sec. 6.5), with matters as complex and subject to rationalizations as this, even when we feel certain, we remain all too subject to being mistaken. So, even when we feel certain, we ought to resist acting upon this belief; even when we feel certain, it would be a bad personal gamble to contravene the above norm. In other words, to discredit the claim that adhering to this norm is always in our best interests, it is not enough merely to produce a "counterexample" about which we "feel certain." Here, as elsewhere throughout this book, the expedient of simply producing a case about which we feel certain—not a fantastic, but a realistic one—will not quite work; this quick refutation is a little too quick.

But, my adversary might continue, if we forego realism altogether and suppose circumstances fantastic enough, we can easily produce a case where we *know* it would not be in our best interests to adhere to this norm. For example, what if there were rings of Gyges, such as Plato spoke of in the *Republic,* rings that made people invisible, and thus (supposedly) immune from detection? Would that not undermine the rationale for the above norm of personal welfare? Perhaps. The point, however, is that *there are no rings of Gyges.* It is reasonable to demand of our norms that they be appropriate for the world as it exists today. Indeed, it is reasonable to demand that they be appropriate for hypothetical worlds that may very well exist tomorrow. It is *not* reasonable to demand, as philosophers all too often do, that they be appropriate for hypothetical worlds that are utterly fantastic.

11.3 NONCOMPLIANCE FOR REASONS OF CONSCIENCE

We now have a partial answer to the question: Why should we comply with the moral norms of our society? We should comply with them because noncompliance, if it is for reasons of greed, is not in our best interests. But what about noncompliance for reasons of conscience? Is it equally against our best interests to fail to comply with society's moral norms when our reason for noncompliance is that we do not think the norms are justified? Say, for example, that society's moral norms sanctioned slavery as did those of the old South, and held that helping a slave escape was equivalent to stealing the slaveowner's property: if then, for reasons of conscience, a person were to help a slave escape would this be likely to be just as much against his best interests as, say stealing the slaveowner's cattle for reasons of greed? In answering this question the first thing to notice is that, for certain kinds of noncompliance for reasons of conscience—that which is peaceful, or destructive but not violent—the reactions people have to it are significantly different from the reactions they have to noncompliance for reasons of greed. Let me explain.

If the noncompliance for reasons of conscience is of a kind that is peaceful—that is, if it involves, at most, only minor damage or injury—then, typically, the reaction to it is not nearly so severe as is the reaction to noncompliance for reasons of greed. Typically, those whose noncompliance is for reasons of conscience, and is also peaceful, are not despised, or scorned, or, in general, held in the low esteem that people whose noncompliance is for reasons of greed are. There will, to be sure, always be some people who do hold such "conscientious objectors" in low esteem. These people will be the arch moral conservatives of society, those with little tolerance for any viewpoint but their own, and prominent among them will no doubt be those who think they have a vested interest in current morality, such as slaveholders where there is a slave morality. But to counterbalance these people there will be others who, even while disagreeing with the conscientious objectors, admire them for their willingness to stand by what they believe. Indeed, some conscientious objectors, if their views manage to gain a certain degree of acceptance, eventually become *greatly* admired, even *idolized,* as have the great moral/religious leaders of the past.

Next, if the noncompliance for reasons of conscience is destructive—that is, if it involves serious damage to, including theft of, property (but not serious injury to persons)—then, typically, people's reactions to it are more severe than their reactions to peaceful noncompliance, but *less* severe than their reactions to equivalent damage from noncompliance for reasons of greed. If, for example, a person steals a million dollars from a rich person so as to buy himself a luxurious yacht he would, I think, be more severely condemned by most than would be the person who believes the society's tolerance of great differences in wealth to be extremely unjust, and who, in Robin Hood fashion, steals a million dollars so as to distribute it to the poor and thereby mitigate what he considers to be this injustice. Both the selfish and the idealistic thief would probably have to suffer to an approximately equal degree from the society's formal (i.e., legal) sanctions; society cannot really afford to make exceptions to its laws for those with high ideals. But I think it fair to say that the idealistic thief would, typically, suffer less than the selfish one from informal sanctions, sanctions such as scorn and ostracism.

Finally, if the noncompliance for reasons of conscience is violent—that is, if it involves serious injury to a person, or death (and I include kidnapping among serious injuries)—then the reaction is typically severe condemnation, in this case just as severe as if the violence had been for reasons of greed. And, incidentally, I think this severity is exactly as it should be; except for genuine self- (or other's) defense (see sec. 6.5), violence should have no legitimate place in anyone's morality; our liability to being mistaken about its necessity, in conjunction with the amount of suffering it is likely to cause, is simply too great. So violence, when committed for reasons of conscience, both is and, in my opinion, should be, as severely discouraged as its counterpart for purposes of greed (and, if I am right, is severely discouraged by the equal consideration system).

But the severe reaction to *violent* noncompliance for reasons of conscience should not obscure the difference between society's reaction to noncompliance for reasons of conscience and that for reasons of greed when the noncompliance is *not* violent. Society's attitude toward noncompliance for reasons of conscience, provided it is not violent, is generally somewhere between tolerance and intolerance; it is, we might say, an attitude of *limited* tolerance.

And there is good reason for this limited tolerance. The current morality of no society is perfect. This is just as true of a society that attempts to implement the EC code as of any other society; it is too difficult to know the full contents of the EC code of morality for any society to hope to duplicate it in every respect. And even if some society did manage to duplicate it in every respect, changes in this society's code would no doubt still be necessary from time to time as a result of changing conditions. In short: a society's current morality can always be improved. There will be no improvement, however, if the society's current morality cannot be changed. This then brings us to one good reason for there being limited tolerance of noncompliance for reasons of conscience; it helps make change, and thus improvement, in current morality possible.

I do not, incidentally, mean to imply that, for a change in current morality to occur, a certain degree of tolerance is necessary. A change in current morality can always occur even if there is no tolerance of noncompliance at all; moreover, I suggest that this change can occur, in theory at least, even without anyone's having to suffer the consequences of the intolerance. To appreciate how this is possible, one must appreciate the distinction between a person's failing to *comply* with his society's current morality, and his failing to *help maintain* it through his praise, blame, and so forth. (It should perhaps be noted that, using my earlier terminology [see sec. 4.2], the distinction is that between, on the one hand, failing to *comply* with the "objects" of society's current "social pressure combinations"—the objects of these social-pressure combinations, or the ones relevant for us now, being moral norms—and, on the other hand, failing to *help maintain* these social-pressure combinations. The terminology of social-pressure combinations, even if more rigorous, lacks familiarity; so, here as elsewhere, I am using ordinary terminology instead, and trust that this does not cause any confusion.) If we assume that there really is, for the most part at least, a distinction between, on the one hand, failing to comply with current morality and, on the other hand, failing to help maintain it, then clearly changes in current morality do not depend upon people failing to comply with that morality, and thereby having to suffer the consequences of intolerance. Changes, and thus improvements, can also occur, although more gradually, through people failing to use their praise and blame for purposes of *helping maintain* the current morality—even while continuing to comply with it until so many others have likewise failed to help maintain it that, for all practical purposes, the change is complete.

In any case, if, instead of no tolerance of noncompliance at all, there is a limited tolerance of that noncompliance which is for reasons of conscience, then changes, and thus improvements, in current morality are likely to occur more rapidly. Limited tolerance of those who, for reasons of conscience, comply with a morality different from society's allows what amounts to limited, direct competition between moralities and, as is well known, improvements are likely to occur more rapidly under conditions of competition, even if very limited competition, then under conditions of monopoly. At the same time, since the tolerance is indeed *limited,* it does not open the door too widely so as to undercut the uniformity of moral behavior, which, as we have seen, any morality must provide. In short: not only is there, in most societies, a difference in severity between people's typical reactions to noncompliance for reasons of conscience (if nonviolent) and their typical reactions to similar noncompliance for reasons of greed, but also, as I have tried to explain, this difference in severity serves a useful purpose. And since changes in the EC code are likely to become necessary from time to time as a result of changing conditions then, for purposes of facilitating these changes, a difference in severity is probably a feature not only of most societies' current social-pressure system, but of the equal consideration system as well.

Another difference between noncompliance for reasons of greed and noncompliance for reasons of conscience that is important for present purposes is the following: noncompliance for reasons of greed is likely to be accompanied by feelings of guilt, sometimes very severe feelings, or by a lessening of self-respect, but not noncompliance for reasons of conscience (since, by definition, with noncompliance for reasons of conscience one is doing what one believes really is morally right). Indeed, for one who believes society's current morality to be unjustified, it is not noncompliance with current morality that is likely to be accompanied by feelings of guilt or by diminished self-respect, but compliance. The only case, it seems to me, in which even noncompliance is likely to be accompanied by feelings of guilt, or something very much like guilt, such as intense regret, is where it results in a serious injury or death.

We thus have before us *two* significant differences between noncompliance for reasons of greed and (nonviolent) noncompliance for reasons of conscience: a difference in the severity with which *others* react to the noncompliance, and a difference in the agent's *own* reaction to the noncompliance. Do not these differences then make a difference in the extent to which these two kinds of noncompliance can be said to be in a person's interests? I am inclined to think so. I argued earlier that, due largely to the way both others and the agent himself react to it, noncompliance for reasons of greed is always a bad personal gamble. But since these reactions are significantly different if the noncompliance is instead for reasons of conscience and is also nonviolent, I do not think that, for this kind of noncompliance, the same argument can be said to be applicable. I do not think, in other words, that noncompliance for reasons of conscience, if also nonviolent, can be said always to be a bad personal gamble as can noncompliance for reasons of greed; rather, sometimes it is and sometimes it is not, depending largely upon how successful the noncomplier is likely to be in defending his moral point of view. So, if I am right, someone interested in doing what is in his best interests must decide whether or not to risk noncompliance for reasons of conscience by considering, as best he can, each case on its own merits; there is no shortcut in the form of a simple, easy-to-comply-with subsidiary norm of personal welfare to which he can turn, a subsidiary norm of personal welfare such as the one applicable to noncompliance for reasons of greed, a norm to which he can appeal for deciding all such cases without having to go each time into what the pros and cons are for him in the particular circumstances at hand.

11.4 AND THE SECOND VERSION OF THE QUESTION

In this chapter I have been attempting to answer the question: Why should we act morally? I distinguished two versions of this question, the first version being: Why should we comply with the moral norms of the social-pressure system that prevails in our society at the present time? My answer to this version of the question was as follows: we should comply with the current moral norms of our society because doing so is always in our (qualified) best interests, but with one possible exception: noncompliance for reasons of conscience if the noncompliance is nonviolent. Let us now turn to the second version of the question, which is: Why should we comply with the moral norms of the equal consideration system? In light of my answer to the first version of the question, my answer to this version should now be apparent: to the extent that the moral norms of the equal consideration system are among those currently prevailing in our society, we should comply with them because, as with any moral norms currently prevailing in our society, doing so is in our (qualified) best interests; to the extent that the moral norms of the equal consideration system are not among those currently prevailing in our society, and our compliance with them would then be for reasons of conscience only, complying with them either may be in our (qualified) best interests, or may not. When complying with them is not in our (qualified) best interests, there may be *no* good reason for complying with them.

I say there "may" be no good reason rather than saying, more strongly, there "is" no good reason because, as will be recalled (sec. 2.1), what we think is in our best interests is not, by definition, identical with what, everything considered, we think we have a good reason to do; a person might therefore conclude that he has a good reason for complying with the moral norms of the equal consideration system, and want to do so, even though he realizes that doing so is not in his best interests. Whether such a reason really *would* be a good reason is a complex matter we need not pursue here.

One final note: even though it may not be in our best interests to comply with the moral norms of the equal consideration system to the extent that they are not part of current morality, we must also remember that, if I am right, there is a standing presumption in favor of our helping bring this social-pressure system into existence (sec. 10.5). And if there is a standing presumption in favor of this, then there is reason to believe that, as time goes by, the moral norms of the equal consideration system will come to be part of current morality to an ever greater extent. Thus, to an ever greater extent, compliance with them will *come* to be in our best interests, even if not in our best interests at present.

12
Utilitarian Standard vs. Original Position

12.1 HOW TO FORMULATE A UTILITARIAN ORIGINAL POSITION

Let me briefly recapitulate where we now stand. I have been trying to show that the utilitarian standard is justified in the sense that the social-pressure system derivable from it—the "equal consideration" system—is, from the standpoint of our self-interest, a better "bet" than any (factually possible) alternative. I could not explicitly compare the equal consideration system with *every* (factually possible) alternative, but in chapter 10 I did compare it with perhaps its most likely competitor—a biased system—and concluded that, as between the two, the equal consideration system is indeed our better bet.

But many philosophers today might consider the most promising alternative to the equal consideration system not to be a biased one, but one derivable from what John Rawls calls the "original position," this original position being a criterion specifically designed for deriving (i.e., justifying) moral norms. So far I have not gone into John Rawls's deservedly famous theory of justice and political morality, except briefly to register some objections to his reflective equilibrium method of justification. Since Rawls is the most renowned and influential of the many present-day opponents of utilitarianism, and since it is a utilitarian theory that I am defending here—although an "indirect" one, rather than the direct variety opposed by Rawls—it is perhaps incumbent upon me to confront Rawls's theory before concluding. And, incidentally, my discussion of Rawls's theory will be directed at his theory as set out in his major work, *A Theory of Justice* (1971), not toward his earlier or later views.

Rawls does not, of course, put forth his original position as a criterion for evaluating what I am here calling "social-pressure systems"; the concept of a social-pressure system is absent from Rawls's theory altogether. Instead, Rawls puts forth his original position as a criterion for evaluating principles of justice, these principles of justice in turn being ones designed only for evaluating basic institutions of society. Thus the role that Rawls allows his original position to play in his book is much more limited than the role I shall be assuming it has for purposes of this comparison. But I see no compelling reason why a criterion, if it is adequate for evaluating principles of justice, should not be adequate for evaluating entire social-pressure systems as well. In fact, Rawls himself suggests that his original position has a far wider use than that to which he puts it (1971, sec. 18).

I have, as I said, tried to make it plausible to claim that the equal consideration system is more in our interests than any alternative by showing the equal consideration system to be more in our interests than a biased one. Here I try to make this claim even more plausible by showing the equal consideration system to be more in our interests than a social pressure system derivable from Rawls's original position. I attempted to show the superiority of the equal consideration system to a biased one by directly comparing the two systems. But in trying to show the equal consideration system to be superior to one derivable from Rawls's original position my strategy will be somewhat different. Although, if Rawls is correct, the social-pressure system derivable from his original position would include at least his two famous principles of justice (see sec. 12.4 below), it is not clear what else this system would include. Since it is indeed unclear what a complete Rawlsian system would be like, I shall somewhat indirectly try to show the equal consideration system to be superior to its Rawlsian counterpart by comparing not the two systems themselves, but the criteria from which they are derived or, in other words, the criteria in terms of which they are justified. The equal consideration system is, of course, derivable from the utilitarian standard, whereas a Rawlsian counterpart would be derivable from the original position. What I shall try to show then is that, as a standard for evaluating and deriving social-pressure systems, the utilitarian standard is superior to Rawls's original position.

Rawls envisions his original position as being made up of a number of hypothetical parties who are gathered together for the purpose of choosing moral principles or (we are supposing) a social pressure system. In order for one of the alternative possibilities to be chosen by this hypothetical group, the parties must agree upon it unanimously. These hypothetical parties are to be thought of as being endowed with those characteristics necessary for a person to be said to be choosing moral norms from an *ideal* standpoint. Since these parties are thus supposed to be making choices from an ideal standpoint, any moral norms they agree upon are therefore, in Rawls's view, *ipso facto* better than any alternatives. And since, in Rawls's view, whether or not a moral norm is justified turns upon whether or not it would be *agreed* upon by ideally situated parties, his approach to justification may be called a *social contract* approach, and the hypothetical parties to the contract may be called *rational contractors.*

Let us now look at the utilitarian standard. As will be recalled, it too specifies an ideal standpoint for choosing moral norms, or a social-pressure system. The difference is that we are to envision an ideal utilitarian choice as being made by just one hypothetical, ideally situated individual rather than by many such individuals, as with Rawls's original position. Thus the utilitarian approach to justification may called an *ideal-chooser* approach, and the hypothetical individual in question may be called an *ideal observer* or *ideal chooser*. I myself prefer the designation "ideal chooser" to that of "ideal observer," the latter designation being, it seems to me, somewhat misleading, given that the hypothetical individual in question is to be thought of not merely as a passive *observer*, but as an active *chooser*.

In any case, what is important is that both Rawls's original position and the utilitarian standard stipulate an allegedly *ideal* standpoint for choosing moral norms or a social-pressure system—a standpoint that is supposed to be such that any two individuals choosing from this standpoint would choose identically. This means that justification in terms of Rawls's original position and justification in terms of the utilitarian standard can both be viewed equally well as *either* a social-contract approach to justification or an ideal-chooser (or observer) approach to justification. As Rawls himself says, we can view a choice made by the parties of his original position as the choice of any *one* of these parties "selected at random" (1971, 139)—in other words, as the choice of an appropriately defined ideal chooser. (In a later publication [1975], Rawls does argue that, although all his parties necessarily would make the same choices, his approach *cannot* be viewed as an ideal chooser approach. But Jean Hampton, in a reply to Rawls on this point (1980), shows, convincingly enough I think, that, even in spite of what Rawls says, the approach can be viewed in this way.) On the other hand, as R. M. Hare has pointed out (1973), a choice made by the utilitarian ideal chooser can just as well be viewed as the choice of parties in a specially defined original position—in other words, as the choice of appropriately defined "rational contractors."

In fact, for purposes of comparing the utilitarian standard with Rawls's original position, let us transform the utilitarian standard from an ideal-chooser criterion into a social contract criterion, and call it the "utilitarian" original position. This is easily accomplished. As we have seen (sec. 3.1), according to this utilitarian ideal-chooser criterion a person is choosing a social-pressure system from an ideal standpoint (and hence is an "ideal chooser") if and only if he has perfect knowledge of a certain sort, assumes that he himself will have to experience all the experiences resulting from his choice, and bases his choice upon and only upon the above knowledge and assumption. To transform this hypothetical ideal chooser into a hypothetical party in an "original position," all we need do is replace the assumption that the ideal chooser will himself experience all the experiences resulting from his choice with the equivalent assumption that the ideal chooser (now to be viewed as any one party "selected at random" from an original position) will himself experience all the experiences of just one of the individuals to be affected by his choice, but does not know *which* one.

The definition of this utilitarian original position differs from the definition of Rawls's original position in the following five ways. I do not claim that these are the only differences; as rich and complex as Rawls's theory is, I would be reluctant to attempt a complete list of the differences between the two definitions. But the following do, I think, include the differences that seem to play the most prominent roles in Rawls's argument—as set out in *A Theory of Justice,* at least. First, admission to Rawls's original position is limited to existing human beings who have reached the age of reason (1971, 146), whereas the utilitarian original position admits all existing and potential individuals of any age. Second, with Rawls's original position there is no general stipulation, as there is with the utilitarian original position, precluding the parties from being influenced by anything other than their stipulated knowledge and motivation. Third, in Rawls's original position the overall objective of a party is presumed to be that of maximizing for himself (and his "nearest descendants") what Rawls calls "primary goods," these primary goods being rights, liberties, powers, opportunities, income, wealth, and self-respect (1971, 142). On the other hand, in the utilitarian original position the overall objective of a party is presumed to be the broader objective of as good a life as possible for himself (as determined by reference to the personal welfare norm set out earlier [chap. 2]). Fourth, the parties in Rawls's original position are (when evaluating alternatives) under a thick veil of ignorance that excludes from them knowledge not only of their own identity, but also of the particular circumstances of present-day society, its economic and political situation, the level of civilization and culture it has been able to achieve, and so on (1971, 137–38 and 155–56). In short, they are to have excluded from them knowledge of nearly all "particular," as opposed to "general," facts about anything. Although Rawls does not spell out his distinction between particular and general facts very precisely, it is nonetheless clear that by excluding knowledge of nearly all particular facts a great deal has been excluded. The parties in the utilitarian original position are, generally, under a much thinner veil of ignorance than excludes from them only knowledge of their own identity. (The utilitarian veil would be made thicker than this only for purposes of enabling the parties [or ideal chooser, as the case may be] to take fully into account the incomplete information and, in general, fallibility, from which real human beings, as opposed to hypothetical parties, suffer [as explained in sec. 2.3].) Fifth, the parties in Rawls's original position are presumed to use Rawls's "maximum" rule for determining which alternative, given their overall objective, it is most "rational" to choose (1971, 152–53), whereas the parties in the utilitarian original position are instead to maximize their expected utility, in the sense of "expected utility" explained earlier (sec. 2.2). I shall argue that each of the above five differences between these two original positions constitutes a reason for favoring the utilitarian original position.

12.2 LESS SIGNIFICANT DIFFERENCES

First, by admitting all existing and potential individuals of any age, rather than, as with Rawls, just those existing humans at the age of reason, the utilitarian original position achieves greater impartiality. The parties in Rawls's original position, by knowing its strict admission requirements (1971, 140), know that they are not, for example, an infant or a fetus; consequently, they might not give fully impartial consideration to the interests of those who *are* infants or fetuses. Rawls apparently tries to gain adequate impartiality in his original position, in spite of its rather strict admission requirements, by endowing his parties with "a desire to further the welfare of their nearest descendants" of at least the next two generations (1971, 128). It is not at all obvious, however, that this would be enough to insure adequate impartiality in questions such as those concerning infanticide and abortion (e.g., see Hare 1973). At the very least the utilitarian position, with its more lenient admission requirements, achieves impartiality much more simply, and less problematically.

We need not, however, linger over this objection; if there were no other way for Rawls to meet the objection he could always, I think, adopt the utilitarian admission requirements himself without thereby doing any serious damage to his own original position.

Second, by stipulating that a party's choices are to be based *only* upon (a) his assumption about his experiencing the results of his choice, the utilitarian thereby precludes the possibility of a party's choices being influenced by disease, superstition, neurosis, or any other irrelevant factor. And by precluding irrelevant factors from influencing a party's choices, this stipulation also serves to assure that all parties will make the same choices and that, therefore, agreement will be reached. The stipulation corresponding to this in the definition of the Rawlsian original position seems to be the stipulation that "the parties are not to be moved by envy" (1971, 143; see also sec. 80). As it stands, this stipulation concerning envy is ambiguous. On the one hand, it could mean that, in choosing norms of morality, the parties are not to be influenced by any envy they might experience *while in the original position;* on the other hand, it could mean that, in choosing the norms, the parties are not to take into account any envy that living according to whatever norms are chosen might engender *in real life*.

If Rawls means that the parties are not to be influenced by any envy they might experience while in the original position, then the stipulation is satisfactory as far as it goes. But it does not go far enough. The appropriate stipulation would be that, aside from their stipulated knowledge and motivation, the parties are not to be influenced by *anything,* be it superstition, prejudice, envy, some sort of neurosis, or whatever. Unless Rawls disallows all irrelevant influences, not just envy, then not only might these influences contaminate the parties' deliberations but, since presumably not all parties will be subject to the *same* irrelevant influence, it is hard to see how they will be able to reach any agreement at all. So if Rawls's stipulation is meant to rule out the influence of any envy experienced within the original position itself, and only this, the stipulation is much too weak. If, on the other hand, Rawls's stipulation is meant to forbid the parties from taking into account any envy that living according to whatever norms are chosen might engender in real life, then the stipulation is much too strong. There is no good reason why the parties, in deciding what norms to choose, should be allowed to take into account *some* of the unpleasant results of living according to whatever norms are chosen, but not *other* such results, like envy. The people who happened to be among those unfortunate enough to have to suffer from the envy that the parties in the original position were, by stipulation, forbidden from taking into account would, I should think, have good reason indeed for objecting to this stipulation.

But we need not linger over this objection either, for it is an objection that Rawls could, I believe, meet by making only a minor change in his theory. Let us turn instead to the next difference between the Rawlsian and utilitarian original positions, this being a difference in what is to be taken as the objective of the parties. (What is to be taken as the objective of the parties largely determines what alternatives they would end up choosing, since conduciveness to this objective is to serve as their criterion for evaluating alternatives.) Here, for the first time, we encounter a difference between the original positions that could hardly be overcome short of a major concession from either one or the other of the two opposing theories.

12.3 PRIMARY GOODS: FIRST OBJECTION

Each party in both the Rawlsian and utilitarian original positions is to be thought of as seeking, above all else, what is in his own best interests. Furthermore, Rawls himself grants that there is no significant difference between his theory and utilitarianism in what, in the most abstract and fundamental sense, counts as being in a person's best interests (1971, 92–93). That which, speaking as abstractly as possible, is in a person's best interests is, according to both theories, living that life—that is, having those "future experiences"—the person would choose for himself, if he were choosing from something like that ideal standpoint for making personal choices specified by the personal welfare norm set out at the beginning of this inquiry (see sec. 2.2 above, and Rawls 1971, 92–93 and secs. 63–64). In view of these points of approximate agreement, one would expect the stipulated objective of each party in both original positions to be living that life he would choose for himself if choosing from a properly defined ideal standpoint. This is indeed the objective of each party in the utilitarian original position but, somewhat surprisingly, it is not the objective of the parties in the Rawlsian original position. Although each party in the Rawlsian original position does seek, above all else, what is in his own best interests, he is not to view what is in his own best interests as being the life he would choose from an ideal standpoint; instead, he is to view it as being that which Rawls calls "primary goods." Thus the objective of each party in the Rawlsian original position is securing for himself as great an amount of primary goods as possible (1971, secs. 15 and 25).

Roughly speaking, primary goods are things anyone would want no matter what else he wanted (1971, p. 92). With the help of some Rawlsian terminology, let me try to explain this more fully. The overall plan of life that is "best" for one—that is, that plan one would choose for oneself if choosing from an ideal standpoint—Rawls calls one's "rational" plan of life (1971, 408). What the rational plan of life is for any one person presumably differs in many details from that for any other person. The only thing that is supposed by Rawls to be common to everyone's rational plan of life is the role that primary goods play in its realization. A primary good is supposed to be a thing such that, the more of it one has, the more successful one can expect to be in realizing one's rational plan of life—that is, in actually living that life which is best for one. Therefore—taking a "rational person" to be one intent upon realizing his rational plan of life—we may define primary goods as things that any rational person would want as much of as possible, no matter what his rational plan of life happened to be. Furthermore, primary goods can be classified as either social or natural: social primary goods (e.g., wealth) are ones the distribution of which is determined mainly by society, while natural primary goods (e.g., native intelligence) are ones the distribution of which is determined mainly by heredity. Since it is only the social primary goods whose distribution we have much control over, they are the only ones that Rawls takes to be appropriate objectives for the parties in an original position. He lists seven social primary goods: rights, liberties, powers, opportunities, income, wealth, and self-respect (1971, 62).

What is Rawls's reason for making primary goods the objective of the parties in his original position? Why does he not (as does the utilitarian) make their objective living that life they would choose from an ideal (prudential) standpoint? At least part of his reason is that the use of primary goods as their objective is, Rawls claims, a "simplifying device" (1971, 95), and as such helps overcome one of the standard objections against ideal-chooser approaches to ethical justification, which is, in essence, what both the utilitarian and Rawlsian original positions are. This objection is that ideal-chooser approaches are too idealistic to be of practical value since we are all in reality mere human beings, not ideal choosers or parties in an original position. As mere human beings, so the objection goes, we have very little idea what choices such ideal choosers would actually make. Thus, it is concluded, the ideal chooser approach to ethical justification is of no practical value. The use of primary goods as the parties' objective is supposed to help overcome this objection by simplifying to such an extent what the hypothetical parties must take into account in making their choices that even we mere human beings will have relatively little difficulty determining which choices these ideal choosers would make. If Rawls is correct about the use of primary goods greatly simplifying matters, this would be a point in their favor. I shall argue, however, that the use of primary goods does not simplify matters after all and that, for this and other reasons, their use is a mistake.

In order to see what is wrong with the use of primary goods as the parties' objective, let us begin by looking more closely at the seven primary goods named by Rawls: liberties, rights, powers, opportunities, income, wealth, and self-respect. How exactly does Rawls define each of these? Unless Rawls specifies rather precisely what these primary goods are, neither we nor the hypothetical parties could know whether one social pressure system would be more successful than another in bringing them about, thus making a choice from Rawls's original position not just extremely difficult, but impossible. In becoming clearer about what these primary goods are, we might look first at what they are not. The primary good of powers is not simply power to get what one desires; similarly, the primary good of opportunities is not simply opportunity to get what one desires, and the primary good of liberties is not simply liberty to get what one desires. If this were all that Rawls meant by the primary goods of powers, opportunities, and liberties, then they would simply collapse into one primary good, namely, the good of being able to get what one desires. And if desire-satisfying ability were a primary good that the parties in Rawls's original position were to take as their objective, then to this extent their objective would be no different than the objective they would be given in an "original position" version of one popular type of utilitarianism: namely, that type which equates utility with maximizing desire satisfaction, a type of utilitarianism I discussed earlier (sec. 3.5), and rejected. Also, I doubt if it would be much easier to determine if some alternative would maximize desire satisfaction than to determine if it would maximize happiness or satisfying experience; so Rawls's claim that primary goods are a simplifying device would obviously fail if they were interpreted in this way. Thus Rawls must give his primary goods a narrower interpretation than one that simply collapses them into the good of being able to get what one desires.

And indeed, Rawls's writings make it fairly clear that he does intend to interpret his primary goods much more narrowly. By the primary good of liberties he is referring not to a general liberty to get what one desires, but rather to a list of more specific liberties, a list that includes political liberty, liberty of speech and assembly, liberty of conscience and thought, liberty to hold personal property, and liberty of the person as protected by the rule of law (1971, 61). The primary good of rights is perhaps redundant since Rawls, it seems, defines our rights in terms of our liberties (1971, 202). The primary good of powers is defined as possibilities for creating "by certain procedures a structure of rights and duties that the courts will enforce. The power to make a will is an example" (1975, 542–43 n.). The primary good of opportunities apparently refers to opportunities to occupy the various offices and positions available in society (e.g., see what Rawls means by "equality" of opportunity on 72–73, and in his second principle of justice, 302). The primary good of wealth Rawls defines as "legal command over exchangeable means for satisfying human needs and interests" (1975, 540). And, according to him, income is closely related to wealth, "income being a flow, wealth a stock" (1975, 541). Finally, the primary good of self-respect "includes a person's sense of his own value" and "a confidence in one's ability" (1971, 440).

But most of these characterizations of primary goods, especially of the ones that are liberties, are still not precise enough to give sufficient guidance. The vagueness of these primary goods, in spite of some effort by Rawls to explicate them more fully (see esp. 1971, chap. 4), is thus a problem. And this problem draws attention to the even more serious problem of how, exactly, one is to go about removing this vagueness. What criterion, in other words, is one to use for deriving these primary goods and defining them precisely enough so that they *are* fully capable of guiding the parties' deliberations? Certainly these primary goods do not stem from the principles of justice that are supposedly derived from the original position. As Rawls himself says (1971, 433–34):

> the principles of justice cannot be used to draw up the list of primary goods that serves as part of the description of the [original position]. The reason is, of course, that this list is one of the premises from which the choice of the principles . . . is derived. To cite these principles in explaining the list would be a circular argument.

Likewise, it can be added, the original position itself cannot be used for clarifying the exact nature of these primary goods either. As Rawls points out above, the primary goods serve as part of the original position's description; thus, to use the original position for clarifying the exact nature of the primary goods would be to use the original position for describing itself, which would be even more blatantly circular than using the principles of justice for describing it. How then is the list of social primary goods to be determined and adequately clarified?

Rawls's own answer is as follows:

> We must assume then, that the list of primary goods can be accounted for by the conception of goodness as rationality in conjunction with the general facts about human wants and abilities, their characteristic phases and requirements of nurture, the Aristotelian Principle, and the necessities of social interdependence. (1971, 434)

By the conception of "goodness as rationality" in the above quotation Rawls is referring to his conception of a person's good which, as we have seen, is similar to the utilitarian conception, where what is in one's interests is what one would choose from a properly defined ideal standpoint. The Aristotelian Principle states that "human beings take more pleasure in doing something as they become more proficient at it, and of two activities they do equally well, they prefer the one calling on a larger repertoire of more intricate and subtle discriminations" (1971, 426). Thus, from goodness as rationality, the Aristotelian Principle, general facts about human wants and abilities, and the necessities of social interdependence, we are able to derive, so Rawls claims, certain goods that anyone would want, no matter what his rational plan of life was, and these are the primary goods. Rawls then goes on to say that he will "not argue the case for the list of primary goods . . . , since their claims seem evident enough" (1971, 434).

Their claims, however, are not evident enough. In the first place, it can very well be argued that Rawls's list of primary goods contains entries that should not be there. It must be remembered that everything on the list is supposed to represent items that *anyone* would (rationally) want, no matter what his rational plan of life; but it is questionable whether, for example, some of the specific rights and liberties on the list would fulfill this requirement. Although I suppose no one would turn down any liberty if he could choose to be the only one to enjoy it, might not many rationally turn down some of Rawls's basic liberties, given that their acceptance of these liberties would, as Rawls says, require them to tolerate everyone else's enjoyment of the same liberty? As H. L. A. Hart writes:

> Some persons, given their general temperament, might reasonably prefer to be free to libel others or to invade their privacy, or to make use of their own property in whatever style they like, and might gladly take the risk of being exposed to these practices on the part of others. . . . Other persons would not pay this price for unrestricted liberty in these matters, since, given their temperament, they would value the protections afforded by the restrictions higher than the unrestricted liberty. (1973, 549)

Are all the liberties that Rawls designates as primary goods really ones that *everyone* of *every* temperament would (rationally) want to see recognized by society? I would certainly doubt it, although I might admit that it is difficult to come to an entirely satisfactory answer to questions such as this until the liberties, and other primary goods on Rawls's list have been made more precise than he makes them.

In addition to the problem of making these primary goods more precise, there is the problem of determining what the priorities among the goods should be. This is the problem of determining which, as between two or more primary goods, is to be given priority whenever they conflict, whenever, that is, the full realization of one primary good can be achieved only at the expense of the full realization of one or more of the others. It is often claimed, for example, that, in underdeveloped countries, the fastest possible rate of economic development—and thus the greatest possible national wealth—can only be achieved if for a certain period of time the country is governed by a benevolent dictatorship. If so then, for a certain period of time at least, the full realization of the primary good of wealth would conflict with the full realization of the primary good of political liberty. What is needed, therefore, is a system of priorities for handling the innumerable different sorts of conflicts, like the above, that might arise among primary goods—a need of which Rawls is fully aware, yet can offer little in the way of advice as to how to fulfill other than to suggest that resorting to our "intuitive capacities" might help (1971, 93–94). But will resorting to our intuitive capacities, or anything else, yield the system of priorities that is, from Rawls's standpoint, needed—namely, a system of priorities that is best for *everyone*, no matter what his rational plan of life might be? I doubt it. That the very same primary goods are best for everyone, no matter what his rational plan of life, is probably false, although it is not preposterous; that the very same *system of priorities* among primary goods is best for everyone is preposterous. Surely some people's rational plan of life would require giving, say, wealth a slightly different priority *vis-à-vis* certain liberties than would other people's rational plan of life. Furthermore, the conflict problem has still another dimension: in addition to needing a system of priorities for resolving conflicts among different categories of primary goods, for some of these categories we need a system of priorities for resolving conflicts solely *within* the category. This need is especially apparent when it comes to the category of liberties since this category is made up of not just one, but a number of different liberties (or rights), any one of which might conflict with any other. For example, were people to exercise their political liberty by voting to abolish the liberty of free speech, there would be a conflict between Rawls's speech liberty and his political liberty; one or the other would have to be curtailed.

12.4 PRIMARY GOODS: SECOND OBJECTION

So far I have argued that Rawls's primary goods have not been defined precisely enough, and the priorities among them have not been and (within the framework of his theory) cannot be worked out completely enough for them to serve as adequate objectives for parties in an original position. I want now to argue that even if the primary goods on Rawls's list were precisely enough defined, with their priorities fully worked out, they still would remain very inadequate objectives for the parties to have. Rawls goes out of his way to make it perfectly clear that once his list of primary goods has been determined, the parties are to take only these goods as their objective, and are never to look beyond them in order to measure the satisfactions people achieve from them (1971, 94–95). Absolutely no questions are ever to be asked about the human satisfactions and dissatisfactions that alternatives to be evaluated from the original position might generate; the parties are to be concerned *only* with maximizing primary goods. I want to argue that this concern only for consequences in the form of primary goods would prohibit the parties from taking into account so much of major importance that choices made on this basis would be intolerable.

To help us see the inadequacy of taking only primary goods as the parties' goal, let us look momentarily at those principles of justice which Rawls thinks would be chosen by men with these primary-good blinders on. The first principle provides for an equal distribution to everyone of the primary goods of rights and liberties. The second principle provides (among other things) for an equal distribution of the primary good of wealth, unless an unequal distribution would result in that class of people with the least wealth having more wealth than they would have were wealth distributed equally; and this principle also provides for all positions in society being open to all, even if this conflicts with there being an optimum distribution of wealth. Finally, the first principle has priority over the second principle in case of any conflict between them. This is, to be sure, only a very rough characterization of these two principles, but a characterization that should do for present purposes. (For Rawls's full statement of these principles, see 1971, 302–3.)

Let us look first at the second principle, which, with the qualifications noted, provides for equal wealth. The first thing to notice is that such a principle might be disastrous for people who, say, were suffering extensively from an agonizing illness, the cure for which was so expensive that they needed much *more* than an equal share of wealth in order to pay for this cure. But, what is still more important, if this principle were indeed disastrous for those with a special need such as this, the parties in Rawls's original position would be in no position to amend the principle so that it did provide for the need. Being forbidden to look beyond primary goods to people's actual sufferings and satisfactions, these parties are therefore forbidden to take into account any special needs arising specifically from these sufferings; and if they are forbidden to take into account any special needs arising specifically from these sufferings, they obviously are in no position to amend any norms of morality so that they do provide for these special needs, or to choose ones that provide for them in the first place. (A similar point is made in greater detail in Barry 1973, 55–57.)

And focusing exclusively upon Rawls's primary goods also precludes the parties from giving adequate consideration to other important matters. According to the second of the two principles that Rawls claims his parties would decide upon, if the wealth of the worst-off class of people in society could be maximized through an unequal distribution rather than an equal one, then this unequal distribution would be mandatory. Thus by means of this principle (often referred to as the "difference" principle) the worst off *seem* to be assured of as great an absolute share of wealth as possible (subject to certain qualifications that need not concern us now). It is worth mentioning, incidentally, that what seems to be so is not really so; with the difference principle, the worst-off might actually end up with a *smaller* absolute share than they would were decisions made instead according to the utilitarian norm, or the general welfare norm (Haslett 1985). Anyway, the parties in Rawls's original position would, according to Rawls, decide upon a principle that provided the worst-off with as large an *absolute* share of wealth as possible even if this were achievable only through providing them with a smaller *relative* (or percentage) share than they otherwise would have had. But a decision concerning which the worst-off should have, as between greater absolute wealth and greater relative wealth, is just the sort of decision that Rawls's parties, with their primary-good blinders on, would be in no position to make. For these primary-good blinders would prevent them from taking certain possible consequences of a smaller relative share into account, which in making this decision *should* be taken into account. For example, a greater absolute share at the expense of a smaller relative share might cause the worst-off more in the way of unhappiness through their *envy* of the rich than they get in the way of happiness through their larger absolute share. (I know that Rawls stipulates envy away, but see sec. 12.2 above.) And it has been suggested that people might derive great comfort and happiness through sharing a similarity of financial status with everyone else, thus being able to feel that everyone is "part of a team where all members sink or rise together equally" (Crocker 1977, 263). Such feelings of "solidarity," as they might be called, would be destroyed through a great disparity in wealth between the best- and worst-off, and even if the worst-off got a greater absolute share as a result of this disparity, their greater absolute share might not even come close to compensating them for this loss of solidarity. Yet, no matter how disastrous the consequences of envy or a loss of solidarity might be, the parties in Rawls's original position are, owing to their concern only with primary goods, forced to pretend that such consequences are of no significance.

Let us now turn from Rawls's second principle, which (roughly) provides for an equal distribution of the primary good of wealth except when unequal distribution benefits the worst-off, to his first principle, which (roughly) provides for an equal distribution of the primary good of liberties. The liberties on Rawls's list of primary goods amount to norms purporting to guarantee that individuals will not be prevented by the state or other individuals from doing certain things, things such as expressing their opinions. Unfortunately, such guarantees may be of little worth to the less-well-off financially who, from lack of wealth, may not be able to take advantage of these liberties. The less-well-off may not, for example, be able to compete with the better-off for access to, and control over, the communication media (newspapers, magazines, television, radio, etc.). Thus, even though the less-well-off may have an equal guarantee that no one will stop them from expressing their opinions, this guarantee may be of little value to them if they cannot gain access to the means by which their opinions can be expressed effectively (e.g., see Daniels 1976, 253–82). Rawls does indeed recognize this problem. He says that, although such things as a person's wealth and education do not affect the extent of his liberties *per se,* such things certainly do affect the extent to which these liberties are *worth* something to him (Rawls 1971, 204–5).

Although Rawls may recognize the distinction between the extent of a person's liberties *per se* and the worth of these liberties, the parties in his original position cannot. What exactly constitutes the "worth" of liberties is debatable, but one thing is clear; the worth of liberties cannot be determined merely by calculating their conduciveness to the primary goods on Rawls's list; there must be more to their worth than this. But whatever more there is to their worth, it cannot be recognized by parties who are prohibited from acknowledging anything to be of value other than these primary goods themselves. Thus with Rawls's original position moral norms are to be chosen by parties unaware of this important distinction between the extent of a person's liberties *per se* and the worth of these liberties to him. I, for one, would not want to be governed by moral norms chosen by parties with gaps like this in their thinking.

Next, how could even the need for such basic moral norms as ones prohibiting physical violence (i.e., assault and battery) be appreciated from the standpoint of parties whose sole objective is maximizing primary goods? Rawls is confident that a prohibition against physical violence would be among the "natural duties" that his parties would choose from the original position (Rawls 1971, 114–15). But to what extent exactly would his parties be able to appreciate the need for such a prohibition? Clearly they could appreciate this need *only* to the extent that a prohibition against violence was necessary for the realization of one or more of the primary goods on Rawls's list since, once again, the parties are prohibited from looking beyond these primary goods. But could Rawls's parties really derive a perfectly adequate moral norm prohibiting violence if their only concern were the realization of opportunities, powers, self-respect, wealth, income, and the various rights and liberties on Rawls's list of primary goods? If, of course, among the various rights or liberties on Rawls's list were the liberty to live without suffering or to live without injury, then there would be little doubt about the parties being able to derive an adequate moral norm prohibiting physical violence. But nowhere does Rawls suggest that any such broad liberty as this is among those on his list. Furthermore, if something like this broad liberty were indeed among those on his list, then his claim that the objective of maximizing the primary goods on his list is simpler and easier to work with than the utilitarian objective would be considerably less plausible. In fact, if something like the avoidance of suffering or injury were a primary good, then, to this extent, the objective of Rawls's parties would be identical to that of one version of utilitarianism—namely, negative utilitarianism, where the objective is not that of maximizing something of general value such as pleasure, but rather that of minimizing something of general disvalue such as suffering or injury. Thus it appears that the easy way of deriving an adequate prohibition against physical violence from the objective of maximizing primary goods—namely, by making the avoidance of suffering or injury itself a primary good—is not available to Rawls.

But might not an adequate prohibition be derived anyway by showing that such a prohibition would be necessary for that realization of some other primary good on Rawls's list? Perhaps some sort of prohibition against physical violence would be necessary for the full realization of, say, freedom of speech, which *is* among the liberties on Rawls's list. But would the parties really be able to arrive at a fully adequate prohibition against physical violence by means of such an indirect route? Would, in other words, a prohibition against physical violence applicable only to those cases where the violence would interfere with freedom of speech or some other primary good on Rawls's list be a general enough prohibition to be adequate? It is difficult to answer such a question without, once again, a more precise characterization of each primary good than Rawls gives us. I would venture to say, however, that, as long as Rawls's parties are forbidden to look beyond primary goods, the derivation by them of a fully adequate prohibition against physical violence is doubtful. Even if, from their very restricted standpoint, they were able to derive *some* sort of prohibition against physical violence, it is doubtful that they would draw the line between the acceptable and unacceptable here in exactly the place it should be drawn, and would be drawn by parties not forbidden to look beyond primary goods.

In short, there are probably many areas where the limited range of values that Rawls' parties are allowed to recognize would prevent them from drawing a line between the morally acceptable and unacceptable that is fully adequate. (For still more on this point, see Hart 1973.) Would we really want the moral norms of our society to be chosen by parties operating under the handicap of having to wear these primary-good blinders? I do not think we would.

Let me now summarize the reasons that primary goods are an inadequate objective for parties in an original position. First of all, primary goods and the priorities among them must meet the requirement of being that which *any* rational person would want, no matter what else he wanted. That some of the goods on Rawls's list would fail to meet this very strict requirement is probable; that any system for determining priorities among them would fail to meet this requirement is certain. Second, Rawls's list of primary goods does not provide the parties with an objective that is broad enough for deriving a social-pressure system from it that is completely adequate. This defect could only be remedied either by adding to the list some very broadly defined primary good—one such as the good of being able to get what one desires—and having this broad primary good serve as a sort of "catch-all" objective for the parties to pursue; or else by adding to the list enough additional, very specific primary goods—goods such as leisure, health, and so on—to ensure that the list contained absolutely no "gaps." But the first alternative of adding a very broadly defined primary good to the list would not serve Rawls's purposes, for any primary good capable of serving as a genuinely adequate catch-all objective would undermine Rawls's goal of keeping the objective of his parties quite distinct from that of the utilitarian. And the second alternative of adding a number of very specific primary goods to the list would only aggravate the already hopeless problem of arranging a system of priorities for these primary goods. With either alternative there could no longer be any doubt but that these primary goods would fail to be simplifying devices, as Rawls intends them to be; they would, if anything, become complicating devices instead. Thus I conclude that the general objective of a good life as both Rawls and the utilitarian might characterize it cannot be adequately simplified by substituting for it some list of primary goods, and that this good life is therefore, as the utilitarian maintains, the more appropriate objective for parties in an original position.

This is not to say that there is no such thing as that which a primary good is supposed to be: something in the best interests of everyone, no matter what his rational plan of life. In fact, use of the utilitarian standard for making certain evaluations is being put forth here as just that, as something in the best interests of everyone. So the utilitarian standard may be said to be at least in the spirit of Rawls's primary good; it is, so to speak, a primary *standard*.

12.5 THE VEIL OF IGNORANCE AND THE MAXIMIN RULE

Let me now continue the comparison of the utilitarian and Rawlsian original positions by turning to the next difference between the two—a difference in the "veil of ignorance" that the parties are assumed to be under. The parties in both original positions are presumed to possess all knowledge relevant for deciding which alternative is in their best interests, except for certain knowledge they are explicitly precluded from having. The knowledge that they are explicitly precluded from having constitutes their "veil of ignorance." The "thicker" their veil of ignorance, the less their knowledge. The relatively thin utilitarian veil of ignorance precludes the parties only from knowing their own identity, and thus from knowing what any of their own personal characteristics are. This is precisely enough of a veil to prevent them from choosing principles designed specifically to favor themselves or people with characteristics they know to be similar to their own. The much thicker Rawlsian veil of ignorance is, of course, also sufficient to insure impartiality, but it goes far beyond what would seem to be the minimal veil necessary for doing this; the Rawlsian veil does not just preclude the parties from having particular knowledge about themselves, but precludes them from having *particular* knowledge about almost anything (Rawls 1971, sec. 24). And, significantly, it even precludes them from having "all but the vaguest" knowledge of probabilities (Rawls 1971, 155). It would seem that the parties in the utilitarian original position, having more knowledge upon which to base their choices, are therefore better situated to choose alternatives that are appropriate for the world as it is in reality. What then can be said in favor of Rawls's thicker veil? In my view (although here again Rawls would not agree—see, e.g., 1975, sec. I) the *most* that can be said in its favor is that, through making so much knowledge off limits, the Rawlsian thicker veil does simplify the evaluation process somewhat. I shall try to show, however, that this simplification is really an oversimplification, and consequently a greater liability than asset. But to try to show this I must turn to the fifth and final main difference between the two original positions—a difference in the rule of rationality the parties are to follow.

As will be recalled, the parties in Rawls's original position are to follow the maximin rule, while those in the utilitarian original position are to follow instead the rule of maximizing expected utility. According to the maximin rule, one is to rank alternatives exclusively on the basis of their worst possible outcome, disregarding all other possible outcomes. Thus the parties in Rawls's original position are required to choose the alternative whose worst possible outcome is better than the worst possible outcome of any other alternative. Disregarding all possible outcomes other than the worst ones does simplify the evaluation process. Consequently, the maximin rule, as well as the thick veil of ignorance that, as we have seen, prohibits the parties from having any but the vaguest knowledge of probabilities, can indeed be said to be genuine simplifying devices.

But these two devices simplify too much; it would be impossible, using these devices, to make any meaningful choices at all. Let me illustrate what I mean. Suppose we were to disregard probabilities altogether and use the maximin rule for making ordinary, everyday choices, such as which mode of transportation to take in traveling from New York to Los Angeles. The maximin rule tells us to choose the alternative the worst possible outcome of which is superior to the worst possible outcome of all the others. The worst possible outcome for us of traveling by airplane is no doubt that of our being killed or seriously injured in a crash. Does this mean the maximin rule prescribes that we, say, walk instead? It does not, since the worst possible outcome of walking is exactly the same, serious injury or death; the very airplane we chose not to take could, after all, come crashing down on us as we were walking alone. That something like this would happen is *highly improbable,* but it is clearly *possible,* and with the maximin rule we are to disregard probabilities (Rawls 1971, 154) and consider only possibilities in making our choice. In short, the worst possible outcome of any mode of transportation is the same thing, serious injury or death; thus by disregarding probabilities and choosing only on the basis of worst possible outcomes, our choice would not be meaningful.

Likewise, we could not adequately distinguish alternative social-pressure systems merely on the basis of their worst possible outcomes either. The absolutely worst *possible* outcome of any social-pressure system would be exactly the same as that of any other, this worst possible outcome being, I should think, the annihilation of all life through the system's failure to constrain nuclear warfare, life-destroying pollution, or something like that (in which case, of course, no one would have any primary goods at all). It is true that the probability of such a disaster occurring would be far less with some systems than with others, but with any system it is surely a *possible* consequence. Since the worst possible outcome of any social-pressure system is thus essentially the same as that of any other (and this would also be true about the *next* worst possible outcome, etc.), in order to make meaningful distinctions between systems it is necessary to take probabilities into account after all.

And, along with these probabilities, *all* the possible outcomes of the alternatives must be taken into account, not merely their *worst* possible one. Just consider, for example, how the relative advantages and disadvantages of flying versus walking from some place to another would be distorted by taking into account only the worst possible outcome of each and its probability of occurring. (For other arguments against Rawls's use of the maximin rule, see Harsanyi 1975.)

Rawls does claim there is an essential difference between choosing, say, modes of transportation and choosing moral norms (or, I assume he would be willing to add, a social-pressure system) in that, with moral norms, some alternatives have possible outcomes "that one can hardly accept," and through the thick veil of ignorance the parties are denied all but the vaguest knowledge of what the *probabilities* of these worst possible outcomes are (1971, 154–55); hence, Rawls concludes, use of his very conservative maximin rule is justified. But, as we have just seen, *all* alternatives from *either* type of choice have *possible* outcomes that one can hardly accept, and therefore, if any meaningful choices are to be made, all knowledge of probabilities must be allowed and taken fully into account. Finally, Rawls claims that the maximin rule is appropriate for choosing moral norms, even if not for other types of choices, since each party in the original position "has a conception of the good such that he cares very little, if anything, for what he might gain above the minimum stipend" that, in choosing moral norms by reference to the maximin rule, he can be sure of (1971, 154). But this will not do either. As commentators have noted (e.g., Nagel 1973), Rawls provides no convincing reason for burdening his parties with such an exceedingly *modest* conception of "the good" as this, and it is doubtful whether such a reason exists.

In sum: to choose meaningfully between alternative social-pressure systems, we must take into account both probabilities and outcomes other than the worst possible ones. Since the maximin rule combined with Rawls's thick veil of ignorance does not allow us to do this fully, whereas the rule of maximizing expected utility combined with the much thinner utilitarian veil of ignorance does, I conclude that the latter combination is preferable, in spite of any simplification afforded by the former. In saying this I by no means wish to minimize the importance of simplification where simplification is appropriate. But where simplification is appropriate—in fact necessary—is with moral and other informal social criteria themselves, rather than with standards for evaluating moral and other informal social criteria (which is what "original positions" are). (On this, see sec. 4.7.)

One final, rather curious feature of Rawls's theory remains to be considered: the assumption of "strict compliance." Rawls tells us that the parties in his original position are to choose moral norms on the assumption that everyone will always *succeed* in strictly complying with whatever norms are chosen (1971, 8 and 145). It might be thought that, owing to this assumption of strict compliance, my claim that social-pressure systems cannot be meaningfully evaluated without taking probabilities into account does not hold for the sort of evaluation Rawls envisions. It does not hold because successful compliance with the norms of whatever system *Rawlsian* parties choose is not merely probable, but (owing to the assumption of strict compliance) is certain. I doubt if this curious assumption of strict compliance really does undermine my claims, but even if it did, it would do so only at the cost of weakening Rawls's position in another, even more vital respect. Requiring that the parties assume strict compliance turns the Rawlsian original position into a criterion for choosing norms, or a social-pressure system, that would be appropriate only for beings that are infallible. What is of interest to us, however, is what would be appropriate not for infallible beings, but *human* beings—that is, beings about whom "strict compliance" with social norms cannot be assumed. If, owing to the assumption of strict compliance, the Rawlsian original position could be used only for choosing a system for beings that were infallible, then the superiority of the utilitarian original position—at least its superiority for choosing a social-pressure system—would be established by this fact alone. All of this is just another application of what is, as I mentioned earlier (sec. 1.3), one of the two underlying themes of this book: that we should focus our moral justification upon social pressure in support of the norms to be justified rather than upon merely the single dimension of compliance with them.

This then concludes my comparison. We have seen that each of the above five differences between the Rawlsian and utilitarian original positions turns out to be a reason for favoring the utilitarian original position. This suggests that the utilitarian original position is in fact superior.

Finally, if the utilitarian original position is, in precisely the ways in which we have been examining, in fact superior, this would, I submit, allow us to conclude that *the social-pressure system derivable from it* must therefore be more in our interests than is its Rawlsian counterpart. In other words, we may conclude that the social-pressure system derivable from the utilitarian original position—namely, the equal consideration system—is indeed a better personal bet. And if the equal consideration system is indeed a better personal bet than its Rawlsian counterpart, this makes still a little more plausible the claim that it is a better personal bet than *any* alternative.

12.6 FINAL REMARKS

The case presented throughout this book for a utilitarian theory of moral justification is now complete. There will, as always, be critics of utilitarianism who remain unconvinced. They will, as always, say that all utilitarian theories are subject to one basic objection: these theories condone the most blatant immorality, the most outlandish injustice, provided only that it maximizes utility. The reason, they will say, is that utilitarianism makes one crucial mistake: it fails to take seriously the distinction between persons. Utilitarianism tells us to choose as if we were one single individual—namely, the "ideal chooser"—while, in reality, we are separate, distinct individuals; for this reason, utilitarianism sanctions any sacrifice at all of the individual for the sake of the group (as represented by this ideal chooser). It sanctions, in other words, any violations at all of an individual's rights provided only that the violations benefit still other individuals enough to more than make up for the costs—that is, more than make up for the costs from the perspective of an ideal chooser who is to experience everyone's experiences. What the utilitarian appears not to realize, so these critics will say, is that, in reality, *there is no ideal chooser;* there are only distinct individuals who are being forced, by the utilitarian, to sacrifice themselves for others *without* getting anything in return to make up for the costs. This, so these critics will conclude, violates one of the most profound moral insights of humankind: individuals are always to be treated as ends in themselves, never as mere means.

The first reply to the objection that utilitarianism fails to appreciate the distinction between persons is that this objection itself is based upon a failure to appreciate an important distinction: the distinction between direct and indirect utilitarianism. With respect to direct utilitarianism, this objection is in fact well taken. Deciding each case directly by appeal to the utilitarian norm—that is, by appeal to what the ideal chooser would choose—might well entail the kinds of individual sacrifices to which these critics object; ones that "intuitively" it would appear to be immoral to force upon individuals. And even if direct utilitarianism did not entail forcing these sacrifices upon individuals, people might all too often mistakenly believe it did (sec. 5.1). The utilitarian theory defended here, however, is a version of *indirect* utilitarianism. According to this version of utilitarianism, moral norms are to be evaluated along not just the usual one or two dimensions, but along three dimensions. As explained in Part I of this book, what this amounts to is an evaluation not just in terms of the consequences of compliance, but one in terms of the consequences of social pressure. And, as I tried to show in Parts II and III, any such evaluation will justify only moral norms according to which any "immorality" as "intuitively" obvious as that which is bothering these critics is explicitly forbidden.

This reply to these critics is perfectly adequate as far as it goes, but there is a deeper reply. Surely a social-pressure system, including the moral norms inherent in it, must be evaluated in terms of people's *interests*. To be sure, some philosophers would argue otherwise but, as far as I know, none have provided us with very convincing reasons for believing otherwise. If a social-pressure system is not to be evaluated in terms of the extent to which it is in people's interests, it is hard to see how it could be evaluated at all. (To evaluate a social-pressure system in terms of some moral criteria would, of course, be circular since, by definition, a social-pressure system is supposed to include all moral criteria within it.) In short, the interesting question is not whether a social-pressure system should be evaluated in terms of people's interests, but is: In terms of *whose* interests should it be evaluated? The answer proposed here is: In terms of everyone's, giving each individual's interests *equal* consideration. If, indeed, a social-pressure system *is* to be evaluated in terms of people's interests, it is hard to see how, merely by insisting that everyone's interests be considered *equally,* the utilitarian could thereby be accused of not taking the separation of persons seriously.

But the critics might press matters still further. *Why,* they might ask, should we consider everyone's interests equally, especially in that sense of "equal consideration" being defended here? With this question we arrive, finally, at the heart of the matter. If what I have argued in Part IV this book is correct, we should consider everyone's interests equally because doing so is in everyone's best interests. It is in everyone's best interests in that, from a standpoint of self-interest, each of us would *ourselves* choose that we do so if fully informed and not subject to irrelevant influences—if, in other words, our choice were made under ideal conditions, the very conditions, I submit, that would have to be met in order for our choice to have been made altogether freely. This is why equal consideration is justified; this is the connection between self-interest and morality; and this is the most profound reply to any who would claim that the utilitarian theory proposed here does not take the separation of persons seriously. For if evaluating social-pressure systems by considering everyone's interests equally is in the best interests of each individual—each *separate, distinct* individual—then how could this utilitarian theory be said to treat anyone as a mere means? I say the moral theory that treats some as mere means is instead any moral theory that does *not,* in the end, come down to what is in each individual's best interests, but that stops rather at "intuition," or "reflective equilibrium," exactly the sort of moral theory likely to be supported by the very critics who claim it is utilitarianism that treats individuals as mere means.

References

Alexander, Larry. 1985. "Pursuing the Good—Indirectly." *Ethics* 95:315–32.
Baier, Kurt. 1958. *The Moral Point of View.* Ithaca: Cornell University Press.
Barry, Brian. 1973. *The Liberal Theory of Justice.* Oxford: Clarendon Press.
Bayles, Michael D. 1981. *Professional Ethics.* Belmont, Calif.: Wadsworth.
Bok, Sissela. 1979. *Lying.* New York: Vintage Books.
Bowie, Norman. 1982. *Business Ethics.* Englewood Cliffs, N.J.: Prentice-Hall.
Boxill, Bernard R. 1972. "The Morality of Reparation." *Social Theory and Practice* 2:113–22.
Brandt, Richard B. 1967. "Some Merits of One Form of Rule Utilitarianism. In *University of Colorado Studies: Series in Philosophy,* no. 3. Denver: University of Colorado Press.
——. 1978. *A Theory of the Good and the Right.* Oxford: Clarendon Press.
Braybrooke, David. 1968. *Three Tests for Democracy.* New York: Random House.
Brody, B. A. 1973. "Abortion and the Sanctity of Life." *Americal Philosophical Quarterly* 10:133–40.
Crocker, Lawrence. 1977. "Equality, Solidarity, and Rawls' Maximin." *Philosophy and Public Affairs* 7:262–66.
Daniels, Norman. 1976. "Equal Liberty and the Unequal Worth of Liberty." In Norman Daniels, ed., *Reading Rawls.* New York: Basic Books.
——. 1979. "Wide Reflective Equilibrium and Theory Acceptance in Ethics." *The Journal of Philosophy* 76:256–82.
——. 1980a. "Some Methods of Ethics and Linguistics." *Philosophical Studies* 37:21–26.
——. 1980b. "Reflective Equilibrium and Archimedean Points." *Canadian Journal of Philosophy* 10:83–103.
Davis, Nancy. 1980. "The Priority of Avoiding Harm." In Bonnie Steinbock, ed., *Killing and Letting Die.* Englewood Cliffs, N.J.: Prentice-Hall.
Delaney, C. F. 1977. "Rawls on Method." *Canadian Journal of Philosophy,* suppl. 3:153–61.
Dworkin, Ronald. 1977. *Taking Rights Seriously.* Cambridge, Mass.: Harvard University Press.
——. 1985. *A Matter of Principle.* Cambridge, Mass.: Harvard University Press.
English, Jane. 1980. "Ethics and Science." *Proceedings of the XVI International Congress of Philosophy.* Amsterdam: North-Holland Pub. Co.

French, Peter. 1975. "Types of Collectivities and Blame." *Personalist* 56:160–69.

Fullinwinder, Robert K. 1975. "Preferential Hiring and Compensation." *Social Theory and Practice* 3:307–20.

Gray, John. 1982. *Mill on Liberty: A Defense*. Routledge & Kegan Paul: London.

Hampshire, Stuart. 1977. *Two Theories of Morality*. Oxford: Oxford University Press.

Hampton, Jean. 1980. "Contracts and Choices: Does Rawls Have a Social Contract Theory?" *Journal of Philosophy* 77:315–38.

Hare, R. M. 1963. *Freedom and Reason*. London: Oxford University Press.

———. 1973. "Rawls' Theory of Justice." *Philosophical Quarterly* 23:144–55 and 241–51.

———. 1975. "Abortion and the Golden Rule." *Philosophy & Public Affairs* 4:201–22.

———. 1976. "Ethical Theory and Utilitarianism." In H. D. Lewis, ed., *Contemporary British Philosophy*. London: Allen and Unwin.

———. 1981. *Moral Thinking: Its Levels, Method and Point*. Oxford: Clarendon Press.

Harris, John. 1975. "The Survival Lottery." *Philosophy* 50:81–87.

Harsanyi, John C. 1975. "Can the Maximin Principle Serve as a Basis for Morality? A Critique of John Rawls' Theory." *American Political Science Review* 69:594–606.

Hart, H. L. A. 1961. *The Concept of Law*. Oxford: Clarendon Press.

———. 1973. "Rawls on Liberty and Its Priority." *University of Chicago Law Review* 40:534–55.

Harward, Donald, ed. 1974. *The Crisis in Confidence*. Boston: Little Brown & Co.

Haslett, D. W. 1974. *Moral Rightness*. The Hague: Martinus Nijhoff.

———. 1980. "The General Theory of Rights." *Social Theory & Practice* 5:427–59.

———. 1984. "Hare on Moral Thinking." *Journal of Value Inquiry* 18:69–81.

———. 1985. "Does the Difference Principle Really Favor Worst Off?" *Mind* 94:111–15.

———. 1986. "Is Inheritance Justified?" *Philosophy & Public Affairs* (Spring 1986).

———. 1987. "What Is Wrong with Reflective Equilibria." *Philosophical Quarterly*, forthcoming.

Heyd, David. 1983. "Is Life Worth Reliving?" *Mind* 92:21–37.

Kupperman, Joel J. 1983. *The Foundations of Morality*. London: George Allen & Unwin, Ltd.

Lewis, C. I. 1946. *An Analysis of Knowledge and Valuation*. La Salle, Ill.: Open Court.

Lyons, David. 1977. *Forms and Limits of Utilitarianism*. Oxford: Clarendon Press.

———. 1977. "Human Rights and the General Welfare." *Philosophy and Public Affairs* 6:113–29.

MacCormick, Neil. 1978. *Legal Reasoning and Legal Theory*. Oxford: Clarendon Press.

McNamara, Robert S. 1979. "Development and the Arms Race." An Address delivered at the University of Chicago, May 22, 1979.

Mill, John Stuart. 1859. *On Liberty*. Many editions.

Murphy, Jeffrie G. 1973. *The Monist* 57:527–50.

Nagel, Thomas. 1973. "Rawls on Justice." *Philosophical Review* 2:220–34.

Nickel, James W. 1975. "Preferential Policies in Hiring and Admissions: A Jurisprudential Approach." *Columbia Law Review* 75:534–58.

Nielsen, Kai. 1963. "Why Should I Be Moral?" *Methodos* 15:275–306.

———. 1982a. "Considered Judgments Again." *Human Studies* 5:109–18.

———. 1982b. "On Needing Moral Theory," *Metaphilosophy.* 13:97–116.

———. 1985. *Equality and Liberty.* Totowa, N.J.: Rowman & Allanheld.

Norton, David. 1976. *Personal Destinies: A Philosophy of Ethical Individualism.* Princeton: Princeton University Press.

Parfit, Derek. 1984. *Reasons and Persons.* Oxford: Clarendon Press.

Plato. *Republic.* Many editions.

Rawls, John. 1971. *A Theory of Justice.* Cambridge, Mass.: Harvard University Press.

———. 1974. "Reply to Alexander and Musgrave." *Quarterly Journal of Economics* 88:633–55.

———. 1975. "Fairness to Goodness," *Philosophical Review* 85:536–54.

Raz, Joseph. 1972. "Legal Principles and the Limits of the Law." *Yale Law Journal* 81:842–54.

Ross, Alf. 1958. "The Value of Blood Tests as Evidence in Paternity Cases." *Harvard Law Review* 71:466–84.

Sartorius, Rolf. 1967. "The Doctrine of Precedent and the Problem of Relevance." *Archives for Philosophy of Law and Social Philosophy* 53, no. 5 (1972).

———. 1968. "The Justification of the Judicial Decision." *Ethics* 78:171–87.

———. 1975. *Individual Conduct and Social Norms.* Encino, Calif.: Dickenson.

Shue, Henry. 1980. *Basic Rights.* Princeton: Princeton University Press.

Sidgwick, Henry. 1907. *The Methods of Ethics.* New York: Macmillan.

Singer, Peter. 1977. "Utility and the Survival Lottery." *Philosophy* 52:218–22.

———. 1978. "Is Racial Discrimination Arbitrary?" *Philosophia* 8:185–203.

———. 1979. *Practical Ethics.* Cambridge: Cambridge University Press.

Sivard, Ruth Leger, ed. 1978. *World Military and Social Expenditures.* Leesburg, Va.: World Priorities, Inc.

Smart, J. J. C., and Bernard Williams. 1973. *Utilitarianism: For and Against.* Cambridge: Cambridge University Press.

Smith, J. C. 1976. *Legal Obligation.* Toronto and Buffalo: The University of Toronto Press.

Strawson, P. F. 1959. *Individuals.* London: Methuen.

Sumner, L. W. 1981. *Abortion and Moral Theory.* Princeton: Princeton University Press.

Thurow, Lester C. 1969. *Poverty and Discrimination.* Washington, D.C.: Brookings Institution.

Wallace, G., and A. D. M. Walker. 1970. *The Definition of Morality.* London: Methuen.

Warnock, G. J. 1971. *The Object of Morality.* London: Methuen.

White, Alan R. 1984. *Rights.* Oxford: Clarendon Press.

Williams, Bernard. 1985. *Ethics and the Limits of Philosophy.* Cambridge, Mass.: Harvard University Press.

Williams, Robin M. 1964. "The Concept of Values." In David L. Sills, ed., *International Encyclopedia of the Social Sciences,* vol. 16. New York: The Macmillan Co. & The Free Press.

Index

Abortion, 105–6, 205
Aid to other jurisdictions, 144–45
Alexander, Larry, 123
Animals, 186–87
Aristotle, 70
Artificial person thesis, 114
Assault, 76–77, 90, 132–33. *See also* Violence

Baier, Kurt, 189
Barry, Brian, 213
Bayles, Michael D., 95
Beliefs that should never be acted upon, 25–28, 117–31, 133–37, 160, 180–82, 184–87, 194–95
Beneficence, 91–94, 101–2
Best interests: term explained, 171
Biased system, 173–84, 201; term explained, 174
Bok, Sissela, 137
Borderline cases: in law, 107–8, 152, 160–62; in morality, 104–8, 165
Bowie, Norman, 15, 95
Boxill, Bernard R., 131
Brandt, Richard B., 11–13, 57, 90
Bridge norm, 108–10
Brody, B. A., 98–99

Capitalism, 126–27
Catch-all legal principle, 161
Catch-all moral norm, 102–4
Censorship, 120–23
Charity, 79–80, 91–94, 101–2. *See also* Aid to other jurisdictions
Cheating, 90, 102
Checks and balances, 136
Children, duty to take care of, 90–91, 101–2
Cole, David, 14
Conflict cases: in law, 152, 160–62; in morality, 100–102, 127–28, 165
Compliance, perspective of, 12, 28, 60, 75, 182–83, 188, 220–21

Compliance decisions, 59, 182–83, 188
Conscientious objection, 195–96
Criteria: defined and classified, 23–25
Crocker, Lawrence, 213

Daniels, Norman, 163–64, 214
Darwin, Charles, 120
Davis, Nancy, 124
Debts, payment of, 76, 90, 92, 100–101, 149
Deceit. *See* Governmental deceit
Delancy, C. E., 163
Desire model, 30
Discrimination, 21, 90–91, 123, 125, 127, 129–31, 172–77. *See also* Reverse discrimination; Biased system
Domain of a norm or standard: defined, 43
Dworkin, Ronald, 22, 63, 123, 129, 152–58

EC code of personal morality, 88–109, 137, 138–39, 150, 161, 169; defined, 67–68
EC code of political morality, 113–63, 169–70; defined, 67–68
EC codes: defined, 67–68; of organizational morality, 149–50
Education, right to, 125, 128
Elitist codes, 94–95
Emergencies. *See* Exceptions to moral norms, for emergencies
Epistemology, 66
Equal consideration, 21–22, 28, 51, 60–61, 63, 67, 80, 129, 140–48, 169–87, 222; defined, 40–43
Equal consideration codes. *See* EC codes
Equal consideration standard. *See* Utilitarian standard
Equal consideration system, 60–65, 67, 75, 76, 149, 169–87, 196, 199–200, 201–2, 220; defined, 63–64. *See also* EC code of personal morality; EC code of political morality; EC codes, of organizational morality
Exceptions to moral norms, 95–100, 128–29,

227

130–31; for consent, 100; for emergencies, 97–100, 102, 128; for preventing wrongful acts, 100
Expected personal utility: term explained, 170–71. *See also* Self-interest
Expected utility: nonmathematical variant of rule of maximizing, 34–36; qualified, 39, 119, 204; rule of maximizing, 32–33, 217; term explained, 42
Experience model, 30
Experiences, 30–36, 41–43, 45–48, 81, 206

Fallibility, human, 27, 78, 82, 95–96, 119, 131–37, 142, 145, 156, 178, 181, 185–86, 193, 204, 220
Falsehoods, 78–79, 90, 97, 100, 169
Fantastic cases, objections based on, 82–83, 131–33, 194–95
Folkways, 64–65
Food, clothing and shelter, right to, 125
Formal norm: defined, 61
Free choice, conditions for, 222
Freedom of conscience, 59–60, 70
Freedom of religion, 118, 123, 125
Freedom of speech, 59–60, 118, 120–23, 125
French, Peter, 114
Fullenwider, Robert K., 131
Fundamental norm of personal welfare. *See* Personal welfare norm, fundamental
Fundamental standard of personal welfare. *See* Personal welfare standard, fundamental
Future generations, 148–49, 184–86

General welfare norm, 67, 138–49, 151, 160–61; initial formulation, 143–44; reformulation, 146
General welfare standard, 139
Golden rule, 40, 49
Governmental deceit, 136–37
Gray, John, 123

Hampshire, Stuart, 163
Hampton, Jean, 203
Hare, R. M., 14, 32, 49, 80–87, 90, 105, 203, 205
Harris, John, 97–98
Harsanyi, John C., 219
Hart, H. L. A., 132–33, 159, 210, 216
Harward, Donald, 137
Haslett, D. W., 14, 87, 90, 151, 164, 165, 213
Heyd, David, 47–48
Human fallibility. *See* Fallibility, human

Ideal chooser: of moral norms, 119, 203–4, 221; prudential, 37–38, 191, 208; theories of, 12, 203–4, 207–8
Ideals, 23–24
Ideal standpoint: implicit in utilitarian norm and standard, 12, 40–42, 49, 51, 202–4; prudential, 29–39, 172, 191, 207
Infanticide, 205
Informal norms: defined, 61
Inter-system vs. infra-system evaluation, 165
Intuitionism, moral, 11, 25–26, 44, 70, 82–83, 91, 125, 132, 170, 211, 221–22

Judicial legislation, 151–63
Judicial reasoning, 107–8, 151–64
Justice, 44, 90, 220; Rawls's two principles of, 212–14

Kant, Immanuel, 113
Killing. *See* Murder
King, Martin Luther, 190
Kupperman, Joel J., 14, 90

Legal counsel, right to, 125
Legislative supremacy, principle of, 152–53, 157–61
Lewis, C. I., 14, 32, 35
Lowest-common-denominator codes, 94–95
Lyons, David, 12, 91, 123

MacCormick, Neil, 152, 160
McNamara, Robert S., 21
Maximin rule, 204, 217–19
Means, treating people as, 221–22
Medical care, right to, 124–25
Metagovernmental decisions, 141, 143–44; defined, 115
Method of moral justification, 52–65, 67–71, 75, 91, 96, 107, 129–31, 165, 169, 221
Mill, John Stuart, 121, 123
Mistakes of fact, 85–87
Moral justification, 14, 25, 28, 52–65, 67–71, 75, 80–87, 88–91, 96, 107, 117–36, 163–65, 169–70, 201–22
Moral philosophy, 66
Murder, 78, 92, 97, 100, 102, 104–6, 110, 169
Murphy, Jeffrie, 102

Nagel, Thomas, 219
Natural facts, 131–33, 178
Nickel, James W., 131
Nielsen, Kai, 163, 189

Index

Noncompliance for reasons of greed. *See* Reasons of greed
Norm conceptions, 69
Norms: distinguished from values, 22–25
Norms of self-interest. *See* Personal welfare norms, subsidiary
Norton, David, 44

Occam's razor, 67
Ordinary language philosophy, 66
Ordinary person test, 97
Original position, 13, 70, 182, 201–20
Other-minds skepticism, 45–46

Page, Edgar, 15
Paine, Thomas, 120
Parfit, Derek, 45
Per accidens and *per se* conflicts: defined, 64
Personal identity, 46–48
Personal morality: defined, 67
Personal welfare. *See* Self-interest
Personal welfare norm, fundamental, 138–39, 170, 183, 204, 206; final formulation, 35–36; preliminary formulation, 31
Personal welfare norms, subsidiary, 12, 181, 190–91, 194–95, 199
Personal welfare standard, 36
Philosophy, nature of, 65–67
Plato, 195
Political morality: defined, 67–68, 113–15
Population growth, 146–47
Practical reasoning, 22–23, 25
Precedents: in law, 153–64
Preemptive moral norms, 156–62
Primary goods, 204, 207–17
Primary norms: defined, 101
Principle of utility. *See* Utilitarian norm
Private property, right to, 125–27
Promises, 44, 76, 78–79, 91–92, 94–97, 169
Prudence. *See* Self-interest
"Punishing" innocent people, 44, 91

Qualified expected utility. *See* Expected utility, qualified
Qualified self-interest. *See* Self-interest, qualified

Rationalizations, 96, 118, 121, 133, 135, 136–37, 178, 181, 186–87, 193
Rawls, John, 11–13, 32, 44, 70, 107, 157, 163, 201–20
Raz, Joseph, 160

Reasons of conscience, 195–99; defined, 190
Reasons of greed, 190–95; defined, 190
Reflective equilibrium methodology, 67, 103, 107, 163–65, 201, 222; in law, 156–58, 162, 164, 170
Relativism, 65–67
Respect for persons, 220–22
Reverse discrimination, 22, 61–62, 129–31
Rights, human, 117–37; positive, 122–25; term explained, 117
Ross, Alf, 26
Rules of thumb, 82, 85, 128–29, 135

Sartorius, Rolf, 77, 152
Schweitzer, Albert, 93
Secondary norms, 101–4, 110, 128, 131; defined, 101
Self-defense, 100
Self-interest, 12–13, 29–39, 87, 93–94, 201–2, 206–7, 220–22; and equal consideration, 170–87; qualified, 13, 36–38, 172–73, 181, 186, 191, 194, 199; and why act morally?, 188–200
Separation of powers, 136
Sidgwick, Henry, 32, 77
Singer, Peter, 22, 98, 129, 193
Sivard, Ruth Leger, 21
Slavery, 25, 44, 123
Smart, J. J. C., 35, 77, 99
Smith, J. C., 155
Social contract approach, 202–3
Social norm: defined, 61
Social pressure, perspective of. *See* Support, perspective of
Social-pressure combinations, 12, 57, 60, 63, 197; defined, 54–56
Social-pressure costs, 56–57, 90, 91, 96, 103, 106, 108, 192
Social-pressure system, 51, 60–65, 77, 80, 165, 169, 201–2, 218–20, 221–22; current, 63; defined, 62–63; formal vs. informal, 192; ideal, 63; total, 192. *See also* Biased system; Equal consideration system
Socrates, 27
Sorensen, Roy, 14
Spatial division of governmental labor, 139–46, 149
Standards: term explained, 23–24
Stare decisis, 152–53, 157–61
Strawson, Peter, 45
Subjectivism. *See* Relativism

Sumner, L. W., 30, 105–6
Supererogatory acts, 91–94, 101
Support, perspective of, 12, 28, 52–63, 75, 182–83, 188, 220–21. *See also* Three-dimensional evaluation
Support decisions, 59, 182–83, 188

Temporal division of governmental labor, 145–49
Teresa, Mother, 93
Terrorism, 58, 196
Theft, 22, 90, 92, 96, 100–102, 169
Theory of law, 63, 156–58, 161–63
Three-dimensional evaluation, 12, 75, 91, 96, 107, 130, 165, 169, 221; defined, 56–57
Thurow, Lester C., 175
Translation thesis, 113–14

Uniformity and predictability, 44, 58, 69–70, 76–80, 84–86, 88–90, 95, 96–97, 101–2, 104–5, 116–17; in law, 159–60
Unqualified self-interest. *See* Self-interest, qualified
Utilitarianism, 50–51, 83, 132, 220–22; act, 12, 77–87, 91; desire, 49–50, 208; direct, 12, 77–87, 201, 221; indirect, 12, 60, 77, 91, 201, 221; negative, 215; preference, 49–50; rule, 12, 77, 91; standard objections against, 43–48, 82–83, 90–91, 131–33, 137, 220–22
Utilitarian norm, 23, 38–39, 40–48, 51, 69, 77–86, 103–4, 106–7, 116–17, 117–20, 124, 127–28, 129–30, 134, 137, 138–39, 161; formulated, 41–43; standard objections against, 43–48, 82–83, 90–91, 137
Utilitarian standard, 23, 50–51, 52, 61, 67–71, 75–77, 79–80, 88, 91, 106–7, 113, 116–17, 124, 130, 145, 148–49, 160, 165, 169–71, 184–87, 188, 201–20; formulated, 50–51; rationale for, 169–87
Utility, 23; cardinal vs. ordinal measurement of, 33–34; term explained, 42

Values: distinguished from norms, 22–25
Veil of ignorance, 204, 217–19
Violence, 196–97, 214–16. *See also* Assault
Virtues, 23–24
Von Magnus, Eric, 14–15

War, 109, 149
Warnock, G. J., 78
Watergate, 96, 136
White, Alan, 117
Why be moral?, 188–99
Williams, Bernard, 60, 90
Williams, Robin M., 24
Wiretapping, 135–36